# *A* CHRIST

# APPOINTED

# MINISTRY

## *The Call of God*

# A CHRIST APPOINTED MINISTRY

## The Call of God

JOHN DEVRIES

CREATION
HOUSE

A CHRIST APPOINTED MINISTRY by John DeVries
Published by Creation House
A Charisma Media Company
600 Rinehart Road
Lake Mary, Florida 32746
www.charismamedia.com

Unless otherwise noted, all Scripture quotations are from the King James Version of the Bible.

Design Director: Bill Johnson
Cover design by Nathan Morgan

Visit the author's website: www.fivefoldministrychurches.com

Library of Congress Cataloging-in-Publication Data: 2012946653
International Standard Book Number: 978-1-62136-097-1
E-book International Standard Book Number: 978-1-62136-098-8

While the author has made every effort to provide accurate telephone numbers and Internet addresses at the time of publication, neither the publisher nor the author assumes any responsibility for errors or for changes that occur after publication.

First edition

12 13 14 15 16 — 9 8 7 6 5 4 3 2 1
Printed in Canada

# DEDICATION

In life, next to our salvation, very few things are of near value. Far beyond material things, the godly people the Lord places in our lives who encourage and steady us with love and knowledge top the list. They encourage us in our eternal faith walk.

Foremost, I thank my dear wife, "Siony," for sacrificially setting me free to devote the many hours involved in writing books. As Solomon pointed out in finding a "woman of virtue," her value is beyond rubies. She does so due to being a godly prophetess, respecting a holy mandate upon my life with a kingdom vision. I also thank my faithful encouraging ministry "Timothys," Pastor Jamie and Sherrie Jenicek, from Idaho, in the United States, who have faithfully stood in the trials.

I am so appreciative of the encouragement from clean and holy-hearted saints whom the Lord has provided in our lives from Canada, the United States, the Philippines, and other countries. A special bouquet of thanks is given in acknowledging those with differing strengths who have taken time to read, critique, and improve the subject content of this book, who include:

My fellow apostle Ernesto Balili, Philippines, who shares my heart.

Brother and prophetic teacher friend, Dr. Kevin, Canada.

Jamie and Sherrie Jenicek, and Salvacion DeVries, Idaho, United States.

Above all, I thank You, my Savior, for the honor of seeing spiritual matters and revelation. Your grace and mercy toward me are higher than the heavens and deeper than the lowest valley. I honor and praise You, my Savior Lord and King.

# Contents

# FOREWORD

*I* HAVE KNOWN JOHN DEVRIES, the author of this powerful book, *A Christ Appointed Ministry,* since 1986. He has blessed many Christian believers and leadership in a number of countries. This is especially true in the many churches I oversee and link with in the Philippines. His apostolic revelation teachings and seminars are filled with fivefold ministry understandings accompanied with the witness of the Holy Ghost.

This book authored by my covenant brother and fellow apostle is uniquely for leadership. It is like no other book I have read, setting forth clear understanding of what is involved when one is truly called and appointed of Christ to the ministry. The numerous revelations of the Holy Word thoroughly set out what the Christ-called and Christ-appointed ministry should know regarding servanthood, ministry truths, and heart focus.

Since the time I was saved in the early 1970s, I have read several hundred Christian books. The knowledge gained has always blessed my ministry. The outflow thereof has affected the leaders, elders, and churches that I serve and oversee. This greatly applies to this book. The mature ministry truths, godly wisdom, and doctrinal understandings herein will enhance any reader for kingdom building.

As I have read, reread, and studied this book; researched the referenced scriptures; and meditated on the holy insights and truths presented, I am challenged thereby. I am so burdened of the Lord to impart these truths to the leaders and all of our churches. This book is not only good for those newly called to ministry, but also for those ministers who are looking for profoundly clear direction in a REAL CHRIST-CALLED MINISTRY. This book is among the few I strongly recommend.

For kingdom expansion,

—APOSTLE E. M. BALILI
PRESIDENT, KING JESUS CHRISTIAN CHURCHES
MINDANAO, PHILIPPINES

# PREFACE

*I*AM CONVINCED THERE must be books existing somewhere written to specifically explain what is "the call of God to ministry." Over the years I personally have found none. I am referring to a blessed understanding of how one thoroughly knows by the Holy Spirit working within whether they are "a called and Christ-appointed ministry" or a zealous Christian. This book addresses that. This writing is a humble attempt to provide scriptural insight leading to a mature understanding as to what every ministry-minded person should know.

We all learn from others and their holy truth revelations, since the body of Christ is blessed with many parts. Over the years the Lord has had me weigh this topic and question this subject intensely. Having found understanding of the answer to this question, I humbly submit this book. There is a huge need for ministry-minded people to understand how the "calling of God to ministry" works.

All mature ministries should be capable and desirous of helping the new ministry generation. They should guide them with understanding about this topic, thereby preventing pitfalls, wasted time, ministry loss, and damage. May we gain in wisdom and understanding of holy doctrine and knowledge, which our Savior would have us know. May we, with the true saints of all ages, build on the foundation of Christ with gold, silver, and precious things, thereby building His church. May we have a clear understanding about the five differing ministry callings and eldership, along with the "must" truths all should understand and present.

*I thank You, O Lord, for Your Holy Word and Your care in providing knowledge and direction. Come, Holy Spirit; we need You. May Your kingdom come within us and use us to reach a dying world.*

# INTRODUCTION

*A Christ Appointed Ministry*

OUR SAVIOR CAME and brought His message by a bloodstained cross. This was the gospel of salvation from sin to a lost and dying world. Christ's words to His followers and to us tell us, "Take up the cross, and follow me" (Mark 10:21). There is a key difference between taking up "the" cross and taking up "your" cross, which He also told His disciples they must do. (See Matthew 16:24.) The committed Christ-loving and -honoring servant will do both. Taking up "the" cross is to proclaim the message of atonement for sin by our lives and words. Taking up "our cross" speaks to our life of self-denial as we follow Christ proclaiming "the" cross.

Our Lord Jesus had a single-minded purpose and vision in His earthly ministry, which was expressed in several points. His mission as the Lamb of God was to accomplish atonement for sin. He continually revealed the Father's glory to all who would receive, speaking of "the kingdom of heaven" (Matt. 4:17). The end of His vision is now His continuing work, beyond the cross and prior to His second coming. Soon He will gather His loved, believing church, His bride, redeemed out of every people and all nations.

When we the ministry take up our cross, we do so by entering into His work and His vision, for without Him we "can do nothing" (John 15:5). We are Christ's appointed ministry, constantly striving to build, mature, and establish His church. We preach the cross, the good news of redemption from sin, until the gospel goes into all the world. True Christ-appointed ministry is linked to the heart of Christ and one with Him, desiring that none shall be lost. We have said, "Yes, Lord, I will feed Your lambs and Your sheep. I desire to be a living sacrifice to You for the love You have given me." (See Romans 12:1.)

Our Lord Jesus said, "I will build my church" (Matt. 16:18). Jesus Christ is our great High Priest, who is constantly engrossed in this work every second of a twenty-four-hour day, year by year as time exists. He is our great constant church-building intercessor (Rom. 8:34). Our ascended Savior gave and is still constantly giving what He termed "gifts to men." These "gifts" are His called and appointed ministries: "And he gave some, apostles; and some, prophets; and some, evangelists; and some, pastors and teachers; for the perfecting of the saints, for the work of the ministry, for the edifying of the body of Christ" (Eph. 4:11–12).

This church, or "body of Christ," is being sought out and established daily throughout the world. These "gift" ministries, and all who enter into ministry should enter into Christ servanthood because of our love for Him who first loved us. Our hearts are captured by Christ. We know what He alone accomplished for us. When He was on the cross, we were on His mind.

This book sets out many of the considerations that all involved in Christ-appointed ministry should understand, demonstrate, and proclaim. Our Lord said the harvest is great and ready. He then told His disciples to "pray ye therefore the Lord of the harvest, that he would send forth labourers into his harvest" (Luke 10:2). This must be our prayer also, a holy desire. This book is written to mature His saints and ministry who desire to enter this work, desiring Christ's appointment.

# THE CALLED

*What glorious works, the mystery, the love of Christ Divine,*
*Your love and grace the cross embraced to make salvation mine.*

*O mighty Father, Son, and Ghost, Your work to me revealed*
*By demonstration, cross, and Word forgiveness now my soul received.*

*Your nail-pierced hands and feet are not what held You to the cross,*
*Your heart of love fastened You there; You saved me from my loss.*

*I've seen Your glory, sun, and moon; the stars by night do shine,*
*But these don't touch my heart as when Your blood has made me Thine.*

*I see Your majesty revealed; Your glorious reign, Your power*
*Have stripped me from my hiding cloak, revealed my dark, sin hour.*

*Thy altar's mercy coal has now forever changed my thoughts and heart,*
*By Christ my Lord, You saved my soul, and salvation did impart.*

*What can I do to worship You, Lord Jesus; what can I give to Thee,*
*I hear, You called, now tell the world, Break*
*chains of sin, set people free.*

*Your heart we'll thrill, Your church we'll build, by service born of love,*
*I will intercede, teach, preach Your Word, win souls, Your bride above.*

*Almighty God, Creator, my Savior Christ, my reigning King,*
*Your covenant redemption brought life from death, new hope did bring.*

*With heart of love I now embrace, love's prisoner now I am to Thee;*
*Honor of honors and joy of all joys, eternity spent, with You to be.*
*I'll tell them, show Your matchless love; I'll go, dear Lord, send me.*

—JDV (taken from Isaiah 6:8; Acts 9:6; Ephesians 4:1)

## CHAPTER ONE

# CHOOSING HIS GLORY

*The Called See Christ by His Salvation Glory*

*T*HE APOSTLE JOHN, under divine anointing, said, "... (and *we beheld His glory*, the glory of the only begotten of the Father,) full of grace and truth" (John 1:14, emphasis added).

Ecstatic joy and glory! What was the glory? He did not shine and was not bejeweled. He was not an idolized handsome Hollywood star. "He hath no form nor comeliness; and when we shall see him, there is no beauty that we should desire him. He is despised and rejected of men; a man of sorrows, and acquainted with grief" (Isa. 53:2–3).

Yes, we are profoundly and ecstatically blessed. We are privileged to look upon Him! The Law, which explains perfection of sinless love in action, is truth. The Law was given by Moses. Christ's coming was with "grace and truth" (John 1:17). The Law demonstrates perfection of love and holiness. The Law demonstrated what we should be and are not. Holiness is the perfection of love, as love does no ill to their neighbor. Every broken commandment of the moral law is a destruction of love (i.e., kill, steal, lie, dishonor). The grace that only comes by Christ is found in His death in our stead, bringing forgiveness for our sins and to them who believe.

To see the holy perfection of truth, immersed in love and forgiveness in Christ, the man of sorrows, is heavenly bliss. To see the light of the world enter our darkness is wonderful. His righteousness united with His divine mercy coming to us is profound. To see our Savior and His love, by mercy dealing with our sin and untruth by the moral righteousness of His cross, is glorious. Forgiveness of sins, compassion, and

1

eternal life by our Lord and Creator God is immensely glorious to those who have seriously "beheld" Him.

## Those Who Saw

The psalmist with holy anointing said it all: "Mercy and truth are met together; righteousness and peace have kissed each other" (Ps. 85:10). The righteousness of the Law that came by Moses was met in Christ. He took our judgment, our sin. Christ, the Word, became flesh. He died on that cross for you and me. (See 2 Corinthians 5:21.) As I stated previously, when He was on the cross, we were on His mind.

Therein lies the understanding of His glory and the righteousness of God. The scales of holy perfection and justice are revealed and met by God's love in Him. Glory!

To the ministering Christian, having the knowledge of one's sins being forgiven and embracing heaven's promise and the Savior's love is glorious. Having received the "Spirit of adoption" births a changed faith and different life (Rom. 8:15, 23). Being an unsaved "religious" Christian, relying on church-administered rites, never produces any godly experience or inner glory. Christian rites do not bring any assurance of salvation, joy, or knowledge that one's sins are forgiven.

Seeing His compassion and love for you and me will cause us to understand that it was not the nails that held Him to that cross; it was His binding love. Seeing the pureness of His selfless love exposes our sin, our lovelessness, and wrongs toward God and man.

Embracing Christ and the cross produced my heart's love and worship for Him who first loved me. All of my goodness, works, pride of personal goodness, or righteousness by works are destroyed. I worship Him, who by His works grants the promise of sins forgiven and life eternal. I receive the down payment deposit of an experiential Holy Spirit: "Who hath sealed us, and given the earnest of the Spirit in our hearts" (2 Cor. 1:22). Should this not be our experience, how can we as ministry lead others into what we do not understand or possess?

The roots to our ministry must be due to an experiential and altered life focus. We do so by having seen this glory, Christ the Lord and King of glory. The living believer is riveted to and captivated by Christ and the kingdom of God. The apostle Paul exemplified this understanding when he described himself as "the prisoner of Jesus Christ" (Eph. 3:1).

We see no visible shackles or chains upon Paul's person as he ministered before His Savior. The exception was the chains Paul willingly accepted at the end of his ministry when he went to Rome. The only constraints that held him in place were the cords of love attached to his heart.

Christ's love has captured me. Now I am a love prisoner of Christ. I see His heart. I am determined to express to all I encounter the gospel, the profound message of salvation.

I bring to those of you loved unbelievers this profound love message of hope. Christ died for the forgiveness of our sins. Be reconciled to God. Receive forgiveness by the cross, the forgiveness of sins and life eternal: "And you, that were sometime alienated and enemies in your mind by wicked works, yet now hath he reconciled" (Col. 1:21; see also Rom. 5:10; 2 Cor. 5:20). All Christian believers must clearly understand this topic to be effective in ministry.

## SEEING CHRIST AS GLORIOUS PRECEDES HOLY MINISTRY

One must know Christ to properly portray Him. Seeing the glory of our God must precede ministry, or we will never portray Him for who He is. He is glorious and beautiful, merciful and mighty, to those who know Him. Many portray Him while never having experienced seeing His glory.

Salvation is experiential. Without this experience one will portray a heavenly judge whom we are to love but cannot draw near to, as a trust bond is missing: "That we should be to the praise of his glory, who first trusted in Christ. In whom ye also trusted, after that ye heard the word of truth, the gospel of your salvation: in whom also after that ye believed, ye were sealed with that holy Spirit of promise" (Eph. 1:12–13).

The sad truth is that many have a dead and boring Christian religion.

Perhaps they have not been shown or they do not understand how to enter into Christ, the door. In Him is life. A living Christian will demonstrate this life. Faith without works is dead. Receiving Christ as Lord and Savior—knowing Him and His mercy, knowing that your sins are forgiven—is the epitome of glorious experience. If this is not your experience, I question your salvation. If the thought of meeting God after experiencing death brings fear to your heart, please be aware. The fearful will be part of the eternal lake of fire (Rev. 21:8). Knowing Christ as Savior deals with this very topic: "There is no fear in love; but perfect love casteth out fear: because fear hath torment. He that feareth is not made perfect in love" (1 John 4:18). When we fully believe in and embrace Christ, His love and accomplished shed blood for our personal sins dissipate our fears. We grow our faith by deepening our knowledge of the Word, believing in God's faithful promises, and knowing Him.

Never having met the queen of England, I can speak of her and tell you a number of things about her person and family. However, should I meet her and talk with her, speaking heart to heart and learning about her, then I may say I know her. May those who have seen and experienced His glory speak of knowing Him instead of knowing "of Him." May all of us who have seen His glory minister His awesome and glorious person to the world from this experiential revelation.

## Salvation's Glory

One's understanding is transformed when they observe even a trace of God's being. Creation declares His power and art. His judgment of sin and wrong declares His moral righteous holiness. His divine plan in redemption demonstrates His glory, love, and mercy. He did not judge mankind who was tempted by the devil as He judged the tempter with his followers. For them there is no grace. He made a way for man, created in His image, to be forgiven. This is why the elders in heaven cast down any crowns earned at His feet, as He is the author of our salvation.

If we do not see His person as the Alpha and Omega, the beginning and the end with eternal omniscience, knowing all things past and future, we will be limited in seeing Him. We must see God through an overlaying film of love, encased in mercy along with a demonstrated revelation of His majesty and power. This will transform us. Our Father is omnipotent (all powerful), which no man should deny. He is a profound God of miracles. This is written in the sky. He alone put the stars in space and the world in place. However, when He saved me and cleansed and made me whole, it was a miracle showing forth His love, mercy, and grace.

A true glimpse of His power and heart, His person, should be the basis for an instant heart transformation. This will instantly affect all of our thoughts and plans in life. We are changed by a glimpse of His glory: "But we all, with open face beholding as in a glass the glory of the Lord, are changed into the same image from glory to glory, even as by the Spirit of the Lord" (2 Cor. 3:18). We must know Him in order to minister Him to others.

## A CHANGED LIFE

Such is the case in my life. From an unusual encounter involving difficulties on a mountainside, I was changed. I was a standard brand religious sometimes go to church heathen. I was bitterly planning a very negative vengeance upon a person in my life who was guilty of corporate betrayal, robbing me of finances and standings in the corporation I had recently left behind. The betrayal involved my provincial manager taking credit for what I had accomplished, thus affecting my finances and corporate standing. Musing on my circumstances while sitting just below the melting snow line on a sunny Saturday morning, I saw a myriad of tiny blue flowers. They were growing where the snow had been present one week previously. This observation amazed me. While thinking on this, my thoughts went to God, the artist Creator.

I looked out over Ross Lake in lower British Columbia and spoke a silent prayer. I said, "God, if I was convinced that You were tuned into me, much like a radio channel receiver, I would have to take a sincere search to understand You." Within a split second much of the anger within me melted away. As I became aware of this, a larger portion of the remaining anger and frustration that had bound me dissipated. The sun became brighter and the lake beneath became bluer.

I became aware that the living God saw me. My instant priority was to gain an understanding of God. This completely changed my life's course. I immediately headed home and started reading my Bible late into the night, long after those with whom I shared my home went to bed. I scoured the pages for understanding as a man dying of thirst.

The Book of Romans gave answers and equally raised many questions. These questions caused me to look up an old background church catechism study, comparing the answers provided to what I was finding in my readings. The results brought about a confrontation within. I did not agree with some of the catechism findings. What did I really believe? The results of my findings greatly affected my future walk. I saw doctrinal truths in a new light. I had a holy meltdown upon seeing the entire plan of God, His faithful nonstop love for mankind and especially Abraham and his natural descendants, Israel, as well as Abraham's spiritual descendants—you and I who believe like Abraham. I believed that our God genuinely wants all of mankind to be saved, although all will not be (1 Tim. 2:4).

This newfound revelation quickly escalated into searching out avenues and implementing ways of sharing the truths of the gospel. I wrote to unsaved family members and found a church to get baptized in water, following the Christ I now had embraced (1 Pet. 3:21). My dead religious past was gone as I started a ministry of giving out gospel tracts and opening a "coffee house" teen ministry.

Early on in my Christian walk I was asked to be an assistant pastor of a newly planted church work. Because of the things the Lord did through my life and efforts, others told me that I was "called of God to the ministry."

As much as I wanted to serve and glorify my newfound Lord, these statements only caused me to struggle deeply within. I only wanted what was real and be whatever the Lord would have me be. I could not accept these statements without receiving an understanding of how this supposed "call of God" to ministry worked. Titles meant nothing to me, unless He wanted me to have a title. I did not want to be presumptuous, and I did not understand what was entailed in being "called of God."

I just wanted to do all I could to cause others to know the living, revealed Christ Jesus whom I had found. After all, should all Christians not seek to witness and do whatever they could for the Lord who saved them? However, in time this statement was reinforced by a known strong ministry who prophetically said, "You are called of God to the ministry; do you not know that?" From that time on I have diligently sought for answers to the question, Who is called to "the ministry"? What makes them so, and what gives them a right to this claim?

## BIBLE ANSWERS

The Bible has all of the answers. In time, after seeing many Bible truths, I understood. All revelation of truth is found in God's time by the seeking. Continual profound truths. Truths that godly heroes over the centuries have found.

The road to genuinely seeing His glory always involves a personal inspection of our person within. This inspection will confront sin before His revealed holiness and throne of majesty. We daily grow in grace by becoming more aware of our lack and His faithful mercy as well (1 John 1:9). Then having faced sin in self, mixed with holy faith in Christ and believing that God in Christ forgave my sin, births worship from the heart. Our love for Him is due to this inner seeing. Then just go from faith to faith with a continuing faith experience (Rom. 1:17), seeing a greater depth and measure of His love and mercy.

Increased faith simply means that the picture of heaven and a sure knowing that sins are forgiven are becoming clearer and brighter. Faith has eyes that grow as we experience His faithfulness in life's trials. God's mercy and love become larger than the shadows and darkness of our unbelief. There are increasing stages of this revelation and a varied understanding of the same, just as the colors of the rainbow are all glorious yet individually unique. Seeing God's glory produces an increased faith within the one who sees. Seeing and placing faith in His purposed salvation produces trust and relationship. Faith in His existence alone will never do this

Only faith in His person allows us to genuinely pray, "Our Father, who art in heaven." Faith in His existence produces a prayer of "Great and mighty God, whom we esteem and revere" (are afraid of). "But without faith it is impossible to please him: for he that cometh to God must believe that he is, *and* that he is a rewarder of them that diligently seek him" (Heb. 11:6, emphasis added). Those who only "peek" at Him with fear, meanwhile hiding behind a song hymnal, will not be capable of grasping this truth. Only those who have diligently sought Him until they see with open eyes will be able to. With our hearts uncovered and standing spiritually naked before Him with our sin exposed, there is nothing left to hide. We will see the glorious revelation of His person. Without having dealt with our sins before His throne, the issue that separates us from God, this is impossible.

## SEEING HIS GLORY

Seeing His glory will draw us into sonship and family relationship. I am family. Heaven is mine because Christ is mine. I see God's greatness in His giving His Son, Christ Jesus, for me. He dealt with my sin at the cross. I see the Sonlight of His glory. All else in life now pales in comparison to this love-bought relationship entered into with my Creator. There is no comparison to His glory. The brightness of His glorious being and salvation diminishes all other aspects of life that now reside in the shadows. "For we preach not ourselves, but Christ Jesus the Lord; and ourselves your servants for Jesus' sake. For God, who commanded the light to shine out of darkness, hath shined in our hearts, to give the light of the knowledge of the glory of God in the face of Jesus Christ" (2 Cor. 4:5–6). This is similar to having that shiny beautiful parked car we purchased and own (Bible), then finally filling it with gas and have it running. Now I experience new worlds as this allows me fascinating travel, secure in Him, due to seeing and knowing my Creator.

The more we see and understand of Christ's glory, the more we will press in to reveal this to others. "God, who at sundry times and in divers manners spake in time past unto the fathers by the prophets, hath in these last days spoken unto us by his Son, whom he hath appointed heir of all things, by whom also he made the worlds; who being the brightness of his glory, and the express image of his person, and upholding all things by the word of his power, when he had by himself purged our sins, sat down on the right hand of the Majesty on high" (Heb. 1:1–3). The called have moved far beyond an initial reverence. They are bathed in His love and mercy; they have entered the grandeur of adoption into the family of God and sonship through Christ. They know with a sure knowledge deep within their hearts that they belong to Christ and their Father in heaven.

## The Glory of God Revealed

One may begin with observing the glory of God by His works. David observed in Psalm 19, "The heavens declare the glory of God; and the firmament sheweth his handy work. Day unto day uttereth speech, and night unto night sheweth knowledge. There is no speech nor language, where their voice is not heard. Their line is gone out through all the earth, and their words to the end of the world" (vv. 1–4). All nature, land, seas, and the heavens declare His wondrous works. The stars and suns echo His time clock perfection. We who smell the fragrance of numerous colored flowers and the green foliage produced from black soil will honor God's awesome creative being. Unfortunately there are many, as Paul pointed out, who will worship His creation but disregard the Creator. They worship the art and deny the artist, missing the entire point, while honoring "mother earth."

Our God expects us to understand His being and presence from Creation:

> Because that which may be known of God is manifest in them;
> for God hath shewed it unto them. For the invisible things of him
> from the creation of the world are clearly seen, being understood

by the things that are made, even his eternal power and Godhead; so that they are without excuse: Because that, when they knew God, they glorified him not as God, neither were thankful; but became vain in their imaginations, and their foolish heart was darkened. Professing themselves to be wise, they became fools, and changed the glory of the incorruptible God into an image made like to corruptible man, and to birds, and fourfooted beasts, and creeping things. Wherefore God also gave them up to uncleanness through the lusts of their own hearts, to dishonour their own bodies between themselves: Who changed the truth of God into a lie, and worshipped and served the creature more than the Creator, who is blessed forever. Amen.

—Romans 1:19–25

We see our holy God's greatness by His creation ability and majesty. If this is all we have seen, we are still blind. This is a limited view of His true greatness. May we proceed to seeing His holy love. The believer has moved from the starting point of insight regarding Creation. They have seen God's heart. He is holy. Our God desires to bring mankind from being satisfied with sin to dissatisfaction with a world of sin. For those who are His, He made the way for them to live with Him in His holy mountain: "Also the sons of the stranger, that join themselves to the Lord, to serve him, and to love the name of the Lord, to be his servants, every one that keepeth the Sabbath from polluting it, and taketh hold of my covenant; even them will I bring to my holy mountain, and make them joyful in my house of prayer" (Isa. 56:6–7). Only those who love holiness and take hold of His covenant will be there. Those who choose the Christian religion believing in both heaven and hell, but only wanting "fire insurance" from hell, with no genuine love for our God, will not dwell in that holy mountain.

David in Psalm 19:7, after stating that the heavens and creation declare God's glory, immediately continues this observation, writing about God's holy, moral glory. He continued with, "The law of the Lord is perfect." The comparison made is profound. The same way that the perfection of harmony in the universe, creation, and a fragrant rose demonstrate

God's creation majesty, God's moral being and beauty are demonstrated by His laws. David continued with, "The law of the Lord is perfect, converting the soul." This by necessity includes perfection in righteousness, or love is broken. This cannot be maintained without holy judgment dealing with sin and the transgression of His holy and just laws of love. There would be no peace in eternity without the perfection of love.

## Holiness

To grasp the understanding of the predicament involved when man lost his relationship with God through Adam's sin, there are several factors that need to be understood. The first consideration is the fact that God is holy, meaning He is the perfection of moral law. Man in sin became a being who continually acts against the holiness described and set forth by God's moral law, the Ten Commandments.

To properly understand God and His nature, we must see the combined factors of love, law, and holiness. God is the perfection of love. The Ten Commandments are not just what we are to do or be, but they are a perfect description of the perfection of love. The breaking of the laws is a breach of love. Picture this. In heaven and the future home for those who trust in Him, there will be perfect honor for all, no murder or hatred, no jealousy. Only love will reign there, as heaven is a place of holiness. Answering the question of laws and greatest law, our Lord said, "Thou shalt love the Lord thy God with all thy heart, and with all thy soul, and with all thy mind. This is the first and great commandment. And the second is like unto it, Thou shalt love thy neighbor as thyself. On these two commandments hang all the law and the prophets" (Matt. 22:37–40).

We will know even as we are known (1 Cor. 13:12). The measuring stick of our heavenly knowing is equal to how our God knows us. We will have an understanding of all with no hidden or negative thoughts: "For there is not a word in my tongue, but, lo, O Lord, thou knowest it altogether" (Ps. 139:4). We will know all fellow heavenly beings and believers without a guard on our communications, as the perfection of love will be our environment. What love, security, and joy we will have with Christ in this new heavenly home. The Ten Commandments are a perfect depiction of what a sinless person will do and will not do. They are the perfection of love. David in awe said, "Shall the throne of iniquity have fellowship with thee, which frameth mischief by a law?" (Ps. 94:20). Holiness is the perfection of love, which our God is.

Sin is the breaking of the laws of love. Our state of sinfulness involves fear and carefulness. Pride, selfishness, jealousy, and wrong thinking are all part of our humanity.

## God's Planned Salvation Glory

Understanding God's plan of eternal salvation and how this fits into our lives is glorious. His plan is the only reason this sin-filled earth still exists. God's plan of salvation was formulated before the world was created. His omniscient knowing of what man would do with his free will and planned salvation remedy is being carried out right now: "Blessed be the God and Father of our Lord Jesus Christ, who hath blessed us with all spiritual blessings in heavenly places in Christ: According as he hath chosen us in him before the foundation of the world, that we should be holy and without blame before him in love: Having predestinated us unto the adoption of children by Jesus Christ to himself, according to the good pleasure of his will" (Eph. 1:3–5).

The omniscient Alpha and Omega planned our salvation before the world was created. One might say, "How is that possible?" I suppose that when we understand how He holds the world in place with precision in relationship to the sun so the world does not freeze or burn, and that for thousands of years, then we will also understand omniscience.

God's holy plan of dealing with sin and forgiveness of same melts my heart. God the Father, Son, and Holy Spirit had a meeting in heaven, knowing what man would do with his free will after being created. Man sinned and had to righteously remedy this. Earth's sinful man could not correct this. The Son said, "I will go at the right time and become as the man We have created." The Holy Spirit said, "After You have been crucified and have paid the price for the sins for those who will receive this payment, I will raise You from the dead. I will also go throughout the world and convict man of righteousness and judgment. I will reveal Your glory until the end of the harvest to those who will believe our love and salvation plan." (See John 15:26.) The Father said, "We are in full agreement to redeem the people We have created in Our image." (See Matthew 25:34.) We can do no less. Our love for them cannot be shortened or hidden by not acting upon it. We long for them to be one with us in glory (John 17:24).

## The Believer's Ministry, the Motivating Love

All genuine ministry efforts should be a result of Christ's love for us. True ministry by a Christian born of the Spirit must be motivated by God's love, our love for Him, and seeing His love for others. The apostle Paul said this so clearly: "I am crucified with Christ: nevertheless I live; yet not I, but Christ liveth in me: and the life which I now live in the flesh I live by the faith of the Son of God, who loved me, and gave himself for me" (Gal. 2:20). The believer knows (not only hopes) that he was included in the crucifixion and death of Christ. He is personally knowledgeable of Christ's love and now lives for our Lord who bought us by His shed blood.

The psalmist, when prophetically speaking of the renewed focus of his life, stated what he now knew to be true after seeking God:

> Behold Philistia, and Tyre, with Ethiopia; this man was born there. And of Zion it shall be said, This man and that man was born in her: and the highest himself shall establish her. The Lord shall count, when he writeth up the people, that this man was born there. Selah. As well the singers as the players on instruments shall be there: all my springs are in thee.
>
> —Psalm 87:4–7

Here we see the fountain of any ministry. This knowledge and vision were the motivation of the author's pursuits. He acknowledges his natural birth being in Ethiopia as well as his spiritual birth in Zion, the City of God, thus being born twice.

He knew of his heritage in the eternal Zion (Heb. 12:22), which the Lord would establish, the heavenly Mount Zion for an eternal habitation (Heb. 8:5). He had left off setting his sights on earthly pursuits and monuments to a self life. He replaced his past vision with eternity in mind. His new enduring passion was summarized with "all my springs are in thee."

He is saying, "Lord! I am consumed by Your holy, eternal person and kingdom. The motivation for whatever springs out of my new life has changed. My joys, desires, and thoughts are now captured with holy focus because of Your love and the glory You have revealed to me. Seeing the glory of what You are doing and what You have done has dwarfed all other ambitions I once held dear. They are now reduced or discarded. Ambitions now dwarfed, I see the glory of Your person and eternal purposes."

Church-attending believers who profess being Christian but do not witness or minister Christ and salvation have a limited understanding of God's grace and glory and little if any genuine joy in their supposed salvation.

## A Boring Topic of Negligible Interest

There are many who may or may not attend church, calling themselves "Christian," to whom this topic will be foreign or of little importance. The reasons for this are several, and the results can commonly be observed. They have no zeal for kingdom or God talk. They never speak of the joy of their salvation. They have a habitual limited and memorized prayer life at best, if they have any at all. Bible reading is a chore for them, due to not desiring to know God intimately. They have not seen His heart and purposes. Basically one can summarize these people with this conclusion: while they believe in both heaven and a burning hell, they simply want FIRE INSURANCE!

They have a firm belief in a heaven to come and a hell to shun. They will do what they deem necessary out of a wrong motive to avoid hell's fires. Consider that many church-attending believers are warned by Christ: "Thou hast a few names even in Sardis which have not defiled their garments; and they shall walk with me in white: for they are worthy. He that overcometh, the same shall be clothed in white raiment; and I will not blot out his name out of the book of life, but I will confess his name before my Father, and before his angels. He that hath an ear, let him hear what the Spirit saith unto the churches" (Rev. 3:4–6). A name has to be placed in the Book of Life, when someone receives salvation, to be capable of this removal. There is a needed overcoming.

These bored Christians have a genuine fear for God but not a holy fear, which is attended with reverend awe, love, and respect. They want forgiveness of sins and heaven but have not seen or desired Him. Perhaps many do not clearly know how to receive this love. Many Christians have never really heard the gospel. They are caught in a death trap of a wrong theological belief system that they rely upon. Those who seek will find their way out of this. Our God will meet those who seek the way, Christ Jesus (John 14:6). Should they not have partaken of His love and grace, this is usually due to a missing step of not understanding how we are to approach God. They have not known what true repentance from sin is, attended with faith in His love and mercy.

Often this is due to the wrong-minded ministry relationship they are looking to while hoping for salvation. Many are blocked and lost by looking to modern-day scribes and Pharisees, who have no knowledge of genuine salvation but do acknowledge the God of Abraham: "But woe unto you, scribes and Pharisees, hypocrites! for ye shut up the kingdom of heaven against men: for ye neither go in yourselves, neither suffer ye them that are entering to go in" (Matt. 23:13).

These leaders need to understand Christ's words regarding those who claim Abraham as their father: "Bring forth therefore fruits worthy of repentance, and begin not to say within yourselves, We have Abraham to our father: for I say unto you, That God is able of these stones to raise up children unto Abraham" (Luke 3:8).

Those who were so sternly addressed by our Lord were the pastors and ministers of His day. These leaders fell short of what needed to be addressed. It's the same now. Look for how these scriptural presentations apply in our day. Some preachers say, "Just accept Jesus and you will be saved." Others say, "You were baptized as an infant and now belong to the church, just keep the laws." They do not fully inform the people that this involves a personal repenting and turning from all sin. Only when one personally kneels before the cross and a merciful Christ, believing in what He accomplished for him by His crucifixion, along with accepting His sacrifice for themselves, will assurance of salvation and the Holy Spirit follow with joy and peace.

Many will say, "This does not apply to me. I am more than a 'fire insurance' Christian. I faithfully sing in the church choir." That may be good and honorable, but your salvation will never be because of singing or church attendance. Many will say "Lord" in that final hour we will all face, and then struggle upon hearing what our Lord said: "When once the master of the house is risen up, and hath shut to the door, and ye begin to stand without, and to knock at the door, saying, Lord, Lord, open unto us; and he shall answer and say unto you, I know you not whence ye are: Then shall ye begin to say, We have eaten and drunk in thy presence, and thou hast taught in our streets. But he shall say, I tell you, I know you not whence ye are" (Luke 13:25–27). Our God desires and demands sonship and a personal relationship.

Ministry should stem from a life in Christ, a life of love for Him. Simply ask yourself the following questions to see your own reality: Are you positioned for ministry?

"Do I love the Lord, proven by my daily communion and thought life toward Him?" Sunday-only Christians do not start their waking hours with prayerful thoughts and seeking His face, thus disproving the genuine Lordship of Christ in their lives.

"Do I care for my neighbor?" If you say yes, then your love for them will be evidenced by prayer, witnessing, and intercession for them.

"Do I believe that those who do not have a Christ "relationship" are heading for a terrible, lost eternity?" If you say yes, your love for Christ and them will be seen by your actions toward unbelievers as you seek to save them from this devastation.

"Do I shrink at witnessing, fearing rejection from them?" If we neglect witnessing, we have several problems pointed out to us by the scriptures as seen from the following.

> For whosoever shall be ashamed of me and of my words, of him shall the Son of man be ashamed, when he shall come in his own glory, and in his Father's, and of the holy angels.
>
> —LUKE 9:26

> I know thy works, that thou art neither cold nor hot: I would thou wert cold or hot. So then because thou art lukewarm, and neither cold nor hot, I will spue thee out of my mouth. Because thou sayest, I am rich, and increased with goods, and have need of nothing; and knowest not that thou art wretched, and miserable, and poor, and blind, and naked: I counsel thee to buy of me gold tried in the fire, that thou mayest be rich; and white raiment, that thou mayest be clothed, and that the shame of thy nakedness do not appear; and anoint thine eyes with eyesalve, that thou mayest see. As many as I love, I rebuke and chasten: be zealous therefore, and repent.
>
> —REVELATION 3:15–19

Beloved believers and saints, please consider the above scriptures spoken by Christ Himself. How do these apply to our personal lives? I very much believe in Christian fellowship and the assembling together as we are admonished to do. However, these efforts do not equate "ministry" unless we are encouraging others in faith and God pursuits. Food, fellowship, and fun are Christian blessings when Christ is glorified and when they include a Christ-centered focus.

A key observation and statement made by our soon coming Lord, King, and Judge of all mankind reads: "He that is not with me is against me; and he that gathereth not with me scattereth abroad" (Matt. 12:30). Our sitting by while doing nothing is a statement that scatters. We thereby say there is no cause and it is not a priority in my life. We must be more than a social church. The genuine issue we must face and ask ourselves, to have "the call of God to ministry" properly addressed, demands taking inventory of our hearts.

Our risen Lord asked Peter to do this with a deep questioning with the same question being asked three times: "Simon, son of Jonas, lovest thou me?" (John 21:15–17). Then Jesus clarified the question in depth by voicing the demanded evidence and testing of this love. The evidence of the genuineness of love for Christ is proven by, "Feed my lambs...feed my sheep." The rest of this question Jesus asked was, "Lovest thou me more than these?" Fishing and the sea was Peter's chosen life. "Do you love Me more than your self-seeking personal life?" is the real question. When this question is asked of those who claim a God-appointed Ephesians 4 holy ministry calling, if this is not answered with, "Yes, Lord," I question their heart and calling status.

Child of God facing eternity, if these scriptures place condemnation and weights of conviction on our hearts, there is hope and an answer. We can repent, as Jesus said we must, by returning to our first love. We can heed the words of the prophet, "Sow to yourselves in righteousness, reap in mercy; break up your fallow ground: for it is time to seek the Lord, till he come and rain righteousness upon you" (Hosea 10:12). Fallow ground is a potential garden that has been neglected or lain idle in winter dormancy. Work up this soil for planting, and be part of harvesting. The fruit of faith and life will follow. Remember how David allowed his land to be placed in dormancy when he was successful against all of his enemies. He placed his eyes on Bathsheba and fell. When confronted by the prophet Nathan, he repented and broke up his fallow ground. He became more fruitful after this experience, being very aware of his failure potential.

## CHAPTER TWO

# HABAKKUK'S CALL
# TO MINISTRY

*Burden of Heart*

$\mathcal{A}$S A YOUNG Christian I was told by several that I was "called of God" to the ministry. I could not accept or deny those words. I expected a night vision or angel visitation for such an honor. Yet I was determined to serve the Lord and be a warrior in His army for His purposes. It took me ten years before I could actually accept this truth, although I had pastored a church and evangelized during this time. I diligently searched for understanding regarding this topic. After several years of prayerfully seeking, the Holy Spirit opened my understanding while reading in the Old Testament prophets. Usually they started their writings with "the burden of the Lord" or "the word of the Lord."

This observation fruitfully blossomed. I understood how these called ministries were strongly impacted by holy truth revealed to them. The Lord shared a revelation of His heart and message that the people needed to hear. They saw the need of preaching the revealed truth as a task of utmost importance and priority. The truths impacting their hearts and minds were of extreme importance and a message their ministry was always to trumpet forth. They became pregnant and weighted with God's message, seeing God's heart revealed. This was the message that needed to be declared to man.

This in no wise eliminates holy experiences those called to ministry may experience. Personally I have experienced particular moments of very emotionally impacting insight. I was searching and reading my Bible for three to four hours per night when others of my household were in bed. As the Lord opened particular portions of the Book of Romans in the first five chapters, I saw God's heart. I would slowly read and reread to understand what was said. I would be so impacted that often I had to stop and bow my head in reverence and pray a "Thank You, God, thank You, God, thank You, God." During this expression of the overflow of my heart in prayer I sensed the touch of and presence of the Holy Spirit. This was the first time in my life that I experienced the tangible Holy Spirit presence or anointing. Then I would read and reread until I fully grasped the awesome plan of salvation, how Abraham fit into this plan, and ultimately how you and I and all believers fit in. Immediately I started looking for ways and wisdom to impact others. How could I share this wonderful faith and knowledge with those around me?

Dreams and visions are not uncommon to called ministers, but most will receive the burden of seeing a truth that must be declared: "The burden of Babylon, which Isaiah the son of Amoz did see" (Isa. 13:1). Upon "seeing," the preacher is burdened to exclaim and speak forth that which now burdens his heart. The ministers are now compelled to speak. I expect that few will see a vision such as Ezekiel did upon the initiation of his ministry. The ministry calling most likely to experience picture "visions" is that of the prophet. However, all genuinely called ministry will and should experience a Habakkuk "burden" within. The response to what they see will cause a volcano thrust of, "I must tell others." If one is called, this built-up volcanic pressure due to the burdening within will erupt. This eruption will be the initiating of the ministry response to the call of God.

## The Habakkuk Experience

Perhaps no Bible writings describe the inner effect of the call of God within a ministry as is recorded by the called ministry prophet Habakkuk: "The burden which Habakkuk the prophet did see" (Hab. 1:1). This verse says so much. What the Lord showed the prophet Habakkuk created a burden upon his person, a weight and sorrow of heart.

Habakkuk saw life through brand-new eyes. He wondered why others did not see what he saw, as our God revealed and shared His vision with him. He saw and was burdened with the weight of the now revealed wrong his eyes saw. He saw the reality of need in the people's circumstances. He saw ungodliness, the unrighteousness of life on the street. He was allowed to receive a glimpse of what our God continually sees while beholding humanity.

Those called of God to ministry will always experience a degree of this seeing, causing a burden of heart. This seeing will always reveal new insight as to humanity's need, sin, the sinner, and unrighteousness in this world.

Those called to ministry will always have a desire to bring righteousness into these circumstances. The advocate of the Lord, the "called," will have a sure knowledge that only the Lord of heaven and earth can bring resolution to humanity's problems. They know the Lord alone to be righteous. All genuinely called ministry will see God's holiness in clear contrast to a sin-diseased world. *All called ministry* (if they are) will relate to Habakkuk.

Holy called ministry will always see the wrongs of people's dealings:

> O Lord, how long shall I cry, and thou wilt not hear! even cry out unto thee of violence, and thou wilt not save! Why dost thou shew me iniquity, and cause me to behold grievance? for spoiling and violence are before me: and there are that raise up strife and contention. Therefore the law is slacked, and judgment does never go forth: for the wicked doth compass about the righteous; therefore wrong judgment proceedeth.
>
> —Habakkuk 1:2–4

Due to what the prophet saw, a burden or weight was placed on his heart, filling his thoughts with struggles—a godly and righteous burden, different from the burden others identify with. The Lord showed the prophet His holy perspective of humanity, as well as specific things of His love and coming judgment that needed to be heralded. Many in his town, his fellow man or family, did not see the injustice and wrong that Habakkuk saw. The prophet's heart and mind reeled due to experiencing this weight, the reality of humanity's revealed need, the result of sin, and the fruit thereof.

This is much like the person who, after ignoring abortion practices, then begins to understand the truth about partial birth abortions. He wakes up the reality of this horrible, ongoing daily occurrence, facing the fact that a small, defenseless human being was murdered. He becomes cognizant of the fact that the mother involved will be subject to emotional scars for life as she will never forget her murdered child.

Coming to grips with this legalized murder of a human being, instead of avoiding and denying it, brings change. The masses may shut out the facts by denial or determining it is someone else's decision and problem, but the called with new eyes will confront and expose sin and wrong. They receive a glimpse of what our holy God is struggling with every minute of every day. They are convicted to do something about it. They will always see the lost on their road to everlasting eternal damnation. They will always want to rescue the lost by salvation.

Those called to ministry will see life's matters through Holy Spirit–altered eyes. This renewed seeing will burden their hearts. This burden will alter their life focus, activities, and priorities. For the called, this seeing will cause a crying out to God. It will wrench out a prayer of intercession from their burdened heart. For those who do not run from this seeing but respond by weighing this reality head-on, a cry of pain and struggle will arise from within.

This seeing and *burdened* heart will respond with a prayer similar to what Habakkuk raised to the heavens:

> O LORD, how long shall I cry, and thou wilt not hear! even cry out unto thee of violence, and thou wilt not save! Why dost thou show me iniquity, and cause me to behold grievance? for spoiling

and violence are before me: and there are that raise up strife and contention.

—Habakkuk 1:2–3

Gray fogged areas of understanding and morality become a stark white and black by clearly revealed truth. A little untruth becomes a great moral lie. Shadowed wrong is now bathed in daylight visibility.

Holy eyes see sin and what is holy. The wrongful matter of sin's effect in man will become clear. Unrighteousness in the actions and dealings of humanity will be seen as never before. "Therefore the law is slacked, and judgment doth never go forth: for the wicked doth compass about the righteous; therefore wrong judgment proceedeth" (v. 4). Holy eyes see the righteous drowning, overwhelmed by the voice of untruth emitted from the unrighteous. Unholy voices drown out the effectiveness of the righteous and their efforts to challenge sin and wrong. The one genuinely called of God to ministry will always become a partaker of a similar understanding as Habakkuk experienced. Habakkuk saw the unholy in a growing clarity, shrinking from the wrong because he was being drawn to the holy.

## THE HABAKKUK EXPERIENCE:
## VISION AND PURPOSE

As the prophet accepted the ministry and purpose of heart to deal with this burden as a yielded vessel, he prayerfully sought the Lord. God caused him to hear His inner voice while seeing. The Lord will always expose His heart and the struggle He has with a rebellious humanity to His people and ministry. He speaks to all who earnestly seek Him. God has always struggled with the sinful state of man and the pain of having sinful man disregard righteousness and His person: "And God saw that the wickedness of man was great in the earth, and that every imagination of the thoughts of his heart was only evil continually. And it repented the Lord that he had made man on the earth, and it grieved him at his heart" (Gen. 6:5–6).

God continually sees: "The eyes of the Lord run to and fro throughout the whole earth, to shew himself strong in the behalf of them whose heart is perfect toward him" (2 Chron. 16:9).

God faces man with a question: "Thus saith the Lord, What iniquity have your fathers found in me, that they are gone far from me, and have walked after vanity, and are become vain?" (Jer. 2:5).

Sinful man desires to be the god of self, denying the first commandment. Those genuinely called of God see God's heart calling out for sons and daughters. They preach the Lord's message of truth balanced with grace. The religious professional clergy only see God's laws. They preach a "must and be" message, believing themselves to have obtained salvation by works, not understanding the grace offered through faith to them and all who believe.

Habakkuk was dismayed by what he saw and cried out to God in passionate prayer. He appealed to the heavens with a holy and righteous pursuit: "How long shall I cry and you will not hear?" He did not realize that the Lord did hear.

The Lord was preparing His messenger for being sent to address the matter. Are we burdened enough to address man's inequity all around us? Do we hear and see? Are we ready to go with God's message? This is the required response to accept and answer the call of God!

Following this, Habakkuk determined to accurately know the purpose for his life—how he could bring righteousness to the wrong observed. The prophet engaged in an intense endeavor of seeking. He determined to know God's purpose for his future, to hear God's direction for ministry. We should likewise respond.

Habakkuk did four things in preparation with a strong and needed determination to hear from God. We also need this type of resolve in order to hear. All called ministry can learn from the man who sought God: "I will stand upon my watch, and set me upon the tower, and will watch to see what he will say unto me, and what I shall answer when I am reproved" (Hab. 2:1). Here are the four things Habakkuk determined to do:

1. I will stand upon my watch.

2. I will set me upon the tower.

3. I will watch to see what God will say unto me.

4. I will determine beforehand what I shall answer when I am reproved.

The result to this model seeking was, "And the LORD answered me" (v. 2).

Habakkuk heard. He then gained holy directions for his future ministry. What did the struggling prophet determine to do that brought heaven's response and voice to his ear?

## 1. I will stand upon my watch.

My watch and watchmen are prepared by the Lord's speaking. God told Ezekiel what watchmen are to do: "Son of man, I have made thee a watchman unto the house of Israel: therefore hear the word at my mouth, and give them warning from me. When I say unto the wicked, Thou shalt surely die; and thou givest him not warning, nor speakest to warn the wicked from his wicked way, to save his life; the same wicked man shall die in his iniquity; but his blood will I require at thine hand" (Ezek. 3:17–18).

Habakkuk determined to observe where the enemy was potentially entering into his life. He did a self-inspection as to his person and walk before God as he defined "my watch."

## 2. I will set me upon the tower.

Our Lord Jesus taught about the value of a tower: "Hear another parable: There was a certain householder, which planted a vineyard, and hedged it round about, and dug a winepress in it, and *built a tower*" (Matt. 21:33, emphasis added). The tower was a defensive observation post from which he observed robbers or destructive animals: "Take us the foxes, the little foxes, that spoil the vines: for our vines have tender grapes" (Song of Sol. 2:15). Wise vineyard owners will construct towers as well. Wise ministries will ascend and spend time there to observe their vineyard with diligence.

Habakkuk said, "I will set me upon my tower. I will see where the enemy may be spoiling my holiness walk and wherever I have allowed him to defile my person or fruit. I will find the little foxes, the small issues of wrong in my life that have allowed damage to the tender grapes and fruit of my God given ministry, hindering a maturity of harvest."

### 3. I will watch to see what God will say unto me.

I am going to listen. My ear is now focused to hear from the Lord. He is my God! All other voices must be silent! Only His voice will be tolerated! I determine to block all voices but His Majesty's voice! I am a bondservant. He has pierced my ear so that I only hear and follow His voice. I am fastened to His abode, and entering in, there will I dwell. "And if the servant shall plainly say, I love my master, my wife, and my children; I will not go out free: Then his master shall bring him unto the judges; he shall also bring him to the door, or unto the door post; and his master shall bore his ear through with an aul; and he shall serve him for ever" (Exod. 21:5–6).

Habakkuk said, "My ear has been pierced to hear one frequency, my Lord and master's voice."

### 4. I will determine beforehand what I shall answer when I am reproved.

I will prepare my mind in surrender and worship so that I will have a ready answer that will be appropriate to my Lord's voice when He speaks. When He calls, I will say, "Speak, Lord," as Samuel did when God called him (1 Sam. 3:10). I will answer Him as an obedient servant in humility, regardless of what He asks of me.

Here we see the heart of faith. God will speak when I prepare myself to hear: "Draw nigh to God, and he will draw nigh to you. Cleanse your hands, ye sinners; and purify your hearts, ye double minded" (James 4:8).

We see the humility of servanthood in the statement "when I am reproved." Habakkuk acknowledged God's Lordship. I always expect God to correct and reprove me when He speaks. I glory in His wisdom. "For as the heavens are higher than the earth, so are my ways higher than your ways, and my thoughts than your thoughts" (Isa. 55:9). I am thrilled by His wisdom, holiness, and being. I love His ways and holiness, and I thrill at His correction, which will always be leading me into an alignment to His person and ways. I love His love, His person, and His ways.

## RESULTS OF PREPARATION

God spoke as a result of this preparation. David and Isaiah understood this truth, having been tested by adversity and coming through to a victorious life of worship and becoming men after God's heart, despite of the failures of humanity: "But they that wait upon the LORD shall renew their strength; they shall mount up with wings as eagles; they shall run, and not be weary; and they shall walk, and not faint" (Isa. 40:31). The Lord gave direction to Habakkuk:

> And the LORD answered me, and said, Write the vision, and make it plain upon tables, that he may run that readeth it.

Our memories will fail us. We should write down what God speaks to us. His words are golden and are meant to be engraved upon our hearts. Value them. Ponder them.

When the Lord speaks, the directions given are usually for a future happening. Usually there is a time of preparation required for us to come to the intended, promised future walk. Many "hear" correctly but never attain to the promised word or directions given. Like Israel of old, many start in their escape from Egypt, but few reach the Promised Land because of their unbelief:

> For some, when they had heard, did provoke: howbeit not all that came out of Egypt by Moses. But with whom was he grieved forty years? was it not with them that had sinned, whose carcasses fell in the wilderness? And to whom sware he that they should not enter into his rest, but to them that believed not? So we see that they could not enter in because of unbelief.
>
> —HEBREWS 3:16–19

The believing will hear and prepare…hear and prepare…hear and prepare.

## ATTAINING THE PROMISE

Ministry must start by doing the immediate shown tasks. We see and minister to the needs we are aware of, whatever they may be. In time, as we wait upon the Lord while obediently walking before Him, the waiting ones will receive an increased vision of what they are to accomplish. One may start with witnessing to a brother or neighbor but in time grow to have a vision, seeing the need to have a church with premises or to evangelize the masses.

Habakkuk was admonished to wait for this promised holy vision, which was now written down, to come into life experience and reality: "For the vision is yet for an appointed time, but at the end it shall speak, and not lie: though it tarry, wait for it; because it will surely come, it will not tarry. Behold, his soul which is lifted up is not upright in him: but the just shall live by his faith" (Hab. 2:3–4).

Faith in God's Word, whether read or imparted by Holy Spirit–revelation, will guarantee the promised results. Faith in the promise will always be demonstrated by preparing for the promise. This waiting on the given word to mature does not mean one should just patiently sit and wait, doing nothing. Rather, the believing hearer will expect this word to happen. He will be busy in preparation while waiting for the fulfillment of this word: "Study to shew thyself approved unto God, a workman that needeth not to be ashamed, rightly dividing the word of truth" (2 Tim. 2:15). Those who heed the promised word and vision will experience "an appointed time."

The directive to Habakkuk to wait upon the vision speaks to focus. We are to consecrate time expenditure with constant preparation. The Hebrew word rendered as "wait" means "adhere to, tarry for it, bc pierced through." Those who receive the call of God must respond with faith. The faith spoken of here, the faith that "the just shall live by," is acted out by taking this vision direction into our hearts. The result will be measurable. This faith will be demonstrated by activity exerted toward preparation for the task.

This waiting involves the practice of hearing with the "pierced" ear, by absorbing God's Word. Faith causes action. A ministry will be limited in experiencing the Holy Spirit bringing all things to remembrance if they do not "eat the roll written within and without." (See Ezekiel 2; 3.) God's Word, when quickened by the Holy Spirit, will be alive. It is He who quickens portions of this scroll. This will be a *rhema*, a living word for God's message to man. If we have not eaten the roll, the Holy Spirit has little within us to bring to remembrance: "But the Comforter, which is the Holy Ghost, whom the Father will send in my name, he shall teach you all things, and bring all things to your remembrance, whatsoever I have said unto you" (John 14:26). The more we digest the Word, the more He has to draw from within us.

Noah did not simply believe in the coming flood the Lord revealed to him. Noah acted upon the shown vision. He built an ark and was ready for it. The one who is "pierced" by the given vision will prepare for it to take place. God always changes the seeing and hearing one. The one who receives the vision will believe for it to come to pass, even if a great amount of time goes by. David, who mightily achieved and overcame, said, "Though the Lord be high, yet hath he respect unto the lowly: but the proud he knoweth afar off. Though I walk in the midst of trouble, thou wilt revive me: thou shalt stretch forth thine hand against the wrath of mine enemies, and thy right hand shall save me. The Lord will perfect that which concerneth me: thy mercy, O Lord, endureth for ever" (Ps. 138:6–8).

The Lord changes and prepares the hearing one. The called are not qualified in themselves. God qualifies, perfects, and matures the called ones.

## KINGDOM VISION MINISTRY

We see the examples of vision throughout Scripture by differing ministries. Paul was moved by seeing with apostle eyes:

> Now while Paul waited for them at Athens, his spirit was stirred in him, when he saw the city wholly given to idolatry. Therefore disputed he in the synagogue with the Jews, and with the devout persons, and in the market daily with them that met with him.
>
> —ACTS 17:16–17

His seeing a city lost in idolatry brought out the preacher in the man. The seeing caused a "therefore." This "therefore he disputed" was due to seeing that the city needed to be changed, and if he did not initiate debate to declare truth, change would not happen.

We see the same in the example ministry of our Lord: "And seeing the multitudes, he went up into a mountain: and when he was set, his disciples came unto him: And he opened his mouth, and taught them, saying, Blessed are the poor in spirit: for theirs is the kingdom of heaven" (Matt. 5:1–3). He saw the needs of the masses and their potential for change. He responded to this, seeing with a heart of compassion, and began to teach.

On another occasion our Lord said, "Go ye, and tell that fox, Behold, I cast out devils, and I do cures to day and to morrow, and the third day I shall be perfected....Oh Jerusalem, Jerusalem, which killest the prophets, and stonest them that are sent unto thee; how often would I have gathered thy children together, as a hen doth gather her brood under her wings, and ye would not!" (Luke 13:32, 34). Jesus saw the multitudes as well as the purpose for His earthly journey. He knew that on the third day He would be perfected, our holy High Priest risen from the dead. We, the called ministry, must always have a vision of eternity and our perfection after death. Eyes of vision are eyes that see all that happens through a lens of eternity. Christ saw beyond the cross when He spoke of the third day. The called ministry who see our third day will gather all they can. With joy they will bring their harvest to heaven's gates.

Ministry vision may start with small beginnings, but vision grows as we enter into it and succeed with what is before us. Believe the vision. Wait and prepare for it. Look for the Lord's opening and guidance to achieve the vision by His hand. A young Christian rightly corrected me after I had spoken about the material cares of life. I had said that you cannot take anything with you to heaven and eternity. He respectfully corrected me with, "You can take another soul!" That is vision.

God, the Lord of the universe, has a divine plan. All ministry must have a kingdom vision. This plan is salvation and an eternity with Jesus for all who accept and embrace Christ's atonement for personal sins. We must see God's purpose and vision. True ministry vision will always enter into His vision.

Our righteous God in mercy determined to redeem believers from sin. God knew those who would seek out His mercy and forgiveness. He is building His church: "I will build my church; and the gates of hell shall not prevail against it" (Matt. 16:18). This is His heart. Hell's gates will be forced open. The prisoners will be released by hearing the gospel. We minister from seeing this. The apostle Peter was one of the foundation stones used in this building. All of the apostles and genuinely called prophets are foundation stones, per Holy Writ (Eph. 2:20).

Our destiny is written and culminates in: "Then we which are alive and remain shall be caught up together with them in the clouds, to meet the Lord in the air: and so shall we ever be with the Lord" (1 Thess. 4:17).

Truly knowing this tremendous vision plan and promise births ministry vision in the ministry. This makes all other priorities fade. We the church are destined to be His bride: "And I John saw the holy city, new Jerusalem, coming down from God out of heaven, prepared as a bride adorned for her husband" (Rev. 21:2).

Ministry vision is seeing the plan of God, a plan formulated before the foundation of the world: "Who verily was foreordained before the foundation of the world, but was manifest in these last times for you" (1 Pet. 1:20). This plan is eternal. Ministry vision has eyes of eternity! Temporal matters fade in the light of this plan because of this vision. We are told important truth by Solomon, applicable to both the saved and unsaved: "Where there is no vision, the people perish; but he who keepeth the law, happy is he" (Prov. 29:18). We see and keep God's ways because of our eternal focus and vision.

How many men and women have personal problems in life because they have no vision? Many do not attempt to improve themselves, their lives, or environment because of this. How many marriages are torn and struggle because neither spouse has a vision? Their marriages and lives are destroyed because they have no vision of a brighter future or possibility thinking. No plan of action is formulated to strive for. This truth is central in a minister's life. A genuine Christ-appointed ministry, while prayerfully waiting on the Lord, will always receive a kingdom vision. We will act because of our vision.

## Born of the Spirit: Kingdom Purpose

We need to preach and teach about the kingdom of God. Our Lord came with a specific message. He continually taught about the kingdom of God, and we need to understand what He taught. Our Savior taught this topic in depth. The kingdom of God is not an earthly kingdom: "Jesus answered, My kingdom is not of this world: if my kingdom were of this world, then would my servants fight, that I should not be delivered to the Jews: but now is my kingdom not from hence" (John 18:36). The kingdom of God does not deal with natural substance, "for the kingdom of God is not meat and drink, but righteousness, and peace, and joy in the Holy Ghost" (Rom. 14:17).

God's kingdom is immersed in absolute righteousness and moral holiness. Seeking and entering His kingdom will result in peace and joy by the work of the Holy Spirit. We are spirit beings inhabiting a body with a soul made up of mind, will, and emotions. God deals with the real us, the real spirit man within, both now and in eternity (1 Thess. 5:23). He constantly focuses on our alignment—His Spirit with our spirit, resulting in righteous reverence and fellowship with our God. We will have perfect direction and peace within as a result of this alignment. In heaven there will be no contentions, division, or debate. There will be perfect unity. There will be no disunity due to limited understanding and lacking love. The soul who is walking in kingdom truth and principles will experience kingdom blessings in this world.

The kingdom of God may seem to be insignificant to some for this time, due to seeing with only the natural eye. However, the truth is, Christ's kingdom will become the only existing kingdom in eternity (Mark 13:31; Rev. 11:15).

Daniel was shown a prophetic vision of the times of man depicted by a statue. The statue depicted four now historic empires, ending with imperialism and democracy coexisting but never joining, as proven by the last seventeen hundred years. (See Daniel 2:43–45.) In this vision the stone that was made without human hands but was made by the works of God ended all other kingdoms: "And in the days of these kings shall the God of heaven set up a kingdom, which shall never be destroyed: and the kingdom shall not be left to other people, but it shall break in pieces and consume all these kingdoms, and it shall stand for ever" (v. 44).

The works of man are always contaminated by sin. Hands always speak of our works throughout the Bible. Dagon, the god of the Philistines, was altered by the hand of God to speak to all who saw this: "And when they arose early on the morrow morning, behold, Dagon was fallen upon his face to the ground before the ark of Lord; and the head of Dagon and both the palms of his hands were cut off upon the threshold; only the stump of Dagon was left to him" (1 Sam. 5:4). Dagon's head, his determinations and thoughts, were shown to be severed with no power. The palms of his hands were removed, showing his inability to perform any works. A useless and disabled stump remained due to God's presence. Our God will destroy this world and all of man's works as well: "But the day of the Lord will come as a thief in the night; in the which the heavens shall pass away with a great noise, and the elements shall melt with fervent heat, the earth also and the works that are therein shall be burned up" (2 Pet. 3:10). This is followed with Christ making all things new: "And he that sat upon the throne said, Behold, I make all things new. And he said unto me, Write: for these words are true and faithful" (Rev. 21:5; see also 2 Pet. 3:13).

Our God reigns.

## GLORIOUS TREASURE VISION

Lastly, of the many kingdom teachings our Lord taught, there is a profound truth understood by those who have tasted thereof.

> Again, the kingdom of heaven is like unto treasure hid in a field; the which when a man hath found, he hideth, and for joy thereof goeth and selleth all that he hath, and buyeth that field. Again, the kingdom of heaven is like unto a merchant man, seeking goodly

pearls: Who, when he had found one pearl of great price, went and sold all that he had, and bought it.

—MATTHEW 13:44–46

The called ministry must respond by buying the field due to the value they have placed on it. Our ministry will demonstrate the value we have placed on the kingdom pearl.

The kingdom of God involves Christ's eternal future reign with His church. His church is made up of people drawn from islands, tribes, and nations (Rev. 5:9). Those who love Christ are not satisfied with simply knowing His history. They will sell all, altering their life pursuits and making kingdom pursuits the first priority in their lives. They will always be salvation conscious when ministering to people. They seek His kingdom glory.

We minister because He is GLORIOUS!

## CHAPTER THREE

# EZEKIEL'S VISION,
# A MUST REVELATION
# FOR ALL MINISTRIES

*Holy Encounter, Ministry Preparation*

*T*HE DIVINE REVELATION of God, His holy glory, revealed to Ezekiel is a minister's lifetime food for learning and teaching. In his first chapter Ezekiel briefly shares with us his circumstances. This is immediately followed by him sharing an intense, detailed, holy and profound divine vision. This vision is for us as well as Ezekiel. We, like Ezekiel, are to note the timing of this vision. It was given in preparation and just prior to the Lord calling Ezekiel to the office of a prophet, God's ordained spokesman.

The seeing of this vision contained the first priority knowledge and understanding that God determined to be necessary for Ezekiel. This vision was a graduate course requirement for the future ministry work to be undertaken. This required understanding must be understood by all who consider ministry before our God. The revelation within this vision portrayed holy insight, which defines the foundation of understanding that should exist between the ministry and God. This vision was given for ministry preparation and insight that the Lord of heaven and earth wanted Ezekiel to know. This was prior to Ezekiel's eating the roll, God's Word and prior to God directing him to his appointed ministry field.

We should study the poetic pictorial meanings of this vision. We must find what insight our Lord intended for Ezekiel and us to gain from this divine presentation and holy encounter. One can be sure that Ezekiel spent many hours weighing the meaning of what the Lord intended to portray. I imagine that Ezekiel's desire to understand all that was depicted can be equated to Nebuchadnezzar's struggling with the vision of the great statue, the result being "his sleep brake from him" (Dan. 2:1).

Our God does nothing without divine purpose. This holy vision was written for all ministry-minded people. We must search out and understand the truths depicted. I cannot overstate this observation.

This God-given vision showed creatures, wheels, and the creatures' activities. These were a demonstration of perfection in ministry. This is a God-given demonstration as to how God expects His ministers to function and conduct themselves. As we ponder this heavenly presentation, we will conclude this provides a glimpse into the reality and answered prayer within His servants, "Thy kingdom come. Thy will be done in earth, as it is in heaven" (Matt. 6:10).

Consider the order of events of God's dealings with Ezekiel. He received this divine confronting vision in chapter 1. In chapter 2 this was followed with being told he was to be sent as God's chosen vessel, an ambassador to God's people. This was followed by the command to "eat this roll" in chapter 3. This vision with holy revelation preceded the calling notification and preparation instructions. It has a priority message.

All who believe that they, like Ezekiel, are called to ministry must digest this vision as well as the roll. Understanding this vision will prepare any called ministry person with a much deeper maturity of insight as to worship, attitude, and holy servanthood.

The directive and prophetic meaning of eating the roll written within and without is not difficult to understand. (Ezek. 3:1). The roll is filled from cover to cover with lamentations and mournings. These writings depict the love of God for man fallen into sin, His plan for redemption, and the pain of man's rebellious not seeking our righteous and holy Creator. We must study ourselves to be approved unto God (2 Tim. 2:15). In so doing we learn of God's righteousness, His history of dealing with man from Creation, and what our future and eternity hold. This study is not a casual matter but an intense absorption of God's holy writings by holy men of old moved upon by the Holy Ghost (2 Pet. 1:21).

The scriptural portrayal of Ezekiel's vision is part of what Paul wrote to Timothy: "All scripture is given by inspiration of God, and is profitable for doctrine, for reproof, for correction, for instruction in righteousness" (2 Tim. 3:16).

The writings within God's Word are a love letter from heaven. Our Creator reveals His deepest heart's desire with us, His created. His letter chronicles His broken heart. These writings include lamentations, mourning, the woe that is to come, and the future reality resulting from sin and death. God boldly states His love for us, including the great promises to those who love and seek Him. His roll also speaks of the judgments awaiting those who despise, ignore, and reject Him.

I will attempt to point out a number of holy depictions from Ezekiel chapters 1 and 2, but I doubt if any man could gain the entire insight. The vision and statements depicted are simply a God-sized grandeur.

## DIVINE ORDER TO THE CALLED

Note the four steps and the order of the steps Ezekiel experienced, which are the common order for God's ministry sending.

1. Revelation of God's glory and salvation

2. Being called to ministry, receiving this directive for our lives

3. Preparing for this sending, attaining wisdom and knowledge

4. Being released by God's hand under His direction

When reading Ezekiel, we start with a holy revelation of Almighty God, His kingdom and authority in chapter 1. We progress to preparation and Ezekiel's God-ordained commission, his mandate to speak on God's behalf to the people of Israel.

At the end of chapter 2 we read of the double directive: Do not be rebellious, and eat the roll in preparation.

> But thou, son of man, hear what I say unto thee; Be not thou rebellious like that rebellious house: open thy mouth, and eat that I give thee. And when I looked, behold, an hand was sent unto me; and, lo, a roll of a book was therein; and he spread it before me; and it was written within and without: and there was written therein lamentations, and mourning, and woe.
>
> —Ezekiel 2:8–10

Many enter into ministry with a presumptive rebellion. They run while not digesting the roll and before they are sent by God. Mature ministry continually digests this roll.

If we have seen God's love, glorious power, and truth, our response should be an overflowing desire to share what He has shown us with those to whom He sends us. We must prepare ourselves with the knowledge of His person and heart. God admonishes the called ministry not to be rebellious like those He is sending them to. Rebelliousness is squelched when we digest His Word. This preparation is by chewing on and digesting the knowledge of God—not just memorizing the Word, but knowing Him, His faithfulness and holy heart. Absorbing His Word, the roll written within and without, should result in more than history and Bible knowledge. All knowledge should lead to a living, experiential relationship, resulting in experiencing God presence!

This absorbing requires waiting upon God and allowing the work of the Holy Spirit within us to bring understanding and revelation. (See Hebrews 5:14.) Obedience is worship, recognizing Christ's Lordship: "So I opened my mouth, and he caused me to eat that roll. And he said unto me, Son of man, cause thy belly to eat, and fill thy bowels with this roll that I give thee. Then did I eat it; and it was in my mouth as honey for sweetness" (Ezek. 3:2–3). Following the digestion of God's given roll, His Word, the sending order came: "And he said unto me, Son of man, go, get thee unto the house of Israel, and speak with my words unto them" (v. 4). Some were sent, and some just went.

## THE MAN

Ezekiel begins his writings with a precise dating of his people and events. He was an observant man. His presence of mind and awareness caused him to reflect on the larger picture of his circumstances and the history involved. Others simply looked at the immediate while groaning and moaning, absorbed by looking at personal need and limitations.

The same applies today. Some will seek to understand the history of how we got to where we are now. Others simply focus on the immediate problem facing us. Salvation comes to those who weigh the bigger picture. Ezekiel sought the Lord with an onslaught of prayer, knowing that Almighty God knew all about this state of captivity and why it was. God always answers the seeking. Ezekiel stormed the heavens, praying, "O Lord, why are we here? Why are You not delivering us from our circumstances? What can we do to be granted mercy and be delivered from this bondage?"

Ezekiel's focus was on God in order to receive the answer to prayer. The Lord showed him how the nation could achieve peace, prosperity, and deliverance from their bondage. Moses had this same desire and was answered when God appeared to him.

Someone who understood the answers to captivity problems needed to tell Israel the truth, leading them into God's marvelous liberty and blessings. You and I who have sought and found the answers are likewise commissioned by Christ. We need to tell the world of His salvation, which is freely received through faith in the Lamb of God. Tell them the only way to liberty. Man must give Him His rightful place as Lord, Creator, and Redeemer. This is the key truth for setting captives free. (See Isaiah 61:1; John 8:32.)

Humility marked the entrance of Ezekiel onto the stage of life in God's servant program. Ezekiel simply writes, "I was among the captives by the river Chebar" (Ezek. 1:1). He made no claim to any special virtue, status of person, spirituality, or heritage. He simply said, "I was a captive by my captors among my people." There was no pretense of grandeur of person. We can learn from this bearing.

Ezekiel was in a very humble setting, just as many other called ministries can relate to. David was as a shepherd boy. Most of us were in a humble environment when the Lord first revealed Himself to us. We were captives in bondage to the slave masters of sin with no hope but God. When we are at the end of self, we are near the door of life, and we thus enable our God to begin.

## The Revelation

Ezekiel in brief said, "I saw visions of God." The amazing fact is that an encounter such as this is available to any and all, for God is not a respecter of persons and meets all who draw nigh unto Him (Acts 10:34; James 4:8). However, there are prerequisites, and Ezekiel most certainly met these for God to reveal Himself in such a unique manner. Our Lord said, "Ask, and it shall be given you; seek, and ye shall find; knock, and it shall be opened unto you" (Matt. 7:7). In the darkness of this difficult bondage Ezekiel found light and liberty. By God's awesome revealed person and grace his chains fell off, albeit his natural location had not changed. When you and I call upon and seek Him who delivers us, we will likewise find: "Rejoice not against me, O mine enemy: when I fall, I shall arise; when I sit in darkness, the Lord shall be a light unto me" (Micah 7:8).

By God's mercy Ezekiel saw the brightness of light in the darkness of his circumstances. Likewise we are shown by this Bible chapter a revelation of God's glory, which always interrupts our world of darkness!

## "Expressly" Revelation

In Ezekiel 1:3 we find this notable statement: "The word of the Lord came expressly unto Ezekiel the priest, the son of Buzi, in the land of the Chaldeans by the river Chebar; and the hand of the Lord was there upon him." This revelation came "expressly" to Ezekiel and not to others. God is always looking through the crowds for that unique individual who is humbly seeking His face to reveal Himself to with divine purpose: "For the eyes of the Lord run to and fro throughout the whole earth, to shew himself strong in the behalf of them whose heart is perfect toward him" (2 Chron. 16:9). One must desire a heart that is perfect toward our God and thus prepare the soil of their heart to receive holy revelation. This "expressly" revelation is in denial to and of all others. The Lord of glory sees and knows who can carry His message. He sees the hearts of all men.

To be called of God to ministry is of a higher order of honor than any other.

We must understand that Nobel Prizes and Hollywood accolades pale compared to the sunshine and honor of being ambassadors of the holy. We are ministers of Christ, His person and kingdom. (See Romans 8:18; 11:36; 2 Corinthians 4:17.)

## Out of the North

Ezekiel 1:4 states, "Behold, a whirlwind came out of the north, a great cloud, and a fire infolding itself." God left His holy throne to reveal Himself to Ezekiel. He left His holy city for this divine encounter with this waiting and praying man to impart a divine revelation. Ezekiel was to be God's voice and message bearer to the most difficult people for him to address, his well-known fellow man.

We know the source and location of the city our God traveled from. His throne is in the heavenly Mount Zion: "Great is the Lord, and greatly to be praised in the city of our God, in the mountain of his holiness 2 Beautiful for situation, the joy of the whole earth, is mount Zion, on the sides of the north, the city of the great King" (Ps. 48:1–2; see also Heb. 12:22).

The glorious thought is that the holy God of the universe will meet with man such as you and me. What an honor to have our Lord visit and reveal His heart and purposes by revealing His person and glory! God always watches all matters on earth, whether in day or night hours (Ps. 139:2, 12). What an outstanding, glorious consideration of insight when we catch a glimpse of heaven's response to Stephen's stoning. The Son of God, seated at the right hand of the Father (Acts 2:34), arose to His feet due to the outstanding response by Stephen at his martyr's death. This brought heaven to its feet: "[Stephen] said, Behold, I see the heavens opened, and the Son of man standing on the right hand of God" (Acts 7:56). God sees and acts; He responds to our actions. David said, "Thou tellest my wanderings: Put thou my tears into thy bottle: are they not in thy book?" (Ps. 56:8).

Whatever we are doing and wherever we are, our God knows. His love discerns our hearts.

## The Revelation Vision: Fire

All of the depictions and components of Ezekiel's vision are a message of learning with distinct purpose to the called man of God.

One needs to understand, "It is the glory of God to conceal a thing: but the honour of kings is to search out a matter" (Prov. 25:2). We are a royal priesthood and kings (1 Pet. 2:9; Rev. 1:6). We need to search out visions—God's veiled speaking by dreams and words. Our Lord Jesus explained what our privileges are when He explained the purpose for veiled communications while teaching in parables. "And the disciples came, and said unto him, Why speakest thou unto them in parables? He answered and said unto them, Because it is given unto you to know the mysteries of the kingdom of heaven, but to them it is not given" (Matt. 13:10–11). It is our duty and privilege to seek out the mysteries of God-revealed dreams, visions, and pictures.

God revealed Himself as a fire and a cloud. He revealed Himself to Israel in their desert journey in as a shade by day and a light in the darkness of night.

The cloud, or Christ, in the wilderness was darkness to the Egyptian enemies of righteousness yet light to those whom our Lord was separating from bondage. "And it came between the camp of the Egyptians and the camp of Israel; and it was a cloud and darkness to them, but it gave light by night to these: so that the one came not near the other all the night" (Exod. 14:20; see also 1 Cor. 10:4). Likewise for us. We see when we escape from a life of sin by His light. Egyptians only see by accepting Christ.

Jesus is the light of the world: "As long as I am in the world, I am the light of the world" (John 9:5). He has commissioned us as His ministers to be a reflection of His light: "Ye are the light of the world" (Matt. 5:14).

God's appearance as fire is also a declaration of warning and authority to mankind, which all would do well to observe: "For our God is a consuming fire" (Heb. 12:29). The Lord our God is a jealous God, and He wants all, not part of us. He demands our all just as He gave His all for us to become His bride. Our God is patient and long-suffering but also very direct in dealings and actions. He is more real and even too real for many people. He is a God of judgment and wrath toward all who deny Him and do not seek Him: "He that believeth on the Son hath everlasting life: and he that believeth not the Son shall not see life; but the wrath of God abideth on him" (John 3:36).

God is holy and the perfection of wisdom and knowledge. There is no indecision or "let me think about it" with Him. He always assesses all matters with instant perfection of understanding. The picture here is of a fire constantly enfolding itself. Fire is unique in that it determines the basic and real qualities of matter.

> But who may abide the day of his coming? and who shall stand when he appeareth? for he is like a refiner's fire, and like fullers' soap: And he shall sit as a refiner and purifier of silver: and he shall purify the sons of Levi, and purge them as gold and silver, that they may offer unto the LORD an offering in righteousness.
>
> —MALACHI 3:2–3

This rolling inward and enfolding fire continuously demonstrates the purifying nature of the holiness of God. This enfolding is comparable to the wheel within a wheel (which I will discuss in more detail shortly).

## MINISTRY REVELATION: THE FOUR CREATURES

These creatures are a demonstration of holy ministry and a pictorial perfection of worship and relationship to the one enthroned above their heads. We read that the creatures came forth from the fire and throne of God: "Also out of the midst thereof came the likeness of four living creatures.

And this was their appearance; they had the likeness of a man. And every one had four faces, and every one had four wings" (Ezek. 1:5–6).

"Out of the midst thereof" speaks of God's creation, His authorship of all creation and creatures. He creates all living entities, for in Him is life. "All things were made by him; and without him was not any thing made that was made. In him was life; and the life was the light of men" (John 1:3–4).

Four is a number demonstrating completion. Hence we have forty years of testing in the wilderness. We know the rain of the flood of Noah's day was forty days (Gen. 7:12). This number also depicts our God as the completion of all that exists by what comes forth from Him. "Thus saith the Lord the King of Israel, and his redeemer the Lord of hosts; I am the first, and I am the last; and beside me there is no God" (Isa. 44:6).

The creatures had the likeness of man, with holy endowed characteristics, depicted by four faces. Here we see the poetic portrayal of prophetic visions, communicating in a manner that we can understand. All the four faces are of His created beings, which we on earth can relate to. Hear as God speaks by visions.

Our God will only surround Himself by those who acknowledge His rightful and glorious power. The rebellious know not His authority. God is the Creator, and we are the created. We are challenged to be like these creatures in attitude and demeanor. They gave perfection of sinless honor, obedience, and worship in their every action.

Ezekiel's vision was a graphic picture of what the matured ministry should be and act like in an attitude of worship. These creatures were under God's firmament on which He is enthroned. Some of those who have gone before us are in the same proximity to the throne of God as the creatures. They loved not their lives unto death, esteeming His person, honor, and glory as greater than their lives. "And they overcame him by the blood of the Lamb, and by the word of their testimony; and they loved not their lives unto the death" (Rev. 12:11). They loved Him, giving their all. Our God holds them intimately and immediately next to Himself. "And when he had opened the fifth seal, I saw under the altar the souls of them that were slain for the word of God, and for the testimony which they held" (Rev. 6:9).

These creatures are also called cherubims in Ezekiel 10:1. They are depicted with the throne directly over their heads as in Ezekiel 1:26. This is a proper God and cherub or God and man relationship. They are a depiction of God's creation under His authority, nature, and being.

### The man

We see the likeness of a man, a holy man in perfection as he was created in the image of God. Only man was created in God's image. We see God's desire to fellowship with man in the depiction of these creatures, just as He fellowshipped with Adam in the cool of the garden, and just as He did with Enoch, who "walked with God: and he was not; for God took him" (Gen. 5:24).

These "creatures" constantly ministered to the Lord, who created them. They ministered with distinct qualities that all ministries should desire to possess and function with as acts of continual worship. All who worship Him in ministry desire Him to be seen and glorified. We desire no glory for ourselves, only His. He is our Father, and holy is His name. His is the kingdom, power, and glory.

### The lion

Lions speak of reigning authority and kingship. This lion face speaks of Christ's power and rule in all matters of life. He is the Lion of Judah. We must possess godly humility in our reigning with Christ, as we are seated with Him in heavenly places. We walk in power and authority, balanced with humility, under God's love and grace toward mankind. "And hath raised us up together, and made us sit together in heavenly places in Christ Jesus" (Eph. 2:6). We must grow to know who we are in Christ. He is our reigning Lord!

### The ox

The nature of the ox speaks of ceaseless and patient burden bearing and works. The ox will patiently work fields in the heat of the sun to accomplish what his master desires. Oxen tend to be strong yet gentle in nature. They patiently and faithfully perform their master's will. May we demonstrate this tireless, faithful, servant heart, prostrating ourselves before our Lord in continuous worship. This becomes clear and less difficult to understand when we observe what the seraphims see while hovering above God's throne. They continuously repeated what they saw. "And one cried unto another, and said, Holy, holy, holy, is the Lord of hosts: the whole earth is full of his glory" (Isa. 6:3).

The seraphims saw unending layers of glory...realms of holiness, with continuous praise and adoration as the result. They in worship understood the realm of holiness, which is righteousness drenched in love.

## The eagle

This face speaks of the ability to attain great heights riding above storms and turbulence. From these heights the eagle has the ability to see with detailed insight. We also are called to rise above the threat of life's turbulence and storms when we are trusting in our God! We are also called to mount up and rise, discerning with wisdom and seeing life from a heavenly perspective.

May we, the ministry of God, attain unto this needed strength, for "they that wait upon the Lord shall renew their strength; they shall mount up with wings as eagles; they shall run, and not be weary; and they shall walk, and not faint" (Isa. 40:31). We must soar high and seek the heavenly kingdom. We as eagles are called to arise to high places (2 Sam. 22:34).

## THE DIVIDED CALF'S FOOT

This is a tremendous portrayal, speaking to what determines the ministry's walk.

The split or cleft foot speaks about our separated walk. We are called to a different walk from that of average humanity. We hear and follow God's voice to minister faith and salvation. We follow the beat of a different drummer as we are separated unto the gospel of Christ. We are servants of the Most High as Christ's ministers. "Paul, a servant of Jesus Christ, called to be an apostle, separated unto the gospel of God" (Rom. 1:1).

The divided foot speaks of an awesome truth. Clean animals, those with the divided foot, can attain unto high places. Our Lord desires us to dwell in and attain unto these: "The Lord God is my strength, and he will make my feet like hinds' feet, and he will make me to walk upon mine high places" (Hab. 3:19). These high places are spiritual plains. God-called ministry is to attain unto greater heights, a making of the Lord. They are destined to arise into high places of hearing and seeing in God's presence.

Recently I learned how mountain sheep can "cling" to rocky slopes and climb seemingly impossible high rocky places. They have a rubber-like growth material that can grasp onto hard surfaces. This material is like a grip pad on the bottom of their hoofs. The ministry of God must likewise learn to overcome. One must cling and stand in adversity. We cling to the sure foundation in our walk, which is a God-provided ability. "For thou hast been a strength to the poor, a strength to the needy in his distress, a refuge from the storm, a shadow from the heat, when the blast of the terrible ones is as a storm against the wall" (Isa. 25:4). We must seek His strength.

> And their feet were straight feet; and the sole of their feet was like the sole of a calf's foot: and they sparkled like the colour of burnished brass.
>
> —Ezekiel 1:7

Our feet are the foundation of our walk and goings. As such we read in the Psalm 119:105, "Thy word is a lamp unto my feet, and a light unto my path." We must understand the beauty of the glory we represent. "How beautiful upon the mountains are the feet of him that bringeth good tidings, that publisheth peace; that bringeth good tidings of good, that published salvation; that saith unto Zion, Thy God reigneth!" (Isa. 52:7).

Our feet speak of where we stand and where we are going in the sight of God, our holy creator Lord. As called ministers we will always publish the gospel, the good news of our salvation. The gospel message brings life and beauty, proclaiming the reign of our holy, living God. Our feet are directed to a separated walk, observing the holy, avoiding Sodom and

Lot's destruction. "Blessed is the man that walketh not in the counsel of the ungodly, nor standeth in the way of sinners, nor sitteth in the seat of the scornful" (Ps. 1:1).

Their goings and their paths in this world bring life from death to those who hear. They bring beauty where ashes prevailed, the oil of joy where mourning resided, and the garments of praise where the spirit of heaviness reigned. This is only because of the Spirit of the Lord being upon His called. (See Isaiah 61:1.) His Lordship must be seen in us by a truthful examination of our ministry endeavors.

The calf's foot is a portrayal of the ministry's walk. This speaks loudly since it is the foot of a clean animal. "And every beast that parteth the hoof, and cleaveth the cleft into two claws, and cheweth the cud among the beasts, that ye shall eat" (Deut. 14:6). All clean animals "chew the cud." They eat and store their food intake for "rumination" in a holding tank, their stomach. Then, before ingesting, they regurgitate this food and chew on it, breaking down their food with a slow ruminating process before passing it to the stomach, where the body absorbs the good vitamins, supporting bodily strengths. We are to understand the picture.

Those who minister should eat food in the same manner as a "clean animal" does. The ministry should chew and carefully weigh whatever they ingest—not physical food, but thoughts, knowledge, and truth of righteous issues. We may hear, but we do not receive statements or expressed thoughts without a slow rumination of these. Prior to receiving and storing as approved in our minds, we digest all thoughts and knowledge. We process all intake carefully prior to receiving the input as fact to walk by and to proclaim.

> But I have said to you, Ye shall inherit their land, and I will give it unto you to possess it, a land that floweth with milk and honey. I am the LORD your God, which have separated you from other people. Ye shall therefore put difference between clean beasts and unclean, and between unclean fowls and clean: and ye shall not make your souls abominable by beast, or by fowl, or by any manner

of living thing that creepeth on the ground, which I have separated from you as unclean.

—LEVITICUS 20:24–25

This diet was a continual daily reminder and sermon speaking to God's people.

This was the Old Testament (covenant) pictorial ceremonial law—not the moral ten laws of perfection in love and righteousness. Note that unclean animals make the soul abominable—they defile the soul. We must see the spiritual values here. After Jesus's crucifixion, resurrection, and ascension, Peter was told that these unclean things can now be eaten as food. (See Acts 10:11.) Consider this truth in the light of physical versus spiritual matters. How can physical food defile the soul realm of mind, will, and emotions? This is a prophetic picture of truth that we are to consider and understand. We are to weigh everything by God's Word. "And Jesus answered him, saying, It is written, That man shall not live by bread alone, but by every word of God" (Luke 4:4). The Law and the events that happened to the Jews in their Old Testament desert journey are prophetic pictures. They were constant sermons to them and are sermons for us to understand and preach.

Today this picture is changed as we see Christ crucified. We see Him who became sin that we might become the righteousness of God. We look to the cross and shed blood. Now we preach that all believers must be born of the Spirit, where the Holy Spirit teaches us and leads us into all truth (John 16:13). The New Testament church lives in a different day and with a different message to the world. However, the clean animal sermon still applies as God-given truth for all to consider daily, especially God's called ministry.

Peter had to adjust his thinking after the cross, resurrection, and atonement. The Lord Himself spoke via a vision.

And [Peter] saw heaven opened, and a certain vessel descending unto him, as it had been a great sheet knit at the four corners, and let down to the earth: Wherein were all manner of fourfooted beasts of the earth, and wild beasts, and creeping things, and fowls of the air.

> And there came a voice to him, Rise, Peter; kill, and eat. But Peter said, Not so, Lord; for I have never eaten any thing that is common or unclean. And the voice spoke unto him again the second time, What God hath cleansed, that call not thou common. This was done thrice: and the vessel was received up again into heaven.
>
> —ACTS 10:11–16

As we see in this passage, the sheet lowered to Peter contained unclean animals, such as crab, reptiles, and all manner of creeping things. God directed Peter three times to "rise, kill and eat" of the contents of this lowered sheet. Creeping things and animals that did not have a split hoof were not to be eaten under the Levitical laws, but they are now eatable. By this prophetic vision Peter was shown that Gentiles could now freely partake of the God of Israel and salvation. Peter could visit the uncircumcised Gentile homes, and they could become part of the Israel of God (Acts 10:34). The New Testament converted Gentile church is now clean. They are cleansed by the Lamb of God and are saints, redeemed by the blood.

John the Baptist understood the values and intentions portrayed in the pictures of the ceremonial laws. John ate locusts with honey. Locusts were part of what was previously not allowed. John saw a new day upon identifying Christ as "the Lamb of God" (John 1:29). This ended all of the pictorial lamb slayings in sacrifice. Our Lord verified this when He said, "The law and the prophets were until John: since that time the kingdom of God is preached, and every man presseth into it" (Luke 16:16).

The new day unfolded with the Morning Star arising. Christ ushered in the light of a new day, delivering us from the night of darkness. "I Jesus have sent mine angel to testify unto you these things in the churches. I am the root and the offspring of David, and the bright and morning star" (Rev. 22:16). We who sat under the shadow of death now can live eternally. "The people that walked in darkness have seen a great light: they that dwell in the land of the shadow of death, upon them hath the light shined" (Isa. 9:2).

The commission after Christ's resurrection is to go into all of the world, to every kindred, tribe, and nation. Remember, Peter was told three times to "rise, kill and eat." The triple vision, never mind a doubled vision, meant it was an established fact (Gen. 41:32). The vision contained established and unalterable truth. Because of this truth, you and I are of a certainty grafted into His tree, as He is the tree of life (Rom. 11:17).

The ceremonial laws and prophetic pictures were fulfilled by God's provided Lamb. It's all right to eat your shrimp and crab now. For those who struggle with this, remember that when God spoke, He did not tempt Peter. He told him to "rise, take and eat" whatever is in the sheet. "Let no man say when he is tempted, I am tempted of God: for God cannot be tempted with evil, neither tempteth he any man" (James 1:13).

## THE BRAZEN HOOF

Lastly, the most difficult picture to ingest is the brazen hoof. This separated hoof made of brass speaks loudly. All God-ordained ministry need to face the truth of what this depicts. Then we must say, "Yes, Lord," upon knowing this truth, when we accept our calling.

Brass in the Bible speaks of suffering. Note the brazen altar:

> And thou shalt make the horns of it upon the four corners thereof: his horns shall be of the same: and thou shalt overlay it with brass. And thou shalt make his pans to receive his ashes, and his shovels, and his basons, and his fleshhooks, and his firepans: all the vessels thereof thou shalt make of brass. And thou shalt make for it a grate of network of brass; and upon the net shalt thou make four brasen rings in the four corners thereof.
>
> —EXODUS 27:2–4

Anything that had to do with the holy offered sacrifices was made of brass. Christ our Redeemer portrayed this, with His feet depicted as of brass that had been through the fire. Suffering and the cross are the foundation of His relationship with His beloved church. We who are blessed to be purchased by His redemption blood see this depiction of holy accuracy: "And his feet were like unto fine brass, as if they burned in a furnace" (Rev. 1:15).

Burnished brass, or fine brass, is brightly polished, speaking of perfection. All of Christ in God is the perfection of holiness—He who has the two-edged sword, His Word of righteousness proceeding from His mouth. He holds the churches in His right hand of blessing. In righteousness He has redeemed His church. He determined His path to pass through the trial of fire by the cross (Luke 9:51). He partook of the cup, the baptism of suffering for you and me (Matt. 20:22). His feet, the foundation of His walk, were pierced for us.

Likewise, the matured minister of God will be altered and strengthened by overcoming in life's trials. We are to reflect Christ's love in a world of suffering and death. Jesus our Lord passed through the fire of affliction for us. "For he hath made him to be sin for us, who knew no sin; that we might be made the righteousness of God in him" (2 Cor. 5:21).

We also will endure suffering when engaged in holy ministry before the Lord and not before man and ego-pleasing pursuits.

> If ye continue in the faith grounded and settled, and be not moved away from the hope of the gospel, which ye have heard, and which was preached to every creature which is under heaven; whereof I Paul am made a minister; who now rejoice in my sufferings for you, and fill up that which is behind of the afflictions of Christ in my flesh for his body's sake, which is the church: Whereof I am made a minister, according to the dispensation of God which is given to me for you, to fulfill the word of God.
> —COLOSSIANS 1:23–25

Christ is the brazen serpent lifted up on a pole in the wilderness journey. When we are dying from the effects of the serpent's poison, we become healed as we look to Him. "And Moses made a serpent of brass, and put it upon a pole, and it came to pass, that if a serpent had bitten any man, when he beheld the serpent of brass, he lived" (Num. 21:9).

Christ-appointed ministry will face and endure suffering as a difficult reality of a holy ministry life. We will also experience times where we cannot open our mouths, either in self-defense or explanation (Mark 15:5). When we stand for truth, we will suffer persecution: "Yea, and all that will live godly in Christ Jesus shall suffer persecution. But evil men and seducers shall wax worse and worse, deceiving, and being deceived" (2 Tim. 3:12–13). Some ministries seem not to be partakers of persecution. There is a reason for this. All will someday answer for that reason. Ouch!

We too are called upon to become living sacrifices. We are alive yet offered up on the altar of God's service. "I beseech you therefore, brethren, by the mercies of God, that ye present your bodies a living sacrifice, holy, acceptable unto God, which is your reasonable service" (Rom. 12:1).

Paul and other ministries described in the letters to the churches shared their experiences of trials and sufferings. Paul described his experiences of facing opposition in ministry:

> For I think that God hath set forth us the apostles last, as it were appointed to death: for we are made a spectacle unto the world, and to angels, and to men. We are fools for Christ's sake, but ye are wise in Christ; we are weak, but ye are strong; ye are honourable, but we are despised. Even unto this present hour we both hunger, and thirst, and are naked, and are buffeted, and have no certain dwellingplace; and labour, working with our own hands: being reviled, we bless; being persecuted, we suffer it: Being defamed, we entreat: we are made as the filth of the world, and are the off scouring of all things unto this day. I write not these things to shame you, but as my beloved sons I warn you.
>
> —1 Corinthians 4:9–14

Some modern-day proclaimed apostles may reconsider claiming this calling due to their avoiding the costs commensurate with confrontation. Some who claim this calling mostly want to be held in visible honor by man. Paul confronted error with truth in love: "Therefore I endure all things for the elect's sakes, that they may also obtain the salvation which is in Christ Jesus with eternal glory. It is a faithful saying: For if we be dead with him, we shall also live with him: If we suffer, we shall also reign with him: if we deny him, he also will deny us" (2 Tim. 2:10–12).

## A Separated Walk

The ministry who desires the Lord, His presence, and anointing has a life and walk of worship. This will always include the acceptance of rejection and persecution. That is unavoidable since darkness opposes light. Can you find one Bible minister who did not face this? Yet they gloried in their God-honored relationship. "I beseech you therefore, brethren, by the mercies of God, that ye present your bodies a living sacrifice, holy, acceptable unto God, which is your reasonable service. And be not conformed to this world: but be ye transformed by the renewing of your mind.... We are fools for Christ's sake, but ye are wise in Christ; we are weak, but ye are strong; ye are honourable, but we are despised" (Rom. 12:1–2; 1 Cor. 4:10).

The servant of the Lord will always walk a path that includes suffering. We willingly continue on this path as a walk of worship, having counted the cost, because of the prize and glory set before us. Like Jesus our Lord we face and overcome, because He is our sufficiency, "looking unto Jesus the author and finisher of our faith; who for the joy that was set before him endured the cross, despising the shame, and is set down at the right hand of the throne of God" (Heb. 12:2).

Those who would argue this should consider this: "He is despised and rejected of men; a man of sorrows, and acquainted with grief: and we hid as it were our faces from him; he was despised, and we esteemed him not" (Isa. 53:3).

Also, Paul shared, "But thou hast fully known my doctrine, manner of life, purpose, faith, longsuffering, charity, patience, persecutions, afflictions, which came unto me at Antioch, at Iconium, at Lystra; what persecutions I endured: but out of them all the Lord delivered me. Yea, and all that will live godly in Christ Jesus shall suffer persecution" (2 Tim. 3:10–12).

May the please-all preachers consider this: "Woe to you, when all men shall speak well of you! for so did their fathers to the false prophets" (Luke 6:26). Those who never suffer for the cross have not fully presented the cross. The cross is more than God's love being presented. The cross speaks to the necessity of dealing with and the judgment of sin due to unrighteousness. The gospel message leading to a God relationship begins with repentance.

The world and the devil cannot stand holiness and righteousness. When holiness and righteousness are presented, some will accept and embrace Christ because they see the justice of this. Those who reject Him will often react by persecuting the standard-bearing messenger. Jerusalem always killed the God-sent and appointed prophets: "O Jerusalem, Jerusalem, which killest the prophets, and stonest those that are sent unto thee" (Luke 13:34). The servant of the Lord must know this and count the cost (Luke 14:28).

The love, grace, and goodness preacher who does not add in the rest of the gospel truths, such as hell, judgment, and damnation, may not understand persecution since he has not presented the offense: "And I, brethren, if I yet preach circumcision, why do I yet suffer persecution? then is the offence of the cross ceased" (Gal. 5:11). Remember, all those who are in Christ Jesus face opposition, as Paul wrote Timothy: "Yea, and all that will live godly in Christ Jesus shall suffer persecution" (2 Tim. 3:12).

## SMOOTH WORD PREACHERS

Our Lord Jesus made a distinction between Himself and His immature disciples. The difference is in what they said. "The world cannot hate you; but me it hateth, because I testify of it, that the works thereof are evil" (John 7:7). Many preachers do not cause offense because they only speak "smooth words." They usually have dry-eyed conversions because they do not bring conviction by confrontation of sin: "Which say to the seers, See not; and to the prophets, Prophesy not unto us right things, speak unto us smooth things, prophesy deceits" (Isa. 30:10). Half-truths are not the truth. Many preach half of the truth.

The servant and called ministry must understand the need to present the love, grace, and mercy of God in their salvation presentation. They must also present the Christ of the cross. The sword of the Word is double-edged. Grace and mercy are applied to self first and then to others, following repentance.

The blessed benefit of this sword being applied is a healing after the surgery of repentance with faith in Christ. Honoring God in Christ avoids judgment.

> Or despises thou the riches of his goodness and forbearance and longsuffering; not knowing that the goodness of God leadeth thee to repentance? But after thy hardness and impenitent heart treasurest up unto thyself wrath against the day of wrath and revelation of the righteous judgment of God; who will render to every man according to his deeds.
>
> —ROMANS 2:4–6

Note this focus on the coming judgment. The last of six doctrines in the Book of Hebrews is eternal judgment.

There are many love, grace, and "smooth word" preachers who do not touch or clearly present this doctrine. In the end they will be guilty of the blood of men. Paul said that he was not guilty of the blood of any man with good reason, while speaking to his fellow ministers: "Wherefore I take you to record this day, that I am pure from the blood of all men. For I have not shunned to declare unto you all the counsel of God" (Acts 20:26–27). May the prosperity preachers know and preach truth, which includes, "And make straight paths for your feet, lest that which is lame be turned out of the way; but let it rather be healed. Follow peace with all men, and holiness, without which no one shall see the Lord" (Heb. 12:13–14).

There is no problem with a balanced message of preaching the truths of kingdom prosperity and blessings. "Let them shout for joy, and be glad, that favour my righteous cause: yea, let them say continually, Let the Lord be magnified, which hath pleasure in the prosperity of his servant" (Ps. 35:27). As long as the blessing truths are balanced with all truth, I believe in God's blessings and prospering of the righteous, since the Bible constantly portrays this.

We must include Paul's holy inspired teachings so the Lord can favor and bless us: "Wherefore, my beloved, as ye have always obeyed, not as in my presence only, but now much more in my absence, work out your own salvation with fear and trembling" (Phil. 2:12). It seems that the grace-only preachers avoid these Bible texts. So many miss the truth. They avoid the Christ-given message and the application of the parable of the sower. The seed that fell among thorns sprouted up but died. Their hearts were detoured by the cares and riches of life, which choked and killed their fruitfulness. These were germinated seeds, which received the Word with joy. They were branches in the vine that are now cut off and burned.

May we remember the apostle Paul's testimony and exhortation: "But I keep under my body, and bring it into subjection: lest that by any means, when I have preached to others, I myself should be a castaway" (1 Cor. 9:27). How many ministers such as Balaam, Saul, Judas, and Demas have destroyed their eternal life walk and ministry? The gospel is preached. God calls. And man decides.

> And the Spirit and the bride [the church] say, Come. And let him that heareth say, Come. And let him that is athirst come. And whosoever will, let him take the water of life freely.
>
> —REVELATION 22:17

## THE WINGS

The completion of four wings speaks of the creatures' unlimited ability to go and be anywhere. The called ministry can do and be all that the Lord desires, including taking rides in Elijah's chariot or Philip's spiritual travels from Gaza to Azotus (Acts 8:40). Our God has not changed! "And they had the hands of a man under their wings on their four sides; and they four had their faces and their wings. Their wings were joined one to another; they turned not when they went; they went every one straight forward" (Ezek. 1:8–9). The apostle Paul shared his knowledge of God-endowed strengths: "I can do all things through Christ which strengtheneth me" (Phil. 4:13). The Lord equips and enables us for any task He has placed before us. We must never turn from a God-assigned path but always maintain a steadfast, straightforward, and determined focus.

## Their Course

They went straight forward: "And they went every one straight forward: whither the spirit was to go, they went; and they turned not when they went" (Ezek. 1:12). The gospel minister must never look back or turn from their course. "And Jesus said unto him, No man, having put his hand to the plough, and looking back, is fit for the kingdom of God" (Luke 9:62). "Not fit" was directed to those who had started out by putting their hand to the plow, pursuing kingdom ministry, but looked back after starting their journey. They longed for the world they had left behind. These are not fit for the kingdom and are eliminated. They lost their kingdom garments, the robe of Christ's righteousness that is required for the wedding (Matt. 22:12; Rev. 3:5; 19:8).

Many believers and preachers have put their hands to the plow but, like Lot's wife, have looked back since Sodom contained their true love. Lot's wife became a cleansing warning to all who would look back, as salt is a preserving and cleansing substance. She became a statue or monument of warning to those in her day and for us as well. Dead people fall and deteriorate. She became a standing sermon. Set not your heart on what God does not love or desire. Love what He loves. Honor what He honors. Desire what He desires. His judgment comes upon the wrong hearted. He desires righteousness and a holy love relationship.

Paul understood and ministered from this knowledge. He knew which truths he followed and what his heart was set upon. He was focused on his course as he was always prayerfully attuned to the Holy Spirit: "For God is my witness, whom I serve with my spirit in the gospel of his Son" (Rom. 1:9). Due to this sensitive listening for and waiting upon the Lord, only moving as his spirit man gave peace and assurance, Paul knew the completion of his course: "I have fought a good fight, I have finished my course" (2 Tim. 4:7). The constantly prayerful and worshipping called ministry will complete their calling and course. Some will not, as our

Lord warned when speaking of Demas, King Saul, and Judas: "The Son of man goeth as it is written of him: but woe unto that man by whom the Son of man is betrayed! it had been good for that man if he had not been born" (Matt. 26:24). Judas was one of Jesus's disciples. Judas was one of the called apostles and an elder (Matt. 10:2, Luke 9:10, Ps. 109:8, Acts 1:20). He allowed his heart to stray by his choosing. His spirit never overcame the flesh, although he had lots of opportunity. He was a thief and covetous of money (John 12:6). May the called ministry know and maintain their God-given course, solely bound by our Lord's will.

One great truth out of many that is found in the Psalms is, "The works of the Lord are great, sought out of all them that have pleasure therein" (Ps. 111:2). David observed the difference in people around him. Some sought out the truths, person, and principles of God, and some did not, although they may have been "religious." Having observed humanity and believers through "God glasses" over the past forty years, I wholeheartedly agree with David's conclusion. Those who take pleasure in God's works and Word seek out all they can know of Him and His heart. These people will not fail but will overcome. They may stumble temporarily, but the Lord will raise them up, washed by the blood of the Lamb (Ps. 37:24). They are the ones who grow from faith to faith and go from strength to strength as they follow their God-given course. "They go from strength to strength, every one of them in Zion appeareth before God" (Ps. 84:7).

## HANDS

Hands always speak of "works" in the Bible, just as feet speak of our goings. We are the sheep of our Lord's right hand. The right hand is the hand of blessing. (See Exodus 15:6; Psalm 17:7; 18:35; 95:7; 100:3.) What this picture teaches the ministry of God is that the creatures were endowed with hands, but the hands were continually covered. Nowhere in this vision did the hands do any works. Rather, they were constantly covered and kept out of sight. Our walk with Him should never deteriorate to a works level. However, our works are always seen by our Lord.

He tells each of the seven churches in Revelation that He observes their works. We the saints are judged and rewarded according to our works. However, we never come into God's presence because of our works. Our salvation is by grace through faith, not works (Eph. 2:8).

All of our works must be worship based and motivated. When we approach God and build an altar to meet with Him, it must be built of natural God-created stones unaltered by our works. "And if thou wilt make me an altar of stone, thou shalt not build it of hewn stone: for if thou lift up thy tool upon it, thou hast polluted it" (Exod. 20:25). We worship and approach Him due to His works and the death of the Lamb. We come to the Father in Jesus's name and His works on our behalf.

Salvation is by faith in the cross and shed blood of Christ. Salvation is achieved by faith in what our Savior accomplished, which has nothing to do with our works. Faith in Him produces works: "But wilt thou know, O vain man, that faith without works is dead?" (James 2:20).

When Jesus was asked the question of what works one must do to attain God's approval and salvation, He answered, "This is the work of God, that ye believe on him whom he hath sent" (John 6:29). The religious hireling has not understood this truth. True faith always produces works! Works do not produce faith. Without this faith we will not please or see God (Heb. 11:6).

"Thus were their faces: and their wings were stretched upward; two wings of every one were joined one to another, and two covered their bodies" (Ezek. 1:11). The two wings stretched upward speak to their continual worship in all of their goings, even as they went "straight forward." "Let my prayer be set forth before thee as incense; and the lifting up of my hands as the evening sacrifice" (Ps. 141:2). The ministry must always be prayerfully listening and acting as the Lord's servants.

The two wings that covered their bodies spoke of a constant awareness of God's glory and our humility (Matt. 6:13). This aligns with kneeling, bowing, and prostration before the Lord. They worshiped in humility while beholding His person, glorifying Him.

## THE LIKENESS

The pictorial sermon to the preacher is found by examining the creatures close to the throne. "As for the likeness of the living creatures, their appearance was like burning coals of fire, and like the appearance of lamps: it went up and down among the living creatures; and the fire was bright, and out of the fire went forth lightning" (Ezek. 1:13). Here we see the appearance and activities of the creatures as lamps, burning coals, and shooting out lightning. The Christ-appointed minister must be a burning, impassioned person, burning up sin and wrong constantly. We must project righteousness and truth as lightning from the heavens. Our God continually purifies us as a refiner with the fire of His Word (Jer. 20:9).

Should we the ministry of our God not be as He who refines us, the sons of Levi and those around us? These creatures were totally pleasing to our God. We the ministry must be ministering His wishes and person and purposes, as living sacrifices in holy worship. We as these creatures must be those who are consumed with pleasing Him. We who have seen Him are changed: "But we all, with open face beholding as in a glass the glory of the Lord, are changed into the same image from glory to glory, even as by the Spirit of the Lord" (2 Cor. 3:18).

We are to be light and salt to the world. God's ministry must constantly examine themselves as to their focus, purity, and brightness of their shining. The ministry's Word and holy God-given revelation will shoot forth as lightning into the darkness of the lost soul's blindness and night. Their understanding of the holy God whom they serve will bring forth the fires of conviction. The Holy Spirit works with them, convicting and consuming sin, bringing repentance unto holiness.

## CHAPTER FOUR

# EZEKIEL'S VISION, MINISTRY RESPONSE

*Instant Response of Obedience*

*I*NSTANT SERVANTHOOD OBEDIENCE was the response by creatures listening for the voice from the throne: "And the living creatures ran and returned as the appearance of a flash of lightning" (Ezek. 1:14). The servant of the Lord who honors Him as Lord will devote himself to developing an instant response and obedience mentality—God speaks, I act. When I run for Him, I instantly return to Him at the completion of the assignment. I will not linger. We see this prophetic picture from the man of God who disobeyed the commandment to go, say, and return. He was killed by a lion after disobeying (1 Kings 13:9, 24). May we learn from this portrayal of disobedience.

As Eliezer, Abraham's trusted servant, responded to the successful mission completion in finding Rebekah, may we say, "Hinder me not...that I may go to my master" (Gen. 24:56). Our ministry effectiveness and accomplishments will be measured against our instant obedience. If we love Him, we make Him Lord of all. We take pleasure in a prostrated position of heart and mind to His will.

We, as the creatures depicted to Ezekiel, must see this ministry prototype vision training. How much have we made Christ our Lord? Our running must be instant, in season and out of season, but always returning instantly to the Lord's side. We must see Him as Lord! Ministry to Him will be measured by our obedience to His authority in our lives. We are bought with a price and are not our own (1 Cor. 6:20). How much we genuinely regard God's authority is a key question in ministry.

The righteous and godly elders depicted in Acts 15 lived under authority. The elders Judas and Silas, who accompanied Paul and Barnabas in verse 22, were in fact identified as prophets. They returned to the apostles, not Jerusalem. "And after they had tarried there a space, they were let go in peace from the brethren unto the apostles" (v. 33).

These prophets were subservient to Christ. They were in obedience to His holy direction and choosing of authority as stated in 1 Corinthians 12:28. They were obedient to God's authority placement and with humility recognized that apostles are to be first in the order of God's governmental placement. Judas and Silas honored their Lord in this demonstration of humility.

May many prophets and other called ministries consider this observed humility. True humility and obedience will be evidenced by following this Christ-given example of submitting to holy authority and governmental order. When they disregard having a personal apostle relationship in their lives, they are denying Christ and His authority. They are in rebellion to God's given authority structure (1 Cor. 12:17, 28).

Consider the loss to the kingdom of God and the church by disregarding this Christ-given authority order and how this is to be applied today. We have an army in disarray, an army that is producing much less than what could be. The result is like a large number of guerrilla warfare groups, lacking centralized focus, supply, and the power of a God-intended structured army, functioning in divisions under generals.

When genuine right-hearted apostles are recognized and received, the result will be that all ministries will flow as they should. This includes churches and eldership, along with ministering fruitful believers.

And may true apostles represent a godly walk and demeanor, with godly humility. Most believers disregard this Christ-stated placement by simply denying they exist, having used their unbelief scissors to this biblical directive. Rather, we should be striving to seek out this truth and how this is to be applied. Many archive this directive to a past church, where there is only one church. Others claim offices that are not theirs to claim because they do not understand the differences in callings. Praise God for His mercy, or we would all be consumed.

We accept the understanding that the evangelist has a great anointing for winning souls, as we consider Billy Graham, Reinhard Bonnke, and others of our day. However, if these souls are not nurtured and fed as babies by pastors, ministries, and other believers, they remain unnourished, and many die as a result. They multiply the numbers of those who become the seed that fell into the shallow soil our Lord Jesus spoke of, which sprung up with joy, yet they perished.

When we disregard the needed in-depth revelation feeding by the teacher and the lack of holy revelation and anointing of the prophet, we rob our newborn babes of growth and the spiritual foods necessary for the journey of faith.

When we deny the overseeing general's eye of the apostle, who sees the bigger picture, and the establishing need of the entire ministry government, much of the harvest is lost. Apostles establish the church in new territory. They also encourage and direct the other callings, guiding these ministries as a harmonious team.

All of these five different callings are to minister in harmony while expanding church growth. They are guardians of doctrine and the holy world vision.

Pastors and teachers are limited in ministering this vision since they have a greater local church vision and burden. Apostles and prophets are equipped with a Christ-given ministry vision, fostering efforts to bring the gospel into all the world. Our Savior said the gospel would go into all of the world, as it is today. The church is not complete and Christ will not come until this is a fact (Matt. 24:14). We must see the necessity and value of fellow ministries. They are just as Christ-called and equally needed as our own.

We must await His voice to do His will. Our Lord Jesus spoke to those He dealt with in life and who were closest to Him, "Wist ye not that I must be about my Father's business?" (Luke 2:49). Yet He obeyed and gave due honor to His natural parents.

When mature and in the Father's time, He was released into full-flight ministry at the age of thirty. These fully shaped truths directed His every act of ministry and speaking. Likewise, we His ministry should fully walk out His words of direction for us. And we must be faithful to our earthly responsibilities. I struggle due to seeing these revelations of truth, knowing it is so, but realize I have not attained unto fully walking in these truths. We thank You, Lord, for mercy on Your servants as we strive to attain unto pleasing You. We worship You, our Father and God.

## Our Times

Our Lord was fully sensitive to the Father's reins (Ps. 26:2). "Then Jesus said unto them, My time is not yet come: but your time is always ready. . . . Go ye up unto this feast: I go not up yet unto this feast; for my time is not yet full come" (John 7:6, 8).

"Your time is always ready" speaks to the god of self and self-determination. This says that we do whatever we want when we want. Our Savior said, "I am different from you. I am fully committed to doing the Father's will at all times when I hear Him speak. This includes facing the cross." (See Luke 22:42.) His disciples were still self-governed while controlling their lives and pursuits (John 7:6). This changed as they matured after Pentecost. "Verily, verily, I say unto thee, When thou wast young, thou girdest thyself, and walkest where thou wouldest: but when thou shalt be old, thou shalt stretch forth thy hands, and another shall gird thee, and carry thee whither thou wouldest not" (John 21:18). Relinquishing to the Master's hand will bless and sustain us even when we are persecuted as Stephen experienced when being stoned. "But he, being full of the Holy Ghost, looked up stedfastly into heaven, and saw the glory of God, and Jesus standing on the right hand of God, and said, Behold, I see the heavens opened, and the Son of man standing on the right hand of God" (Acts 7:55–56).

## OUR WORDS

Love for our God and servanthood are measured by our words as well as our works. "He that loveth me not keepeth not my sayings: and the word which ye hear is not mine, but the Father's which sent me" (John 14:24). What is the topic matter that commonly proceeds from our mouths? Does this match our works?

Our Lord was always in perfect union with the Father and the Holy Spirit. He spoke forth heaven-given truths of righteousness in all communications. For those who only preach grace and love, consider this: "The world...me it hateth, because I testify of it, that the works thereof are evil" (John 7:7). We must preach about sin, damnation, and judgment with a future hell—just as we must preach both love and grace to help the hearers avoid this place. Humor is an acceptable trait, but may our conversation be seasoned with godly understanding: "Only let your conversation be as it becometh the gospel of Christ" (Phil. 1:27). Our fellow man judges us by our words and conversation.

Jesus spoke His Father's words. Should we not do likewise? "Walk in wisdom toward them that are without, redeeming the time. Let your speech be always with grace, seasoned with salt, that ye may know how ye ought to answer every man" (Col. 4:5–6).

## OUR WORKS

"I can of mine own self do nothing: as I hear, I judge: and my judgment is just; because I seek not mine own will, but the will of the Father which hath sent me" (John 5:30). Our Lord said, "My judgments and what I do are perfectly in tune with My Father in heaven. I go, speak, minister, and work as He desires." O Lord! We your servants desire to attain unto this!

We desire to see God's miracles flow through us to others, bringing faith and salvation by our ministry: "I must work the works of him that sent me, while it is day: the night cometh, when no man can work" (John 9:4). May we, the called ministry, be aware of the brevity of time available to us. Night is coming, when we can no longer labor for Christ.

May we attain unto Christ's ministry, both in words and works. I claim the promise of greater works, because Christ has all power since He went to the Father (John 14:12). I believe the truth of Mark 16:17–18, which is an eternal relevant truth for today: "And these signs shall follow them that believe; In my name shall they cast out devils; they shall speak with new tongues; they shall take up serpents; and if they drink any deadly thing, it shall not hurt them; they shall lay hands on the sick, and they shall recover."

## THE WHEELS

These wheels and their components are a much-needed ministry picture of truth. They are a must understanding for those who seek to walk with the Lord and not simply attend a Sunday service. They speak to the truth and reality of what Paul said: "The grace of the Lord Jesus Christ, and the love of God, and the communion of the Holy Ghost, be with you all" (2 Cor. 13:14). These wheels are a picture that depicts the central foundation of a holy walk with God the Holy Spirit. These wheels speak of an experience lived out and a constant awareness of God's presence. They speak of the reality, the results of praying without ceasing (1 Thess. 5:17).

> Now as I beheld the living creatures, behold one wheel upon the earth by the living creatures, with his four faces. The appearance of the wheels and their work was like unto the colour of a beryl: and they four had one likeness: and their appearance and their work was as it were a wheel in the middle of a wheel. When they went, they went upon their four sides: and they turned not when they went. As for their rings, they were so high that they were dreadful; and their rings were full of eyes round about them four. And when the living creatures went, the wheels went by them: and when the living creatures were lifted up from the earth, the wheels were lifted up. Whithersoever the spirit was to go, they went, thither was their spirit to go; and the wheels were lifted up over against them: for the spirit of the living creature was in the wheels. When those went, these went; and when those stood, these stood; and when

those were lifted up from the earth, the wheels were lifted up over against them: for the spirit of the living creature was in the wheels.

—EZEKIEL 1:15–21

These wheels constantly attended and were inseparable from these creatures.

Every inch of these rims was full of eyes. Everywhere they traveled, they totally and infinitely observed and discerned all matters wherever they went. The creatures did not go anywhere without the wheels full of eyes. Eyes see. Many have eyes and ears yet do not see or hear. (Mark 4:23; Eph. 1:18; Rev. 2:29). Discernment is such a needed strength in ministry. In Ezekiel 1:20 we see the completion of this picture: "Whithersoever the spirit was to go, they went, thither was their spirit to go." Their spirit (moral referee, conscience, examining all thought) went wherever the Spirit went. The ministry's spirit should always go, speak, and minister as the Spirit desires and leads, because the Spirit is God the Holy Spirit.

Wheels are a picture of motion and going places. There is no wheel that is intended to stay stationary without function. The wheel rims were full of eyes. Their four sides speak to their perfection and completeness in their travels, awareness, observation, and vigilant discernment.

The rims full of eyes are a pictorial message to you and me. Vigilance in the ministry is imperative. We must use discernment, weighing all that we partake of. We must examine every step of our walk, discerning our motives and directions under God.

This is why we see Gideon's overcoming army was only made up of three hundred men. They lapped up water as a dog habitually does (Judg. 7:5). A dog will always have his eyes fix on the horizon while drinking, guarding against potential danger. This is why Peter said, "Be sober, be vigilant; because your adversary the devil, as a roaring lion, walketh about, seeking whom he may devour" (1 Pet. 5:8).

The spirit of the living creature was in the wheel with the rings full of eyes, going and moving only as the Spirit would have them go, stand, and return. We the ministry need the Holy Spirit for holy direction! The learning of this truth continues until the day we graduate. I am in my sixties, and I have learned so much over the last two years. Learning is a constant, nonstop must. Our learning of Him will lead us into a continually greater walk with the Holy Spirit.

## Wheel Within the Wheel

What a mighty tremendous truth depiction is deposited in this inner wheel part of the vision: "And their appearance and their work was as it were a wheel in the middle of a wheel" (Ezek. 1:16). The servant ministry constantly has two functions in their walk through life. They walk before God and walk before man as well. There is an inner walk and outer walk. These manlike creatures did not go anywhere separate from both the wheel and the wheel within the wheel.

Our inward walk, our hearts before the Lord is of key importance, since this will determine the outer walk, which God and man both see. As the wheel on the outside was full of eyes, we see the same eyes and seeing ability functioning in the wheel within the wheel. The spirit of man measures and weighs all actions from within, which should govern our external walk. "The spirit of man is the candle of the Lord, searching all the inward parts of the belly" (Prov. 20:27). The conscience approves or disapproves our decisions and actions. "Which shew the work of the law written in their hearts, their conscience also bearing witness, and their thoughts the mean while accusing or else excusing one another" (Rom. 2:15). We also need to constantly go as these: "Whithersoever the spirit was to go, they went" (Ezek. 1:20).

Their travels and whatever they did had a constant inclusion and presence of God and His presence. This is a central point in true worship. Do we desire God's presence wherever we go and no matter what we are doing? Should we not be capable of saying yes to this, then we are still retaining the god of self. Surrender includes love and trust, a believing that wherever a complete Holy Spirit presence walk takes us will be a greater walk. This will be attended with peace, love, joy, and fulfillment in life.

Why a searching of the "inward parts of the belly" and not the heart or mind? The picture is clear. The belly contains the digestive food intake that feeds every cell in our body. Likewise our spirit man monitors what we take in and digest, affecting decisions, words, and actions in our walk before God. To summarize:

We must constantly search our hearts and motives within, affecting our goings through life. "Let a man examine himself" is a holy directive given to us as we partake of Communion (1 Cor. 11:28). Is our Christ relationship real before God and lived out in our walk?

The outer wheel constantly observes, taking in what is happening around us. We weigh and discern what we hear and what we see in the natural dealings on life's road. This wheel full of eyes depicts the intake that we discern, what is holy and righteous in all matters. Pharisees were people who had physical eyes, yet our Lord said they were blind in their understanding (Matt. 23:16). The righteous will see holy and spiritual realities, matters of faith just as Elisha's servant saw God's army in 2 Kings 6:17. We will see the spiritual reality of our environment and circumstances.

The world sees our travels and outward wheel. May the outward wheel be a true reflection of the inward wheel. The world and church are tired and worn out with expressed empty words, exposing a visible misalignment to the obvious inner reality. This is seen when someone says to you, "I love you and have missed you," yet he or she has never called. Or, "I was concerned about you and have been praying for you," but you have never heard from them. Or how do you feel when a church tells you, "Cheerfully give us your tithes and offerings, but go to the government welfare system when you have needs." How much do we suppose God is dismayed by our words, when we sing, "I love You, Lord" in church and then ignore Him until the next Sunday?

We see the inner and outer wheels at the same time. The bigger challenge on life's road is to demonstrate the reality portrayed here. The truth of the inner wheel must be reflected in the truth of the outer wheel travels. Our God exposed both simultaneously in Ezekiel's vision. The challenge is for ministry to be truthful and transparent. Our outer walk and actions must demonstrate our inner being with no hypocrisy. The world and church are waiting for the manifestation of the "sons of God" (Rom. 8:19).

David's prayer was a function of the wheel within the wheel. May we pray, "Search me, O God, and know my heart: try me, and know my thoughts" (Ps. 139:23).

We must *take heed unto* ourselves before we touch the blood-bought flock of God (Acts 20:28).

## THE FIRMAMENT

And the likeness of the firmament upon the heads of the living creature was as the colour of the terrible crystal, stretched forth over their heads above.

—EZEKIEL 1:22

These ministering creatures that ran and returned as lightning were under the throne pavilion. They moved as the throne directed. They were inseparable from the throne and the throne's directives and intentions. They knew their place, with the throne pavilion above their heads. These creatures had crowned and enthroned our living God as Lord of their lives. They constantly lived a God-directed life and ministry.

May we learn from this vision, given to us as well as to Ezekiel. Our God reigns. "Therefore let all the house of Israel know assuredly, that God hath made that same Jesus, whom ye have crucified, both Lord and Christ" (Acts 2:36).

May we know this truth: the firmament of crystal is above our heads. Our God is enthroned. He sees every thought. He hears every word spoken. Crystal is a transparent material, as glass is. However, crystal has a greater density and transmits light and colors much better than glass. The ministry is always to know that all of their works are transparent before our Lord. We are to reflect His brightness, light, and glory. "For God, who commanded the light to shine out of darkness, hath shined in our hearts, to give the light of the knowledge of the glory of God in the face of Jesus Christ" (2 Cor. 4:6). We are to be salt and light to the world, reflecting the light of the One upon the throne.

## The Posture of the Wings

> And under the firmament were their wings straight, the one toward
> the other: every one had two, which covered on this side, and every
> one had two, which covered on that side, their bodies. And when
> they went, I heard the noise of their wings, like the noise of great
> waters, as the voice of the Almighty, the voice of speech, as the
> noise of an host: when they stood, they let down their wings. And
> there was a voice from the firmament that was over their heads,
> when they stood, and had let down their wings.
>
> —Ezekiel 1:23–25

The wings or goings of these creatures were one with the voice of God.
The Almighty spoke, and they simultaneously responded and went.

Two wings constantly covered their bodies and hands in humility and
worship. They only wanted to worship the Lord for His works. As the
elders in heaven's future, they cast their crowns at Jesus's feet (Rev. 4:10).
Their only posture was one of worship.

Wings speak of our goings and travels, a flight ability beyond our
feet limitations. Two wings were always raised in worship as they went
wherever the Spirit led them. The only time they lowered their raised
wings is when they stood upon returning from their Lord's assignment.
They stood while waiting to hear and fulfill the next desire of their God.
When they stood, the voice from the throne spoke to them.

We the ministry must stop and stand, breaking from our works.
God's ministry must learn to stop and wait before Him to hear His
voice. We cannot be Spirit led unless we hear from Him before moving
to our next act of worship, a new assignment.

## The Throne of the Almighty

> And above the firmament that was over their heads was the likeness
> of a throne, as the appearance of a sapphire stone: and upon the
> likeness of the throne was the likeness as the appearance of a man
> above upon it. And I saw as the colour of amber, as the appearance
> of fire round about within it, from the appearance of his loins even

upward, and from the appearance of his loins even downward, I saw
as it were the appearance of fire, and it had brightness round about.
As the appearance of the bow that is in the cloud in the day of rain,
so was the appearance of the brightness round about. This was the
appearance of the likeness of *the glory* of the LORD. And when I saw
it, I fell upon my face, and I heard a voice of one that spoke.

—EZEKIEL 1:26–28, EMPHASIS ADDED

The firmament above the creatures was the platform of God's throne.
God is enthroned above all in heaven, in the earth, and in eternity to
come, when time shall be no more. Only those who know and understand this will be party to this heavenly kingdom.

Lucifer, who desired to have a throne equal to God, was cast down,
as all who have not enthroned God will be. All who have not enthroned
Him are in rebellion and will be eternally separated.

How art thou fallen from heaven, O Lucifer, son of the morning!
how art thou cut down to the ground, which didst weaken the
nations! For thou hast said in thine heart, I will ascend into heaven,
I will exalt my throne above the stars of God: I will sit also upon the
mount of the congregation, in the sides of the north: I will ascend
above the heights of the clouds; I will be like the most High. Yet
thou shalt be brought down to hell, to the sides of the pit.

—ISAIAH 14:12–15

Ezekiel heard a voice from the throne. We note the timing and initiation of this voice. The throne spoke when Ezekiel "fell upon my face"
(Ezek. 1:28). This is the great understanding required in order for us to
hear Him speak. He is the omnipotent Lord God Almighty. He is our
Father Creator. When we in humility reverence and prostrate ourselves
before Him, when we come by the blood of Christ, He will speak.

The figure on the throne was as the likeness of a man. Note it was not
a man but the *likeness* of a man. The love of God is portrayed in this, as
Christ identifies with us by this depiction—God in flesh, Immanuel, our
Redeemer. Here we see the awesome reality Paul spoke of. Our Creator

and Savior put aside His glory to take upon Himself the form of man and is now glorified (Acts 2:36; Heb. 2:9).

The glory of God was shown in the Son of man, Christ Jesus. His holy glory is that He, as the Lord of the universe, with a holy incomparable love, took flesh and blood to redeem His beloved, us. (John 1:14; Phil. 2:5–7). We are honored to observe and reveal this glory.

Heaven gave this vision, and the appearance is glorious to the mind's eye. However, the true glory depth of this vision is revealed in this. His love for us is shown in identifying with us. Those who resist this knowledge must be advised of this truth imbedded in the rest of this vision:

> See that ye refuse not him that speaketh. For if they escaped not who refused him that spoke on earth, much more shall not we escape, if we turn away from him that speaketh from heaven: Whose voice then shook the earth: but now he hath promised, saying, Yet once more I shake not the earth only, but also heaven. And this word, Yet once more, signifieth the removing of those things that are shaken, as of things that are made, that those things which cannot be shaken may remain. Wherefore we receiving a kingdom which cannot be moved, let us have grace, whereby we may serve God acceptably with reverence and godly fear: For our God is a consuming fire.
>
> —Hebrews 12:25–29

Our eternal picture is completed when He appears wearing a vesture with the name only He can bear: "And he hath on his vesture and on his thigh a name written, KING OF KINGS, AND LORD OF LORDS" (Rev. 19:16).

## A Must for the Called Ministry

"I fell upon my face, and I heard a voice of one that spake" (Ezek. 1:28). God always:

- Reveals His glory to the "called": Do not speak of Him unless He has revealed His glory. He is glorious to us who have seen His glory. This seeing has enabled us to become the sons and daughters of the living God! "But as many as received him, to them gave he power to become the sons of God, even to them that believe on his name: Which were born, not of blood, nor of the will of the flesh, nor of the will of man, but of God. And the Word was made flesh, and dwelt among us, (and we beheld his glory, the glory as of the only begotten of the Father,) full of grace and truth" (John 1:12–14).

• Speaks only to those who bow before Him, in reverence prostrating themselves.

• Asks us to stand at attention and be alert as He speaks (Ezek. 2:1–2).

• Sends all believers, but especially the called ministry, into dangerous territory: Jesus sent the seventy, commissioning them with, "Behold, I send you forth as lambs among wolves" (Luke 10:3).

• Grants His hearing and love-bound believers wisdom with knowledge—both of whom they are and whom they are sent to: "And he said unto me, Son of man, I send thee to the children of Israel, to a rebellious nation that hath rebelled against me: they and their fathers have transgressed against me, even unto this very day. For they are impudent children and stiffhearted. I do send thee unto them" (Ezek. 2:3–4).

• Tells us to speak in His stead: "And thou shalt say unto them, Thus saith the Lord GOD" (v. 4).

• Expects us to speak, whether they will hear or not: "And they, whether they will hear, or whether they will forbear, (for they are a rebellious house,) yet shall know that there hath been a prophet among them" (v. 5). Our wisdom must discern appropriate speaking, knowing what a word "in season" is to the hearer, as well as not casting pearls before swine (Isa. 50:4; Matt. 7:6).

- Will cause the sent ones to know whom we represent without fear: "And thou, son of man, be not afraid of them, neither be afraid of their words, though briers and thorns be with thee, and thou dost dwell among scorpions: be not afraid of their words, nor be dismayed at their looks, though they be a rebellious house" (Ezek. 2:6).

- Wants us to speak His words, not ours: "And thou shalt speak *my words* unto them, whether they will hear, or whether they will forbear: for they are most rebellious" (v. 7, emphasis added).

- Expects us to walk and speak in obedience: "But thou, son of man, hear what I say unto thee; Be not thou rebellious like that rebellious house" (v. 8).

- Will give us the words we need to speak: "Open thy mouth, and eat that I give thee" (v. 8).

- Fills the called with His Word: "And when I looked, behold, an hand was sent unto me; and, lo, a roll of a book was therein" (v. 9).

- Gives a revelation to the called ministry of God's heart— sorrows and the pain of seeing the lost and rebellious: "And he spread it before me; and it was written within and without: and there was written therein lamentations, and mourning, and woe" (v. 10). God's Word describes His heart's sorrow and is a love letter. God reveals His intentions and desires for man within this Holy Book. His Word also shows the rejection of our God by man and God's eternal judgment to come for the lost—and the rewarding of the saved as well.

- Asks those to whom He has revealed Himself to enter
  into His service: He gave a firm statement of fact to
  the disciple and people—"Whosoever therefore shall be
  ashamed of me and of my words in this adulterous and
  sinful generation; of him also shall the Son of man be
  ashamed, when he cometh in the glory of his Father
  with the holy angels" (Mark 8:38). Being silent about
  His kingdom truths and revealed glory, especially in
  the face of opposition, speaks to our lack of love for
  Him. Wrongful silence shows disrespect for His person,
  exposing a fear of man more than God. "The fear of man
  bringeth a snare: but whoso puts his trust in the LORD
  shall be safe" (Prov. 29:25).

There will always be a testing of our love for Christ, often in the face of ridicule (John 18:25). Our love will be tested by the same question our Lord placed before Peter: "Do you love Me?" (See John 21:15.) If we do, we will feed and oversee His sheep with a shepherd's heart. We will love the unlovable. We will embrace the outcasts. We will become knowledgeable and strive to be all of what our Lord would have us to be. We will prioritize leaving our fishing nets and ships behind, while embracing the fishing of men.

We the ministry, honored and called to the highest office in the world, are continually asked this question: "Do you love Me?" May we continue in our walk before Him as Abraham, the father of our faith, was directed to walk: "Walk before me, and be thou perfect" (Gen. 17:1).

## CHAPTER FIVE

# CHRISTIAN SALVATION, GLORY MINISTRY

*Our God Vision*

*I*N SALVATION ONE must see God's heart, plan, and future determinations. We must understand God and know His person. He is the God of the Bible, the God of Abraham, Isaac, and Jacob (Mark 12:26). He is the only eternal and existing God (Isa. 44:6). Our holy God reveals His person in Deuteronomy 6:4: "Hear, O Israel: The LORD our God is one LORD." Yet a careful study of Scripture will demonstrate God revealing His person as Father, Son, and Holy Spirit, or what we term "the Trinity," being three in one. Our Lord Jesus is the second person of the Trinity. Christ, in unity with the Father and Holy Spirit, determined to take upon Himself the form of man (Phil. 2:7). He purchased our salvation, fulfilling divine justice for those who genuinely believe. His nature and being are described by four attributes:

1. *God is holy* and without sin (Isa. 6:3). He always acts in perfect love and righteousness, including righteous judgment. The Ten Commandments describe the perfection of love.

2. *God is omnipotent.* He is all power, having created all things (John 1:3). Isaiah said, "Hast thou not known? hast thou not heard, that the everlasting God, the LORD, the Creator of the ends of the earth, fainteth not, neither is weary? there is no searching of his understanding" (Isa. 40:28).

3. *Our God is omniscient*, meaning He knows all things at all times, including the past and future (Heb. 4:13, 2 Chron. 16:9). This is proven by His prophetic words in Scriptures. No comparable book exists. No book like the Bible shows prophesied current and future events.

4. *He is omnipresent*, being in all places at all times. "Whither shall I go from thy spirit? or whither shall I flee from thy presence? If I ascend up into heaven, thou art there: if I make my bed in hell, behold, thou art there. If I take the wings of the morning, and dwell in the uttermost parts of the sea; even there shall thy hand lead me, and thy right hand shall hold me. If I say, Surely the darkness shall cover me; even the night shall be light about me. Yea, the darkness hideth not from thee; but the night shineth as the day" (Ps. 139:7–12).

Our heavenly Father's love and mercy in salvation's plan is glorious and wonderful. Seeing this plan captivates the genuinely called ministry. This knowledge will capture our hearts. We have no greater pleasure or satisfaction than to proclaim His glory.

When our days are over, all we will see is God, His will and works. There will be no atheists or agnostics in the soon coming eternity events, when every knee shall bow and every tongue confess that Jesus Christ is Lord (Phil. 2:11)!

## MATURING MINISTRY

Sadly, so many well-meaning Christians and ministries preach a "love" message that is defiled. A message of love without the balance of truth will minister much death. John the Baptist spoke of Christ's coming with grace and truth. The truth he spoke of is the reality of who Christ is. He is our sin bearer. Receiving Christ must be commensurate with a repentance of any and all sin. This is evidenced by desiring to please Him and love holiness. A changed life will be the immediate result.

John the Baptist refused to baptize those who did not demonstrate a life of repentance from sin. "But when he saw many of the Pharisees and Sadducees come to his baptism, he said unto them, O generation of vipers, who hath warned you to flee from the wrath to come? Bring forth therefore fruits meet for repentance" (Matt. 3:7–8).

A love message without presenting the offense, the root cause of what has separated man from God, is a bastardized truth or another gospel. The balanced message includes repentance, which is central to receiving salvation. Repentance is confronting sin within one's personal life. This happens by acknowledging we are lost. Without Christ we have no claim to any right of unity with a holy God! The true love message includes the necessity for the cross. I must identify with the cross and need thereof. My sins placed Christ there. Also, as a believer, I am crucified with Christ (Gal. 2:20). The cross speaks of the judgment Christ took upon Himself for His believers.

The gospel message must include an escape from divine judgment, acknowledging salvation from an eternal hell by Christ. Hell lies directly ahead for all who deny Christ. He is the only way, truth, and life, and those who deny Him His rightful place will perish. Eternal judgment faces all who do not seek Him as their Lord and Savior. "He that believeth on the Son hath everlasting life: and he that believeth not the Son shall not see life; but the wrath of God abideth on him" (John 3:36).

Hell, judgment, and damnation are part of the gospel message. These are just as much a part of the gospel as forgiveness of sins. Yes, the preaching of the cross and the blood that washes our sins and repentance of sin for salvation is offensive to many. Yes, this is the same offense that some avoid preaching, that Christ is the only way to God (John 14:6).

Paul spoke of offense in preaching: "And I, brethren, if I yet preach circumcision, why do I yet suffer persecution? then is the offence of the cross ceased" (Gal. 5:11). Holiness preaching will always offend some. The holy and obedient servant of the Lord has a "full banquet" message. As my apostle friend Ernesto Balili so aptly states, Christ preached more about hell than heaven. Why should His servant ministers differ in their message? Preaching half of the truth is not preaching the whole truth and counsel of God. Partial obedience is still disobedience.

One of the best prophet and preacher examples in the Bible is John the Baptist, who prepared the way of the Lord. He preached more about damnation, judgment, hell, and religious hypocrisy than "sugar-coated" love sermons in comparison to all Bible preachers. Jesus our Lord and the holy Bible writings never rebuked, critiqued, or corrected him. Rather, our Savior named him the greatest among all prophets. "Verily I say unto you, Among that are born of women there hath not risen a greater than John the Baptist" (Matt. 11:11).

## UNCONDITIONAL LOVE

Should we preach a message of complete and radical forgiveness being made available in and through Christ, that would be good truth and theology. There are conditions to benefiting from this complete forgiveness.

Partaking of salvation and God's glory requires decisive actions on the believer's part. We all relate to the scripture "For God so loved the world, that he gave his only begotten Son, that whosoever believeth in him should not perish, but have everlasting life" (John 3:16). Herein we see the profound love of God for all mankind. We also know that our God's desire is that all men might be saved: "The Lord is not slack concerning his promise, as some men count slackness, but is longsuffering to us-ward, not willing that any should perish, but that all should come to repentance" (2 Pet. 3:9). We are assured of this being God's heartfelt desire.

The Christian who is walking with Christ in salvation may rejoice in the knowledge that his sins are eternally forgiven by Christ's shed blood. By his acceptance of and believing in Christ as his personal Savior is this accomplished. Such believers have met the gospel conditions. They repented and believed, with a commitment to shun sin and love Christ. This repentance and avoidance of sin is a continual repentance throughout our Christ-following lives.

Preaching an unconditional love of God, which some preach, is not truthful. There is no such thing with God. God greatly loved the man He created. However, for God to walk and to live with man, there were conditions. Man was told of these when he was directed not to eat of the tree of the knowledge of good and evil. Man broke this condition, and death entered in—an immediate spiritual death and eventual natural death.

An unconditional love message trumpets out untruths about God's love, mercy, and grace. Preaching a half-truth is always untruth! The other half of John 3:16 includes the truth of what man needs to hear and do in order to be recipients of God's love and grace, which are that man must repent and believe. May we not leave out the textual truth of man's responsibility, as stated by "whosoever believeth in him should not perish" and "that all should come to repentance." Without our repentance and believing, we will never be associated with or recipients of God's love. The receiving of God's love is very conditional. I fear for those who preach an unconditional love and have responsibility over others in their ministry. The next stop is God.

## CONDITIONS TO RECEIVING CHRIST'S LOVE

Unconditional love does not exist! How in ignorance can some present this supposed "unconditional" God love? God loves us but hates our sin. The condition for dwelling with God is becoming holy, because He is holy. We become holy, both positionally in Christ due to His death in our stead and by desiring personal holiness. Those who preach an unconditional God love state God's heart for people, but then ignore man's responsibility and the conditions to receiving His love. Christ and the cross is a crossroad monument. We either go to the left or right, as the horizontal cross timber points us to. "And he shall set the sheep on his right hand, but the goats on the left" (Matt. 25:33).

Denial of the cross and what it stood for, with a belief in or presentation of an "unconditional love," is a horrible blight and ignorant denial of truth. Presenting this fallacious untruth is an undermining of gospel truth. Without an encounter with the cross, mankind remains under the shadow of death! "The people that walked in darkness have seen a great light: they that dwell in the land of the shadow of death, upon them hath the light shined" (Isa. 9:2).

Yes, the preaching of the cross and the necessity for same is more offensive than preaching a message that God "unconditionally" loves you. Those who do not seek for or receive faith in the Lamb of God whom the Father sent abide under the shadow of death and the wrath of God. "He that believeth on the Son hath everlasting life, and he that believeth not the Son shall not see life; but the wrath of God abideth on him" (John 3:36). The sincere receiving and believing on the Son of God is the "very conditional" truth. This needs to be preached, heard, and applied to meet the conditions of being partakers of eternal life. Those who do not meet these conditions "shall not see life."

Receiving God's love and mercy is a narrow way and gate. Christ and the cross are that way. Only upon repentance of sin, by living and loving a life without sin, while seeking holiness, will salvation be applied to a limited people. This limited people, the born of the Spirit church, are admonished as to holiness and their need to overcome in life, or be overcome: "For if after they have escaped the pollutions of the world through the knowledge of the Lord and Savior Jesus Christ, they are again entangled therein, and overcome, the latter end is worse with them than the beginning" (2 Pet. 2:20).

Many teach that upon the acceptance of Christ, they have already overcome and have arrived. This is so contrary to what our Lord told the Christians in all of the seven churches. He gave promises to the churches, with an exhortation. They needed to overcome to receive these promises. "He that overcometh, the same shall be clothed in white raiment; and I will not blot out his name out of the book of life, but I will confess his name before my Father, and before his angels" (Rev. 3:5). All Christians are exhorted to work out their salvation. "Wherefore, my beloved, as ye have always obeyed, not as in my presence only, but now much more in my absence, work out your own salvation with fear and trembling" (Phil. 2:12).

Unfortunately many teach there is nothing left to work out, and that no matter what one does, if saved, they have already overcome. The truth of this "work out with fear and trembling" is directed to beloved Christians. We must weigh what we are to work out. The Bible and Paul's words are, "our salvation." This working out of our salvation is the overcoming our Lord Jesus tells us we need to do in order to receive the promises to the churches. If upon our initial receiving of Christ our salvation standing is accomplished, then there would be nothing left to work out. An unalterable possession of salvation would only require a works-resulting-in-rewards belief, as many preach.

Should that be the case, there be nothing left to work out, especially with "fear and trembling."

The apostle Peter also spoke to this topic, addressing the believer and church. He said that we are to add virtues to our faith to make our election sure. Peter followed this with teaching us that when the brethren do this, they will ensure they will not fall and will have an abundant entrance into the kingdom of our Savior. "Wherefore the rather, brethren, give diligence to make your calling and election sure: for if ye do these things, ye shall never fall: For so an entrance shall be ministered unto you abundantly into the everlasting kingdom of our Lord and Saviour Jesus Christ" (2 Pet. 1:10–11).

Not to fall or fail needs to be considered. What if we do not heed his exhortation and do not add these virtues and then fall?

To those who overcome, there is the assurance and promise that He will not remove the overcomer's name from the Book of Life. He will remove the names of those who do not overcome. This applies to those who fall, due to not adding to their faith after the initial gaining of same, and are blind having no eyes to see: "But he that lacketh these things is blind, and cannot see afar off, and hath forgotten that he was purged from his old sins" (v. 9).

The church is admonished to seek holiness or not see God: "Follow peace with all men, and holiness, without which no man shall see the Lord" (Heb. 12:14). These are holy love warnings. They are to exhort us to make sure our hearts are right, that we meet the conditions of abiding in God's love and not become branches that are cut off from Christ, who is the vine (John 15:2). Only believers are grafted into Him. The world and unbeliever are not branches in Him. These branches are we who believe, as Jesus said, "Ye are the branches" (v. 5). We are cautioned by Christ to abide, or stay in Him, or be cut off and be burned. Branches that are burned are those who were made part of the vine but bore no fruit.

The burning of these branches that were in Christ is a terrible judgment they will experience, the same as unbelievers. The unbeliever faces an eternal judgment where the fire is not quenched and the worm does not die. Deny this truth, and one denies a foundational doctrine of the Christian church.

Those who preach, teach, or embrace an unconditional love have eradicated the conditions and truths of the Beatitudes. These attitudes to be embraced are all contingent upon and conditional to what we do. The blessing promises are to those who act out their will to be these:

> And he opened his mouth, and taught them, saying, Blessed are the poor in spirit [contrite, small self esteem]: for theirs is the kingdom of heaven. Blessed are they that mourn [over a world of sin]: for they shall be comforted. Blessed are the meek [humble]: for they shall inherit the earth. Blessed are they which do hunger and thirst after righteousness: for they shall be filled. Blessed are the merciful: for they shall obtain mercy. Blessed are the pure in heart: for they shall see God. Blessed are the peacemakers: for they shall be called the children of God. Blessed are they which are persecuted for righteousness' sake: for theirs is the kingdom of heaven. Blessed are ye, when men shall revile you, and persecute you, and shall say all manner of evil against you falsely, for my sake.
>
> —MATTHEW 5:2–11

These exhortations are encouragement to us to determine to be this way. We control our decisions. All of these texts give blessing promises to those who choose to be these blessed people.

God so loved the world that He was willing to and did come in the form of Christ. He paid for our sins and made the way to heaven and eternal life possible. The receiving and participating in this love is conditional and conditioned upon our efforts—our seeking, hearing, repenting, and believing. Where in the Bible does one find forgiveness without repentance? Even between mankind and believers, repentance of wrongdoing is involved, for forgiveness is to be applied. "And if he trespass against you seven times in a day, and seven times in a day turn again to thee, saying, I repent; thou shalt forgive him" (Luke 17:4).

Clergy and elders must teach this greatest of salvation truths. Learning the six foundational Christian doctrines as listed in Hebrews 5:12–6:2 will bring much change to any church nursery babies, maturing believers and preparing them for useful ministry. This knowledge equips believers for the task. Having a clear knowledge of the church foundational doctrines will evaporate clouded understandings. These doctrines, when learned to the degree that one can explain each one with some limited textual basis, takes a baby to maturity. These are:

- Repentance from dead works: What is repentance of dead works?

- Faith toward God: What kind of faith is needed?
  Describe God, the deity of Christ, the person of the Holy Spirit, and the doctrine of the Trinity.

- The doctrine of baptisms: What are the three clearly taught distinct plural baptisms? Who is doing the baptism, and into what? When do these take place? (1 Cor. 12:13; Rom. 6:3; John 1:26, 33).

- Laying on of hands: Who does this, and what is involved?

- Resurrection of the dead: How do the two different resurrections work? (Rev. 20:4).

- Eternal judgment: What are the two separate differing judgments? (1 Cor. 3:13–15; Rev. 20:12).

We must preach all of these holy truths, including the topic of holiness and maintaining our first love, to not have our candlestick (church and believer) removed: "And hast borne, and hast patience, and for my name's sake hast laboured, and hast not fainted. Nevertheless I have somewhat against thee, because thou hast left thy first love. Remember therefore from whence thou art fallen, and repent, and do the first works; or else I will come unto thee quickly, and will remove thy candlestick out of his place, except thou repent" (Rev. 2:3–5).

Preaching the conditions to receive God's love is extremely important. Removed candlesticks no longer possess light. This topic is central to the outreach, growth, sustenance, and governance of the church.

The true church, made up of the "redeemed from every kindred tribe and nation," is the epitome of treasure in God's heart, when we consider all that the universe contains. You cannot love Christ without having a heartfelt love for this true church. We must love the religious and unsaved unbelievers as well. We minister to bring them to Christ. Understanding this foundational knowledge enables one to excel in the call of God to ministry. This understanding is as basic a need as the alphabet is to enable reading and numbers to understand mathematics.

Salvation would not be possible if God did not in mercy meet the results of and conditions imposed by His own righteous judgment of sin. Man's sin brought death. "Wherefore, as by one man sin entered into the world, and death by sin; and so death passed upon all men, for that all have sinned" (Rom. 5:12).Christ met the conditions imposed by the judgment of sin in order to redeem man from sin:

> But not as the offence, so also is the free gift. For if through the offence of one many be dead, much more the grace of God, and the gift by grace, which is by one man, Jesus Christ, hath abounded unto many. And not as it was by one that sinned, so is the gift: for the judgment was by one to condemnation, but the free gift is of many offences unto justification. For if by one man's offence death reigned by one; much more they which receive abundance of grace and of the gift of righteousness shall reign in life by one, Jesus Christ. Therefore as by the offence of one judgment came upon all men to condemnation; even so by the righteousness of one the free gift came upon all men unto justification of life. For as by one

man's disobedience many were made sinners, so by the obedience of one shall many be made righteous.

—Romans 5:15–19

Christ met the conditions of righteousness by His cross. We are also to meet our conditions of righteousness by repentance of sin and believing in His atonement. The many who became righteous are so because they received this payment in their stead. Not all received. What happened to those who were not made righteous? Eternal judgment is ahead when the dead shall rise.

The reason why many and not all are made righteous by the obedience of one is because this granting of righteousness has only been given to those who have met the conditions required, for man to partake of God's love. This text starts with the largest word in the Bible—*IF*.

As Jesus preached, "*IF* ye keep my commandments, ye shall abide in my love; even as I have kept my Father's commandments, and abide in his love" (John 15:10, emphasis added). Many do not abide in His love.

The many who do abide have continual repentance from sin. They continually desire holiness because He is holy. They desire Him, the holy Son of God. They have met the conditions to receiving God's conditional love. These are righteous in Christ.

Many start with an explosion of love, but do not abide and fall away: "They on the rock are they, which, when they hear, receive the word with joy; and these have no root, which for a while believe, and in time of temptation fall away" (Luke 8:13).

In conclusion, ask yourself this question: If God's love is unconditional, why do more people wind up in the lake of fire than in heaven? May the conclusion hasten the messengers.

## CHAPTER SIX

# MINISTRY FROM REVEALED GLORY

*The Truth in Ministry*

*T*HOSE WHO HAVE experienced a dimension of the genuine call of God to ministry will know this is always preceded by a holy encounter and revelation of the person of Christ. We see this exemplified by Saul of Tarsus, who later was renamed Paul. Paul was called of Christ to be an apostle. He is a Bible man of fame as he wrote almost half of the New Testament. His scriptural introduction is inglorious, due to being a man of infamy. Saul was party to those who stoned Christians. He looked after the removed outer garments of those who killed the martyr Stephen.

Paul aggressively continued in this pursuit by obtaining authorization letters from the high priest to grant him the legal rights to imprison Christ followers (Acts 7:58; 9:2; 26:11). He tortured and murdered many of those who belonged to Christ. Perhaps our Lord Jesus saw this passion of Paul's pursuit as the product of lacking knowledge rather than that of a corrupt mind.

While in high-speed pursuit of this endeavor, Saul was abruptly halted by a life-changing event.

The risen Christ Jesus confronted him with a blinding bright light. Paul heard a voice emanating from this light personally addressing him. His natural strength failed due to being touched by Holy Ghost–slaying power. He fell to the ground, much like the soldiers accompanying Judas when our Lord responded to their questioning of who He was with "I AM" (John 18:6).

From this prostrated position Paul humbly asked, "Who are You, Lord?" Our Lord identified Himself as Jesus and accused Paul of persecuting Him because he was harming His children.

Upon digesting this statement, Paul asked a second question, "What will You have me do, Lord?" This question was the direct result of his new realization as to who Christ is. This shocking revelation of the living Christ, His person and glory, resulted in a radical turning point and change of direction in Paul's life.

Likewise we, in response to receiving a holy revelation of Christ and His Lordship, should respond with "Lord, what would You have me to do?" This key question should be asked by all of us who have received similar revelation. Seeing Christ as our eternal God, Creator, Redeemer, and our imminent coming King of kings and Lord of lords is confronting. Knowing the mystery Isaiah revealed is life changing— the revelation that the baby Son given unto us is also the Everlasting Father (Isa. 9:6). This realization demands change within us commensurate with this awareness!

"What would You have me do, Lord?" is a humble, loving, and grateful response to our seeing. A true enlightening revelation—seeing our Lord's life-giving glory, commensurate with embracing Him as our personal and holy Savior—will remove the darkness of our past lost existence. This should always result in making Him the Lord of our lives.

This revelation of Christ's glory, now understanding who Jesus is, brought about a transformed Paul. This aggressive persecutor was now instantly changed into a magnificent preacher and soldier of the cross. What Paul said in response to our Lord Jesus after absorbing Christ's identification, His person and Lordship, is a great demonstration of what the only reasonable response should be from every Christian believer.

The progression of communications in this historic encounter is so revealing. Reading this account, we observe Paul's mind spinning with a multitude of thoughts. He responded after concluding this observation.

He had greatly persecuted those whom Christ loved, and he responded to Christ's question after having come to terms with this realization.

Our similar realization equally demands response from us, or we are unworthy of having seen this greatest of all truths.

Years later Paul still carried the effects and awareness of his past history of error. He told the church of Corinth that he felt unworthy to be called an apostle due to his history of persecuting the church (1 Cor. 15:9).

Having to discard and undo conclusions reached, undoing the results of many years of learning, was mind staggering. Our Lord graciously allowed him three days of blindness to weigh these matters. Likewise He graciously allows all of us time to consider who He is and what our resulting decisions will be after we have received a revelation of His person. Embracing new truth contradicting the values of his past and peers and his erroneous religious beliefs greatly affected Paul. The change was instant and radical. It was the result of a true heart now following the glorious truth he now saw.

Paul now maximized his efforts and potential for good, just as he had in his zeal in past erroneous pursuits. Our God observes and seeks those of this kind of material. This is a perfect example as to what our normal response should be. We too were on a road of denying Christ in our past. We thereby damaged Christ and His people by our journey in unbelief. We were a testimony by our denial to a dead or nonexistent God. Our Savior made this clear when He said, "He that is not with me is against me, and he that gathereth not with me scattereth" (Luke 11:23).

When we see the bright light of truth...the revelation of Christ's person and atonement by the cross...this light of understanding must birth change. This light exposes and destroys our past life of death, religiosity, and darkness. This encounter knocks our feet out from underneath us. This is always cause for a reassessment of our entire worldview. When we become aware of and digest the thought of who Christ is, with Him being revealed as the Lord of the universe (if indeed we have genuinely seen this fact), the response of "What will You have me do?" is a natural normal progression. Seeing the reality of substitutionary atonement, seeing how Jesus died on a cruel cross for my sin, pierces my heart.

Later Paul described his resulting response that was initiated by this experience. Paul wrote to the church of Galatia regarding his changed life: "I am crucified with Christ: nevertheless I live; yet not I, but Christ liveth in me: and the life which I now live in the flesh I live by the faith of the Son of God, who loved me, and gave himself for me" (Gal. 2:20). Paul simultaneously saw his sin and the cross, identifying with both. He was confronted by the living God.

Experiencing a temporary blinding to life's natural circumstances bore results. Paul's eyes were being focused on the supernatural and the greater spiritual realm. This caused a complete reassessment of his actions, direction, and tomorrow. Likewise we, upon having had a Christ encounter, should be caused to reflect and consider how this affects all of our life's pursuits.

Ministry is birthed from this encounter, or it is entered into from a wrong basis. When one confronts the unrivaled truth and greatness of Christ, as God in flesh having clothed Himself as man for the sole purpose of reconciling man to Himself, it is mind staggering. When we understand the glory of His holy love for our person, as demonstrated by the cross, this act of His holy love is spell binding and life changing.

A clear revelation of sins eternally forgiven, commensurate with an eternal heavenly future with the King of kings and Lord of lords, must capture our hearts. It is finding the pearl of great worth; therefore I will sell all and purchase this pearl. I embrace Him and a glorious future where time shall be no more, where all tears are wiped away (Rev. 21:4). Those who have genuinely experienced this revelation will see a changed life and focus as a result. They now live with eyes of eternity with less focus on the temporal.

Ministry will always be part of this changed focus. What young man is ashamed of the girl he dearly loves? Who finds a treasure and does not rejoice? Who embraces the Savior and does not tell? Who, upon knowing they were lost and heading for an eternal death and damnation...after experiencing this grace and finding the light of the way...who will not direct others to this road of life?

## CALLED TO MINISTRY

By study I found where Paul wrote to the church of Ephesus that upon Christ ascending, He gave five differing ministry gifts to mankind and the church. These are Christ-given men and women of God, appointed by Christ, the Lord of the church, for ministry. They are called of God to minister revelation of His person and holy Bible truths. God Himself names these gifts unto man, or mankind. "Wherefore he saith, When he ascended up on high, he led captivity captive, and gave gifts unto men....And he gave some, apostles; and some, prophets; and some, evangelists; and some, pastors and teachers; for the perfecting of the saints, for the work of the ministry, for the edifying of the body of Christ" (Eph. 4:8, 11–12).

These are a Christ-given and Christ-appointed people. They are given to reveal God's heart and redemption, His love for man.

Somehow many have concluded several of these appointed gift callings are given for a limited, brief time period, to the early church. Somehow they have concluded this Christ giving to mankind was only for the early first- or second-century church. I have not found any scriptures that differ from Christ's giving to mankind for the entire church age. This truth is fortified and clear when one reads this topic in context, including the purpose for this giving.

Those who erroneously conclude that some of these five callings and this giving is for a limited time period never have a scriptural answer for this limiting opinion. They are silent if asked why they uphold some and deny other callings.

Those of this wrong limited time giving opinion always disregard the scripturally attested giving of numerous named apostles beyond the original twelve. To understand the complete and timeless giving of these ministry gifts, one will need to understand what determines the identification of these differing gift callings, and then study the need for these back then and now.

Most Christians are not Christ appointed to these callings, although all Christians are called to minister Christ and salvation to the world, both in and outside of the church. However, Christ after His ascension gave some specific and differing ministry callings. Unfortunately, the common understanding of Christ's giving, along with a clear discernment of who these callings are and what makes them so, has mostly been lost. Today the lost understanding of this subject is being renewed and revealed progressively under what we term fivefold ministry teachings.

This giving was not speaking about the gifts of the Spirit described in Romans chapter 12, which are given to those whom our Lord Jesus has baptized in the Holy Spirit (John 1:33; Acts 1:8). These Christ-termed gift ministries given to the church have differing ministry wiring, affecting their focus and grace strengths. All of them, although different as to makeup and function, were given to do the work of the ministry. They are all given to proclaim salvation, teach, and govern the church. All of these called and appointed by Christ ministries should grow to being capable of fulfilling the ministry office of the other callings. However, they will all differ in their heartfelt burden toward what they are really called to be. They maximize their potential when they flow in their own unique calling.

This declaration of truth begs the questions: How do we identify these ministry gifts, and what is the call of God to ministry? How do we know if we are one of these five Christ-appointed ministries? In my life this has been a burning question since my initial salvation experience some forty years ago. Over the following years the understanding of this question has unfolded, with a continuing increase of revelation. How I wish that a teaching book had been made available to me in the years gone by to enlighten me on this topic. With much seeking I found answers to this question in the Bible. Our faithful God answers all sincere questions in time. The Holy Spirit is the teacher of all teachers. I share with you the holy insights I have found and enjoyed.

All believers are called to be fruitful in God's church and kingdom pursuits (John 15:8). We must consider our future accounting to be given in our Christ confrontation by all believers at Christ's throne. We will be asked for an accounting before Christ as to what we did with our talents (Matt. 25:19; 1 Cor. 3:13). The Master gave gift abilities to all of His servants, although different in quantity.

He does not give these gifts to strangers and the unsaved, but only to His servants. He has no expectation from strangers. This normal expectation from the redeemed is a reasonable response. We owe a debt of love. This love for Christ will affect our thoughts, lips, and actions. What our focus is and what we project in this life will demonstrate our love for Him. The unprofitable servant, after squandering his talents, was cast into outer darkness, where there is weeping and gnashing of teeth (Matt. 25:30). The tree that looked good but bore no fruit was visited in an untimely fashion and was cursed to die (Matt. 21:19). Our master will come for us in an hour when we do not expect (Matt. 24:44). All who genuinely love Christ must be kingdom and fruit focused. This labor of love will be effortless for those who love our Lord. And to the contrary, this will be a burden of weight to those who are working to earn their salvation while attempting to pay their dues to receive fire insurance. Salvation is not of works (Eph. 2:8–9).

However, only some are called by Christ to the distinct and set apart five ministry callings the apostle Paul listed in Ephesians 4:11. These "some" are called by Christ and are appointed to fill the five unique and differing ministry offices that Paul listed. These Christ-appointed ministries will receive a greater revelation insight of the Word of God. These who are called to these five callings will constantly be burdened to minister the burden that consumed Christ's heart in ministry. Jesus was the epitome of all of these five callings. He was the great apostle, prophet, teacher, evangelist, and pastor. Called ministry will carry a burden of heart to fulfill that which their Lord has imparted within them. This holy impartation by the Holy Spirit will differ in the five callings. However, the differing burden of heart will always be a vein of the burden of Christ's heart for His people and church. This burden and holy vision will always involve what our Lord has revealed to them as to needs in humanity. Physical needs will be part of this seeing, but the greater observed need will always be spiritual.

All Christ-appointed and called ministries will see these needs due to receiving a Holy Spirit–impartation of insight and burden. As they mature, the differing ministry callings will naturally gravitate their focus and ministry to the particular need of humanity that has been imparted to them. They will incline toward shepherding, teaching, evangelizing, doctrine, and church planting, or to the realm of the Spirit in the prophetic revelation and presence matters. All of this is brought about by holy revelation, a work of the Holy Spirit within the believer (Phil. 2:13).

The young Christ-appointed minister Timothy gained maturity and growth with the help of Paul, due to this apostle father's heart ministry and guidance. We will all benefit from apostle father figures. Although Timothy was directed to do the work of an evangelist as part of his ministry training, all of his ministry efforts eventually brought him to the maturity of his Christ-given calling, which was apostle (2 Tim. 2:5; 1 Thess. 1:1; 2:6). Timothy demonstrated this calling when the matured man of God accompanied Paul in travels or Paul-directed assignments (1 Tim. 6:11; 1 Thess. 1:1; 2:6).

Those who are not called to a distinct fivefold Ephesians 4 calling will also be guided in ministering Christ to others by receiving a burden. If we have no burden to touch souls or edify fellow believers in faith matters, an immediate inventory of our truthful Christ relationship is mandatory. Lacking this will certainly disqualify us from claims of being of the five "called" or raise sincere questions as to our salvation. One may have the heart of an elder, which is open to "any man" (1 Tim. 3:1), and have a burden for the flock to teach and oversee, yet still not be of the five "called" and Christ-appointed ministry.

The question of "Am I alive in Christ?" needs to be answered daily by all of us. "But if the Spirit of him that raised up Jesus from the dead dwell in you, he that raised up Christ from the dead shall also quicken your mortal bodies by his Spirit that dwelleth in you" (Rom. 8:11). A holy burden of heart will lead us to teach Sunday school, enter into intercessory prayer, or witness to a lost soul and family members.

We will always be looking for avenues to reach others, to win them to Christ. We will have a genuine continual life of prayer, while walking with our Lord. Perhaps we may be janitors as a service to Christ, or look after other people's children to free parents to partake in ministry or a church service. We must have a servant heart.

The Holy Spirit always imparts a holy burden that motivates the believer to fulfill His purposes in reaching and drawing humanity (John 6:44). Those who are never burdened to minister Christ in some capacity have a dead faith. Ministry that stems from other reasons without a burden of heart may gather people but will produce very little holy life within them. Numbers are of value, but they are a limited measure in weighing ministry results. Maturing of the saints to a stronger faith and knowledge of God principles is very valid in measuring ministry effectiveness. We must have a prayerful revelation of God-directed need and purpose as we minister. Our true ministry growth should include a growing revelation of our God, His being, and eternal purposes.

Genuine ministry growth will cause one to wear and see life and people through what I call "God glasses," glasses, so to speak, that allow us to see life and people with a God view of blessings and righteous holy need. These glasses will daily be bathed in continuous layers and depths, a deepening immersion in Christ and His glory.

## CHAPTER SEVEN

# LOVE'S RESPONSE, NOW SERVE

*Ministry Anointing Roots, Waiting on God*

*A*FERVENT CHRIST-APPOINTED AND directed ministry must have a great love for God and man. The genuine call of God working within these ministries should always have an underlying foundation to their ministry walk. This will be much like the roots of a large tree. Their roots should be strong and spread wide. Their ministry roots become strong by waiting on the Lord. These roots take time to grow. Little may be showing aboveground, but the foundation for the future and ministry effectiveness is being formed. This growing process is always achieved by waiting on the Lord and spending time in His Word. Failed ministry will become fruitful even after many years of emptiness, simply by stopping and aggressively waiting on the Lord.

We, the servants and Christ-appointed ministry, must never be anxious to get visible fruit or accomplishments for self-image. The flesh has a tendency to become impatient and anxious to jump into the battle prior to being sent. The wrong start without God's signal and sending is usually due to wrong ambitions, leading to a self-image-focused ministry. Often this is the result of the desire to revel and bathe in the accolades of people: "You are so elegant, wise, and talented." These words easily become a death trap to the anointing and holy presence. Bathing in the allurement and sunshine of these words generates ministers who at heart are pursuing spiritual visibility instead of a Christ and His kingdom vision.

The anointing comes to those who die to self, those who have a radical pursuit of revealing Christ as Lord. The roots of a righteous servant-hearted ministry will focus their eyes on Jesus, His person, glory, works, and kingdom. Their ministry will result from the overflow of their love for Christ. They will demonstrate a Christ heart for the lost in the world. They will cherish the church and believers, His people. Their love for Christ will be demonstrated by their love for man. They burn with a passion for the souls of men. They totally see Christ's heart and possess a spiritual dynamo within, fueled by a radical love for humanity. Redeeming the church, His blood-bought bride will be our joy. Their ministry foundation will be a deep love for Christ and seeing the gospel as the only God-provided answer to humanity's needs. No greater time or ambition can be pursued than a constant pursuit of this deep heartfelt focus.

## MOSES, PREPARATION AND RESPONSE

Moses started out in a basket floating wherever the water currents would take him. He was placed in the waters of the unknown when his parents saw no other answer. God always sees what is unknown to us and has the answers. The content of this basket was ultimately transformed to be used of God in a mighty way. We never know our limits under our God, because He is unlimited. Likewise all called ministry are equally candidates for great accomplishment, but only if we surrender to our Lord's work within us.

Moses was a child destined for Pharaoh's orchestrated death sentence, but the God of Israel intervened. Moses grew into the man with whom God spoke to face-to-face (Exod. 33:11). We may be assured that his parents sought the heavens for deliverance from the oppression of the Egyptian whip and brick kilns. During her pregnancy, Moses's mother and father would greatly hope this new baby was a girl so as not to face the enforced death of this child. Sometimes that which may seem like a huge struggle or difficulty may turn out to be a great blessing under God for our deliverance. This basket baby was a part of the Lord's answer to the situation. We may well ask, "Lord, what can I do, and where can I be an answer to prayer to bring deliverance to the captives?" (Isa. 61:1).

Several times in my past life, as I look upon certain people and ministry separations that were so painful, I now see what the Lord saved me from. After Abraham endured the painful separation from his nephew Lot, whom he loved, he heard the Lord's voice. "And the Lord said unto Abram, after that Lot was separated from him, Lift up now thine eyes, and look from the place where thou art northward, and southward, and eastward, and westward" (Gen. 13:14). Note this promise was released by our Lord "after that Lot was separated from him." Note the words *after* and *now*, which came subsequent to a difficult choice and dealing in Abraham's life. We constantly learn and are tested in our heartfelt decisions and choices.

While being raised in Pharaoh's court as a youth, Moses somehow realized he was born of the Israelite nation. He became grieved while observing the slavery abuse of his heritage people. Moses responded with a righteous and protective heart of love for his people, but in his own wisdom. He killed an abusive Egyptian. In time the Lord showed him how to deal with the entire nation.

Paul wrote with holy insight regarding Moses: "By faith Moses, when he was come to years, refused to be called the son of Pharaoh's daughter; choosing rather to suffer affliction with the people of God, than to enjoy the pleasures of sin for a season; esteeming the reproach of Christ greater riches than the treasures in Egypt: for he had respect unto the recompense of the reward. By faith he forsook Egypt, not fearing the wrath of the king: for he endured, as seeing him who is invisible" (Heb. 11:24–27).

Moses made tough decisions accompanied with strong actions. Due to his faith in our eternal God and the concern he had for his people, Moses acted. His heart placed confidence and trust in his Creator, the God of Israel. His insight and resulting actions were due to seeing the need, which the Lord of heaven revealed within his heart. There were eternal consequences to this response and Moses's actions. The attempts to right that which was wrong were the roots to his eventual great ministry. This will also be the roots to our ministry. Seeing must be accompanied with actions, but these actions must be under God and in His time.

Moses had "respect unto the recompense of the reward." This was the foundational motivation to his actions. These spoke of his respect for the God of Israel. Likewise the wise and correct ministry will also have respect for the eternal reward our God will give to all who see the eventual end of their journey and ministry. The quality and dedication of a ministry can be observed by the depth of their respect for "the recompense." Do we see our eternal recompense, measured by our works?

Moses was raised as Pharaoh's daughter's son. His standing in Pharaoh's family offered great prominence in the royal court, attended with riches and power. He had all that Egyptian royalty status provided. He did not look to wealth or the allurement of status and personal comforts as he made his decision. This is the potential our omniscient God foresaw within the heart of this basket baby. Our Lord preserved him for a higher purpose in His program.

He also saw a shepherd boy who was not esteemed, whom Samuel anointed. He became a great prophet and king. Our God always discerns the heart of man.

Moses left Egypt on a journey that took forty years of his life. He dwelt in a desert-like terrain where the Lord shaped his life in this unique workshop. This was the isolated Bible school where the Lord shaped his character. He became a man of God. It takes time to form a man of God. Timothy started out in different circumstances while being mentored by Paul. Eventually Paul bestowed upon him these words: "But thou, O *man of God*, flee these things; and follow after righteousness, godliness, faith, love, patience, meekness" (1 Tim. 6:11, emphasis added). These words Paul bestowed on Timothy were a great compliment. Timothy held steady as a servant, a humble, tutored minister who accepted the honor of being mentored by God's provided overseeing apostle ministry, Paul.

Moses, Elisha, and John the Baptist likewise received a huge education as they were Holy Spirit–trained in the quiet unseen, the none applauded desert Bible school. These were molded by God's mighty hand until the Lord said, "You have attained." No certificates. No doctorates. Just God!

This was no different with Joseph. His feet were bound in shackles until the word of the Lord came to move him forward into a new walk (Ps. 105:18). The real molding is the heart within, resulting in a yielded spirit.

Moses became a transformed man prior to leading Israel out of Egypt. The self-assurance of a young man had long ago left him. Like Jacob he leaned on the Lord, who became his rod and staff as he entered into his called ministry. "By faith Jacob, when he was a dying, blessed both the sons of Joseph; and worshipped, leaning upon the top of his staff" (Heb. 11:21).

The intervening change in Moses was due to this God-orchestrated forty-year-long desert dealing.

Moses focused his heart heavenward while in a place of solitude. "Now the man Moses was very meek, above all the men which were upon the face of the earth" (Num. 12:3). Moses knew all actions undertaken in his own strength had failed. He waited for and humbly yielded to the voice of a higher wisdom.

Moses had depicted his greatness of heart in desiring to free his people. He had demonstrated this by putting his life on the line—only this had been attempted in his own strength. Now this would be achieved as he was sent by the hand of God. In God's time and hour of readiness a prepared Moses had a holy and God-orchestrated encounter. He was a changed man, yet the same. He had never forgotten his enslaved people, his roots. He just got to a place where he accepted that only the Lord of heaven, the God of Israel, could deal with this task of freeing His people.

May we never forget our enslaved people or roots. May we, as Moses, demonstrate a heart for the people around us, proven by a heart to defend our people from their slavery and bondage. That heart focus never left Moses and should always be within our hearts. In time Moses was altered as he yielded to the Lord to accomplish what he personally could not do. He now looked to the God of Abraham, Isaac, and Jacob. Likewise the called ministry, regardless of rejection and difficulties faced, will always want to affect God's people for good. To deliver them from bondage, now knowing the Lord must lead us, we must follow.

## A BURNING BUSH

Moses's life was changed in a moment of time. God may show us His glory as well in a multitude of different ways. Our lives can instantly be transformed.

> And the angel of the LORD appeared unto him in a flame of fire out of the midst of a bush: and he looked, and, behold, the bush burned with fire, and the bush was not consumed. And Moses said, I will now turn aside, and see this great sight, why the bush is not burnt. And when the LORD saw that he turned aside to see, God called unto him out of the midst of the bush, and said, Moses, Moses. And he said, Here am I. And he said, Draw not nigh hither: put off thy shoes from off thy feet, for the place whereon you stand is holy ground. Moreover he said, I am the God of thy father, the God of Abraham, the God of Isaac, and the God of Jacob. And Moses hid his face; for he was afraid to look upon God.
>
> —EXODUS 3:2–6

Note: The God of Abraham often shows Himself as an angel, three men, a burning bush, or enthroned in glory (Gen. 18:1; Isa. 6:1). More commonly His sermon and revelation to us are by creation's glory and His Holy Word. The greatest glory is seen by Christ's love in redemption (Ps. 19:1; John 1:14). Should we see His glory revealed, this will be due to having received eyes that see and ears that hear from God's mercy storehouse. The awesomeness of this seeing will likewise cause us to turn aside as well. We will be caused to take a detour from our normal course of direction. We are intrigued with and desire to see more closely, to understand the miracle of the revelation. This revelation of our God, His glory and might, should bring instant change to the course of our lives.

Change always involves what the burning bush revealed. It burned and was still alive. Likewise in us, our God is a consuming fire (Deut. 4:24). True seeing will change us into becoming living sacrifices. "I beseech you therefore, brethren, by the mercies of God, that ye present your bodies a living sacrifice, holy, acceptable unto God, which is your reasonable service" (Rom. 12:1).

True revelation will always cause us to see and stand on holy ground, because our God is holy. This will cause us to take off our shoes, so to speak. This depicts us presenting ourselves before our holy God, with a walk void of our works, an unsheathed, uncloaked, and transparent determination. We stand spiritually naked before a transforming God, who knows our all with nothing hidden, yet loves us.

## PRAYERS ANSWERED IN TIME

> And the LORD said, I have surely seen the affliction of my people which are in Egypt, and have heard their cry by reason of their taskmasters; for I know their sorrows; and I am come down to deliver them out of the hand of the Egyptians.
>
> —EXODUS 3:7–8

I believe Moses often thought of and besieged the heavens regarding the bondage of his people back in Egypt. After all, he killed a man to demonstrate his heart in the matter. His prayer result now being answered is comparable to the time frame Zacharias experienced. The angel of the Lord told Zacharias, "Thy prayer is heard" (Luke 1:13)—a long-forgotten prayer from a young couple, offered for a desired child. This prayer was answered when he and his wife, Elizabeth, were old. God always hears and never forgets. Our greatest ministry may be after many years of preparation.

Our God knows and sees the suffering and pain of all. He alone knows the brokenhearted and weariness of the soul under the whip of the taskmaster, whatever this may mean in our lives. In His wisdom and time He answers our prayers. I suspect that most likely it is us who are withholding the God answers we are waiting for. This is due to our inaction and unbelief. After all, Israel could have reached the land of promise in twelve days, should they have believed and acted on God's promises.

Twelve is the number of government. God's governmental representatives of Israel were sent out to view the Promised Land. The unbelieving ten spies destroyed faith, much the same as wrong, unbelieving leadership will always destroy faith. When we believe and get under God's called believing government, and then believe His giving and ways, blessings will always flow quickly.

## THE SENDING

> Now therefore, behold, the cry of the children of Israel is come unto me: and I have also seen the oppression wherewith the Egyptians oppress them. Come now therefore, and *I will send thee* unto Pharaoh, that thou mayest bring forth my people the children of Israel out of Egypt.
> —EXODUS 3:9–10, EMPHASIS ADDED

God always shows us His glory before sending His messengers. After we see Him and His glory, He will show us the need to be addressed. Then He sends! Did He send, or did we "went"? Love for God and man accompanied Moses in his sent journey. The Lord was with him.

Many people run and attempt to do God's works long before genuinely being ready for the Lord's sending. They do not wait or allow for their God-intended preparation completion. Then when they fail, they get disillusioned and confused, whereby many quit their entire ministry efforts. These people "went" and were not "sent." They were zealous and full of good intentions, but they did not wait for the Master to initiate their journey into His ministry, direction, and plans. Unfortunately, few have apostle-hearted ministry to prepare and mature them. Both Paul and Barnabas were called apostles. They would naturally have a desire to travel into new territory due to their growing apostle wiring within. They had progressed through differing ministry responsibilities, having taught and functioning as elders for several years (Acts 11:26). They waited and were successfully sent when the Holy Spirit directed them.

## ISAIAH SEEING GLORY, NEED, THEN SENT

The prophet received a vision showing God's heart. This included seeing his and the people's sin. He saw the need for a preacher to tell them of

God's love, to bring the answers to their sin that was leading them to sorrow and death, both now and eternally.

> The vision of Isaiah the son of Amoz, which he saw concerning Judah and Jerusalem in the days of Uzziah, Jotham, Ahaz, and Hezekiah, kings of Judah. Hear, O heavens, and give ear, O earth: for the LORD hath spoken, I have nourished and brought up children, and they have rebelled against me. The ox knoweth his owner, and the ass his master's crib: but Israel doth not know, my people doth not consider.
>
> —ISAIAH 1:1–3

The called minister will always see God's broken heart for man entangled in sin. Likewise we will see His love in redemption and His desire that all men would be saved (1 Tim. 2:4). We respond from our genuine love for God and man. Love is the fuel to the dynamo within. Ministry is a direct result of seeing God's love and receiving His mercy. Simultaneously Isaiah saw his sin and man's predicament, that all are heading toward an eternal judgment. Isaiah saw this need with a heart to preach and tell them about their salvation potential.

This revelation was of God's majestic reign, glory, mercy, and person:

> In the year that king Uzziah died I saw also the Lord sitting upon a throne, high and lifted up, and his train filled the temple. Above it stood the seraphims: each one had six wings; with twain he covered his face, and with twain he covered his feet, and with twain he did fly. And one cried unto another, and said, Holy, holy, holy, is the LORD of hosts.
>
> —ISAIAH 6:1–3

## REVEALED STEPS TO MINISTRY

Isaiah saw and was greatly impacted by this realization or revelation: "The whole earth is full of his glory" (v. 3). Our God reveals His glory with divine purpose from His heart of divine love. When we receive a revelation of His majesty and throne, the gods of wood, silver, and gold die a natural death. This death includes our gods of sports, hobbies, or continual entertainment without a God focus. Seeing Him always causes the natural man to hide. Adam responded in similar fashion to Isaiah. Upon experiencing the sight of holiness, Isaiah responded with, "Then said I, Woe is me! for I am undone; because I am a man of unclean lips, and I dwell in the midst of a people of unclean lips" (v. 5).

Seeing Him and His holy pure glory always reflects our unclean unworthiness, "for mine eyes have seen the King, the Lord of hosts" (v. 5). We see God, holy and reigning, yet in mercy reaching out to our needs. "Then flew one of the seraphims unto me, having a live coal in his hand, which he had taken with the tongs from off the altar: And he laid it upon my mouth, and said, Lo, this hath touched thy lips; and your iniquity is taken away, and thy sin purged" (vv. 6–7). We see Christ, the eternal coal from God's burning and purifying altar, who touches our lips and what comes out of us, thereby cleansing us.

Subsequent to our cleansing He always asks this key question. Then He eagerly waits for our response, and He judges us accordingly. Are we worthy of our received cleansing? Our Lord Jesus made this clear: "And he that taketh not his cross, and followeth after me, is not worthy of me" (Matt. 10:38). "Whosoever therefore shall be ashamed of me and of my words in this adulterous and sinful generation; of him also shall the Son of man be ashamed, when he cometh in the glory of his Father with the holy angels" (Mark 8:38).

Heaven pours out grace and love but equally demands a love response. "Also I heard the voice of the Lord, saying, Whom shall I send, and *who will go for us?*" (Isa. 6:8, emphasis added). "WHO WILL GO FOR US?" The divine Trinity—Father, Son, and Holy Spirit—is intently watching for a love response to His love.

Will we tell others about the altar coal availability? NOTE: God always asks us. He always waits for our answer, requiring us to exercise our will. Then He judges and holds us accountable for our choices.

God never orders or enslaves His ministry with force. He respects our will in all matters. He always appeals, allowing and demanding that the ministry respond as an act of their will. Our response must be a reverent act of worship—never by the law of you shall and must, but a heartfelt response. This prophet's response placed him in God's Hall of Fame. "Then said I, Here am I; send me" (v. 8). The heart that has been healed from being "undone" responded with "send me." This was love's response from a heart overflowing with grateful thanks and adoration, the result of having been made whole. We are still undone and broken if this is not the case.

## PROFOUND TRUTH

The profound truth applicable to godly and ministry-minded people is found in Luke 7:44–47: "And he turned to the woman, and said unto Simon, Seest thou this woman? I entered into thine house, thou gavest me no water for my feet: but she hath washed my feet with tears, and wiped them with the hairs of her head. Thou gavest me no kiss: but this woman since the time I came in hath not ceased to kiss my feet. My head with oil thou didst not anoint: but this woman hath anointed my feet with ointment. Wherefore I say unto thee, Her sins, which are many, are forgiven; *for she loved much: but to whom little is forgiven, the same loveth little*" (emphasis added).

Unfortunately the phrase "little is forgiven" is often read as applicable to the fairly good person with little sin needing forgiveness. The truth is, this scripture refers to the depth of forgiveness any person has perceived themselves to have received. We all need a huge ocean of forgiveness. We are self-righteous or blind when we do not see the chasm full of sin that has separated us from our God, our loveless self-righteousness and pride. We do not need a history of murder, drugs, or immorality to need much forgiveness. We all need the cross and blood. "I am pretty good" has to die.

The depth of our personally received forgiveness will be revealed. This will be made visible by the depth and the fervency of our ministry. How deeply do we see the mercy of His forgiveness? The eternal judgment He has saved us from? His love and forgiveness of our sins, now placed under His cross-shed blood? This will now be demonstrated by our life's focus.

Our needed prayer is this: "Lord God, in mercy strengthen us. Help us Your ministry to respond in like manner. May we be holy sacrifices sent from Your altar, poured out with love, vision, and a ministry desiring to tell all. May our love response be lived out, with a willingness to speak Your words."

> And he said, Go, and tell this people, Hear ye indeed, but understand not; and see ye indeed, but perceive not. Make the heart of this people fat, and make their ears heavy, and shut their eyes; lest they see with their eyes, and hear with their ears, and understand with their heart, and convert, and be healed.
>
> —Isaiah 6:9–10

Judgment comes to all who do not seek.

Our commission is to go and tell. We speak forth of His glory and mercy. It is not for us to save man. That is the work of the Holy Spirit (John 16:8). Furthermore, should few listen or respond, do not be discouraged. Noah was listed in God's Hall of Fame in Hebrews 11. He preached for many years, while only seeing his family getting saved. The faithful prophet John the Baptist was beheaded at the end of his very brief ministry. He is now waiting in the closest place to God Himself, under God's throne (Rev. 6:9). Glory!

## MICAH, THE WORD OF THE LORD

The word of the Lord. The holy revelation of what God wanted this ministry to know and see. The revelation that filled and burdened his thoughts and heart. The insight and message Micah was to proclaim. "The word of the LORD that came to Micah the Morasthite in the days of Jotham, Ahaz, and Hezekiah, kings of Judah, which he saw concerning Samaria and Jerusalem" (Mic. 1:1). Micah was shown God's words and desire for mankind. In obedience he ministered this. The called ministry will always be shown God's seeing, heart, and thoughts if they wait upon Him. Ministry is a declaring of God's heart, as we are His ambassadors. Waiting to hear, spending time in His Word, and quiet time prayerfully hearing promote the receiving of this.

The message was an awareness of impending judgment, God's coming and dealing with sin. This message is to be proclaimed to all of the earth and the inhabitants thereof. We are to proclaim this God-ordained and unchanging message as well.

> Hear, all ye people; hearken, O earth, and all that therein is: and let the Lord GOD be witness against you, the Lord from his holy temple. For, behold, the LORD cometh forth out of his place, and will come down, and tread upon the high places of the earth. And the mountains shall be molten under him, and the valleys shall be cleft, as wax before the fire, and as the waters that are poured down a steep place.... Woe to them that devise iniquity, and work evil upon their beds! when the morning is light, they practice it, because it is in the power of their hand. And they covet fields, and take them by violence; and houses, and take them away: so they oppress a man and his house, even a man and his heritage.
>
> —MICAH 1:2–4; 2:1–2

God's messengers will ALWAYS SEE SIN and CONFRONT SINFULNESS, or they are become servants of man, not wanting to offend man. They demonstrate their being content and comfortable while doing so, but while ignoring the offending of God!

## SAUL CALLED TO BE PAUL

The apostle Paul is a beloved Bible storied person. We see so much of his heart and passion for God after a Christ confrontation, bringing about a change to his name. Immediately after this encounter we see his life depicted as the living sacrifice he became—a prisoner of love responding to Christ, His Lordship, and mercy. Few are the serious Bible students who do not admire his teachings and exploits. He is a great New Testament gospel hero of heroes, much as David is in the Old Testament gallery of God's most famous warriors.

The transition from Saul to Paul took place at a specific time with holy purpose: "And when I could not see for *the glory of that light*" (Acts 22:11, emphasis added). The "brightness of that light" was God at work in two differing realms. One was in the natural realm, the blinding of natural eyes for a time with divine purpose. The other was the spiritual truth impact upon seeing "the glory." Often one needs to be blinded to our natural realm before he can look to the spiritual realm. In my case, several hospital trips, along with corporate betrayal in my absence due to an injury while on the job, shook me with a blinding to my past pursuits and blindness. Like Paul, although not as graphically, I was confronted by the risen Lord of glory (1 Cor. 2:8).

This holy confrontation evoked one question: "Who are You, Lord?" I have to know and understand the one whom I now see as relevant to my life. Many come to Christ after having been shaken in their natural lives.

Understanding the graciously given answer Christ gave when identifying His person, especially in the face of being confronted with the persecuting of His beloved, brought instant change. "I am Jesus whom thou persecutest" (Acts 9:5). Understanding Him to be the Lord of glory instantly changed Paul's direction and purpose, his mission and life focus.

Paul was zealous beyond his equals prior to this revelation (Gal. 1:14). He was fervent in the belief of and in defense of his traditions. He was hot and not cold, but in pursuit of the wrong hot direction. This Christ confrontation, the revelation of His person and glory, evoked the only correct response any called servant should have: "Lord, what wilt thou have me to do?" (Acts 9:6).

Likewise, the one called to ministry, upon seeing "the glory" of God's person and salvation, must ask the same question beginning with the term "LORD." Christ either becomes Lord of all in our lives, or He is not Lord at all.

## Believer's Ministry

All believers must enter into ministry. All true believers are part of the "WE" company who have seen His glory.

In the beginning was the Word, and the Word was with God, and the Word was God. The same was in the beginning with God. All things were made by him; and without him was not any thing made that was made....And the Word was made flesh, and dwelt among us, (and *we beheld his glory*, the glory as of the only begotten of the Father,) full of grace and truth.

—JOHN 1:1–3, 14, EMPHASIS ADDED

I question the salvation status of those who do not share or speak of their love for Christ. Many genuinely believe in heaven and hell, having a belief in their needing salvation. Many of these will do religious duties. They respect and fear Him but are not filled with love for Christ.

All true believers, upon having seen His glory, have experienced Christ's love, grace, and forgiveness of sins. They will continuously act. Our ministry to others must always rise from this experience and an ongoing Christ relationship. If one has not seen Jesus as glorious, he is not born of the Spirit and only has a dead Christian church-attending religion of choice, a chosen Christian religion instead of a Buddhist or a Muslim affiliation and attendance. All believers are to be living messages and messengers. "Ye are our epistle written in our hearts, known and read of all men" (2 Cor. 3:2).

If others cannot read you and me, it is with understandable reasons. We are a blurred writing, and the reason will be because Jesus has not been made Lord. He must reign and be enthroned in order for our writing to be clear to all. May all believers and ministers be saturated with the love of Christ. We are called to be His friends: "Ye are my friends, if ye do whatsoever I command you" (John 15:14). What if we do not do what He commands? We are commanded to go into all of the world to preach the gospel (Matt. 28:19).

Note the big *if* word. Seeing an eternal judgment ahead for those who do not believe will cause us to act out of our love for them. What kind of friends are we when we have no heart to introduce Him to all whom we meet? Shame of Him now will be met with eternal shame: "Whosoever therefore shall be ashamed of me and of my words in this adulterous and sinful generation; of him also shall the Son of man be ashamed, when he cometh in the glory of his Father with the holy angels" (Mark 8:38).

Our introducing of Christ to others is THE LOVE AND TRUTH RESPONSE OF THE CALLED!

## CHAPTER EIGHT

# NEEDED TRUTH IMPACT

*Revelation Impact*

*I*T IS SO piercing and convicting when one sees great truths but is aware of his personal limitations in living these out. We are convicted by our limitations due to not having achieved a walk that matches the revealed knowledge. This is comparable to us seeing the holiness of God's laws and then being aware of our inability, knowing we are incapable of fully keeping these holy commandments.

We cannot perfectly love God or our neighbor. If we did, we would arrest all unbelievers with tears, imploring them to know Christ to save them from hell. We would be in prayer for them every waking hour. When not involved with intercession, we would be praising and worshipping Him every waking hour. No, we have a limited love. We are limited due to our humanity and the "flesh." This understanding and awareness applies to this writing, and these truths are presented with a keen knowledge of this reality.

I personally struggle when I see the truths I share in the following pages. I see and know their beauty. I strive toward living out these truths but realize I have not attained unto them. I am convinced that this is the truth experienced by many sincere believers and ministers. Regardless of our limitations we press toward the goal. We share the blessed glorious Bible truth revelations we possess. We also strive to make these revelation truths we rejoice in, part of our experiential walk through life, despite our failures.

We personally lean on God's grace as we preach. We will always be aware of our personal failures in attaining unto the awesome truths we hold out as righteous. We are on dangerous ground when we preach when we are not aware of our personal lack in meeting the perfection we preach and strive for. Many preachers, while portraying truth, fall into this trap. They as standard-bearing leaders become deceived, pretending they have achieved in a walk matching their preaching of holy perfection.

Christ confronted the Pharisees, who were a walking minefield of this deception. We are blind to our true selves and have become self-righteous when we preach and say "you should" as opposed to "we should." Only God has the right to say "you should," while we humbly say "we should."

This truth is scripturally emphasized as to the attitude a spiritual person should have when addressing a brother overtaken by failure. The apostle Paul taught, "Brethren, if a man be overtaken in a fault, ye which are spiritual, restore such an one in the spirit of meekness; considering thyself, lest thou also be tempted" (Gal. 6:1).

Herein we see the appropriate heart attitude of all mature and balanced ministries. The textual inclusion of "considering thyself" speaks to this truth. I can also be tempted. We must know that all of us are capable of failure. All of us are constant recipients of God's preservation and grace. May the one who thinks "I would never do that" be aware of God's gracious preserving power, as He demonstrated to King Abimelech when Sarah, Abraham's wife, was involved: "And God said unto him in a dream, Yea, I know that thou didst this in the integrity of thy heart; for I also withheld thee from sinning against me: therefore suffered I thee not to touch her" (Gen. 20:6). May we give glory to His name. His grace restrains us from sin and keeps us by His holy power in our lives, but we still have the ability to ignore His restraining.

This truth principle applies to the called-of-God ministry. God uses imperfect people to do His perfect will. However, knowing our limitations should never stop our walk and growth. Our patriarch Jacob started out as a "supplanter." Over time he overcame and won a victory, an overcoming within himself. Jacob the deceiver spent time in a God-orchestrated school. He was personally victimized by his uncle Laban, who was a master at deceiving. The results brought about a graduation of change. Our God is all wisdom.

Upon his graduation, the Lord said that Jacob's name was now changed to Israel. Our Lord said that "as a prince," after wrestling with the angel, he now had power with God. Jacob had refused to let go in this wrestling until he received a blessing (Gen. 32:34). Are we wrestling with the angel? Are we holding on to God, refusing to let go until we receive His blessing?

When introduced to Pharaoh by Joseph, this matured prince with God gave a changed Jacob answer. He humbly confessed, "The days of the years of my pilgrimage are an hundred and thirty years: few and evil have the days of the years of my life been, and have not attained unto the days of the years of the life of my fathers in the days of their pilgrimage. And Jacob blessed Pharaoh, and went out from before Pharaoh" (Gen. 47:9–10).

Yet he blessed the greatest leader of his known world. Jacob ended his journey by leaning on his staff and worshipping. With prophetic revelation and promise he blessed his heritage. The stature and greatness of this transformed giant were defined by his humility under God (Gen. 49:1; Heb. 11:21).

We see that we positionally possess righteousness due to what Christ has done for us. We achieve this righteousness by the grace of God and the shed blood of Jesus as we believe. We name this substitutionary atonement. He did for us what we could not do. This is hugely important. We still fight a sin nature. The flesh and natural man still fight with the spiritual, the new man within (Gal. 5:17). Humility must always prevail in our teaching and preaching.

Always remember who is God. We must avoid the gross error of a wrong understanding. This is commonly demonstrated by the pope and many high up in the Roman Catholic and other churches. They accept obeisance and people bowing to them, as if they are deserving of such. They thereby dishonor our holy God by claiming the status of mini gods on earth. Only God in His throne deserves obeisance.

Many other ministers will not allow this form of obeisance, yet in reality they demand and expect this in a portrayal and expected attitude. May we avoid this, as demonstrated by the apostle Peter, the man whom the pope claims himself to be in the succession of. "And as Peter was coming in, Cornelius met him, and fell down at his feet, and worshipped him. But Peter took him up, saying, Stand up; I myself also am a man" (Acts 10:25–26). I wonder how these so-called ministry people will answer our living God when experiencing God's inevitable judgment day? He alone deserves worship, while we may receive love.

The apostle John was also corrected in this behavior by the angel who gave him the insights to the now written Book of Revelation. The angel refused to accept John bowing to him, directing John to bow to Christ (Rev. 19:10). We must bow to Christ and His Word. He is God! May we yield our hearts and thoughts to scriptural truth principles, denying all writings that contradict Holy Writ. We must esteem Him and be holy leaders, enriched by the Word of God. When we lack the mentoring of wise mature ministry, we waste so much time. May we become God-provided mature and wise spiritual mothers and fathers in Israel.

A wise listening ear will steady our walk with mature counsel. Unfortunately Paul was correct in what he told the believers: "For though ye have ten thousand instructors in Christ, yet have ye not have many fathers" (1 Cor. 4:15). We will experience a greater level of ministry frustration and be limited when we lack the wisdom availability of receiving mature counsel. Pete Beck, a modern-day apostle, has a great book on this topic entitled *Not Many Fathers*. Mature fathers in the Lord will guide us, due to their God-given experiential paths they have traveled. This guidance especially applies to our recognizing and understanding the workings of the Holy Spirit within us. May we help and mentor others wherever we can.

## Ministry Gifts but Not a Fivefold Calling

To the genuinely saved believer and ministry, the church and all souls should be precious. Our hearts are flooded, and should be, with the awesome love our Savior has shown for us and all mankind. We will desire to see all new babes in Christ come under the protective shelter of true and genuine God-ordained ministry leadership. How do we discern the called ministry from the professional "nice guy" who, whether saved or not, has chosen ministry as a professional career?

Sometimes it helps to portray a truth by exposing what it is not. This certainly applies when we consider the "call of God" to ministry. A person may be endowed with desirable gifts, eloquence, knowledge, and people skills, yet not be called of God to the holy Christ-given "called ministry" of an apostle, prophet, teacher, evangelist, or pastor. These callings have a holy impartation gifting and strengths. They minister because of the heart of Christ within them and their love for His people in Christ's stead. Learning and knowledge attended with credentials will in itself not produce this heart burden. This is Holy Spirit given and Christ imparted.

This is more than being "big hearted" and having empathy for the wounded or the hurt of humanity. I have met some wonderful considerate and sacrificial people in life's journey who have no saving knowledge of Christ. More than being "good people," genuine Christians see life as an opportunity to obtain a creator God relationship. These want more than a superficial religious knowledge of Him. All knowledge of Him should lead to a deepening relationship. This relationship will bring about a holy impartation and cause one to have what we will describe as "God glasses." In life there are sunglasses that are "polarized." These glasses allow greater visibility in rain, water, and glare. The "polarization" of "God glasses" is the holy treatment that causes one to see people and life through the cross and salvation, fostering our ministry to lost humanity.

While others have sunglasses that protect from the sun's brightness, the believer with God glasses will always see the spiritual need in humanity. These needs are always solved by salvation accompanied with the believer's growth stabilization. They see the great need of providing a secure ministry safety structure for all. The provision of knowledge impartation is so very important. Bringing them under the umbrella of a mature mentoring fellowship...protecting and mentoring them by believers and a godly eldership ministry...will be a result of wearing our "God glasses."

This seeing will cause ministry to address the need of learning to hear God's voice...the guiding of the church to be in God's presence...learning to become sensitive to the Holy Spirit…ministering healing to hearts…bringing understanding to holy experiential dealings.

Different callings will naturally gravitate to and focus, as they impart, toward their differing ministry calling burden. This is due to their Holy Spirit wiring. The teacher will naturally focus on knowledge impartation more than the pastor, who will focus on binding up the wounded. The evangelist will naturally focus toward the souls of unredeemed humanity. Yet all should demonstrate an elder's heart meeting whatever needs they are confronted with. Do not expect these other callings to be as we are when they differ from us.

Any knowledge and gained maturities, learned skills, and talents will benefit the ministry abilities of any believer. Our skills and strengths will always be tools of blessing. They enable us with an increased capability and greater communication skills when ministering to people— skills of knowledge, wisdom, and discernment. We must develop talents and strengths while being engaged in ministry pursuits. However, these strengths do not prove one is called of God to the five Christ-given gifts, the ministries listed in Ephesians 4:8–12:

> Wherefore he saith, When he ascended up on high, he led captivity captive, and gave gifts unto men. (Now that he ascended, what is it but that he also descended first into the lower parts of the earth? He that descended is the same also that ascended up far above all heavens, that he might fill all things.) And he gave some, apostles; and some, prophets; and some, evangelists; and some, pastors and teachers; for the perfecting of the saints, for the work of the ministry, for the edifying of the body of Christ:

Most believers have coined the name "fivefold ministry" in the description of a church government headed up by these five callings.

When we attain and receive a certificate of completion from a Bible school, the knowledge gained may be of great value. However, this certificate may simply be proof of having completed a course of studies. This study completion does not mean one is called of God and set aside for the unique "call of God" to the five ministry callings. Unfortunately this truth is little understood by many. I personally am acquainted with people who have completed a doctorate in theology and have an "ordained" minister status due to their scholastic achievements, bestowed by man, *while they are not called of God to a fivefold* ministry calling. Their training and equipping will certainly help in personal witnessing, or eldership functions, in some believing church body, should they desire to flow in this responsibility.

All five of the called ministries are automatically destined to mature to being an elder. However, they should still not be ordained to ministry until they have matured beyond the novice status (1 Tim. 3:6). However, all elders are not fivefold called ministries (1 Tim. 3:1; 1 Pet. 5:1). God equips the called. May we respect learning and studying, but may we always be aware that many of the greatest ministers of our time have a limited education, never having studied in a Bible school or seminary. They just sought the Lord. It is so important for the church to understand what genuinely constitutes the call of God to the ministry, independent of formal education.

Just recently I heard of a young man considering attending a Bible training ministry center. To my discernment, the young man is looking for direction in life and personal fulfillment, having natural abilities. This learning will doubtless be of value, but I question the discerning of the "call of God" to a fivefold calling. He is being encouraged by a preacher who is limited in understanding of what the call of God entails. I would look for a young man who has received and demonstrates the wearing of "God glasses." This will be evidenced by a deep need to minister to people's needs. Bringing people to salvation is an initial evidence of this. One must discern their person and ministry direction by weighing the evidenced work of the Holy Spirit within them. We must not make conclusions or determine directions for others by what we personally desire them to become. Allow the Lord to reveal this.

If a person does not demonstrate Christ's heart and see people through "God glasses," do not mislead or claim a fivefold calling title for them. This must be evidenced by a deep burden from within. This burden will be demonstrated by a continual striving to see souls won to Christ, by witnessing to the lost. We would expect to see a heart burden—their desiring to teach others the principles of God's Word, not a ministry evidence based on accolades for speech and communication abilities. "God glasses" always see a need to minister to the needs of humanity, ministering with holy insight, knowledge, and compassion. Accolades, abilities, and acceptance of one's person are the wrong basis for entering into ministry or claiming a fivefold calling. The call of God involves a demonstrated burden and vision resulting in dealing with souls for eternity.

## Blind Ministry

We must discern the limited and genuine "call of God" to a fivefold ministry calling. Any life giving Christ glorifying ministry will always experience and be preceded by a God burden and heart vision. All true believers have an experiential seeing or revelation of God's glory upon their receiving Christ as Savior. The seeing by the genuinely called five gift ministries appointed and given by Christ, spoken of in Ephesians 4:11, will be a much deeper and far more powerful experience: "And he gave some, apostles; and some, prophets; and some, evangelists; and some, pastors and teachers." These ministries will experience a continuing and heavier burden of heart to minister the truths they see to others as they accept and pursue their Christ-appointed calling and vision.

They see that people need the very thing the Holy Spirit has burdened their hearts with.

They see the glory of God in the truths they have been made partakers of.

They are burdened with the desire to minister to needs, to set people free.

They badly want and need a venting of their burdened hearts, to share and minister the revealed glory. If the opportunity to minister to people is not provided, they will feel like a shaken soft drink bottle under pressure and needing to vent.

If mature ministry does not recognize those who are Holy Spirit–burdened and guide them, regardless of their immaturity, they will move out in ministry even when unprepared. They need discipling. Do not criticize them for their lack unless you are of a guidance and mentoring mind-set. Embrace them. Impart knowledge and wisdom while preparing them for ministry.

Be aware that we like Jonah are capable of running from a God-given assignment. Be aware. There are those who preach and teach Bible truths without having seen the glory of our God. They will be doing so, but with much error. This is a scripturally attested truth. Some preach Christ out of a wrong motive. Identify and help those who are followers of and limited by these wrongful ministers. Paul wrote: "Some indeed preach Christ even of envy and strife; and some also of good will: The one preach Christ of contention, not sincerely, supposing to add affliction to my bonds: But the other of love, knowing that I am set for the defence of the gospel. What then? notwithstanding, every way, whether in pretence, or in truth, Christ is preached; and I therein do rejoice, yea, and will rejoice" (Phil. 1:15–18).

Paul could have added to this statement with, "Many preach Christ because of a ministerial status." Others do just because they like to work with people, due to being "people persons." May we encourage all. Perhaps some of these "people persons" should mature in Christ and prepare to become elders. However, this in itself does not qualify them for a fivefold ministry calling. True called ministry will have a deep heart burden to bring salvation, impart knowledge, and bring Christ as the answer to the wounds needing to be bound up, wounds both physically and mentally. Christ, His person, kingdom, and majesty will be a consuming fire within their hearts and minds.

Many hold ministry positions with a wrong basis for doing so. To apply this statement and to prove this is more than mudslinging, or statements stemming from a critical spirit. May we test this statement, in the light of Scripture, and look at our church and world circumstances. Just consider the numerous churches and preachers who do not understand or preach that a person must be born of the Spirit to see and enter the kingdom of God. They have unsaved clergy. As a young Christian I personally experienced being excommunicated from the church I grew up in. This was due to getting water baptized after seeing my need to answer God (1 Pet. 3:21). The "pastor" demanded that I recant from having done this, and I could not do so. In my last communication with this gentleman, I asked him if he knew for sure that he would personally be in heaven if he were to perish that night. He responded with, "You cannot know that until you are judged."

How many millions of seeking Christians are under this type of leadership? Generally these so-called "ministers" are not saved and, like the Pharisees of old, are whitewashed, good-looking tombs. They are walking tombs, full of dead man's bones within, never having experienced new life. They refuse to enter the kingdom of God and block the door to those who seek to enter (Matt. 23:27, 13).

Many of these "ministers" are the product of wrong theology leading to spiritual death. They are part of the "My people" God spoke of in Hosea 4:6: "My people are destroyed for lack of knowledge: because thou hast rejected knowledge, I will also reject thee."

Millions are trapped with and under a wrong theological direction by those who lack an experiential salvation. Wrong doctrinal beliefs will usher in death. Wrong knowledge limits the attaining of a genuine spiritual God connection for many. Countless people are bereft of the knowledge they need to be "born again."

Perhaps this is being somewhat redundant, but due to the gravity and huge proliferation of this wrong, let us reason this out. Huge numbers of denominational churches will teach their adherents that by virtue of being a baptized baby, they have already received the Holy Spirit. They hereby teach that a human being can cause another person to be "born of the Spirit," when these are not party to communication or understanding what is involved. They teach that God the Holy Spirit will come to unknowing people, due to second-party actions.

Perhaps study the level of godliness and God seeking in these children when they are aged six to sixteen. How many demonstrate a love for and faith in Christ? What an erroneous and horrible untruth, causing masses of spiritual manslaughter. They need to hear the gospel and make personal decisions. This affects mega millions. We must minister to the victims of this.

## KEY BIBLICAL IMPORTANCE

One must be born of the Holy Spirit to see or enter the kingdom of God (John 3:3, 5). Since this is the key prerequisite to having any entrance into God's kingdom, our theology of how this works must be impeccable. Our Lord prefaced this statement with "verily, verily," meaning trustworthy firmly, and of a truth. He chided the Pharisee Nicodemus for not knowing this, and He would chide and rebuke many who claim ministry standings today.

> There was a man of the Pharisees, named Nicodemus, a ruler of the Jews: The same came to Jesus by night, and said unto him, Rabbi, we know that thou art a teacher come from God: for no man can do these miracles that thou doest, except God be with him. Jesus answered and said unto him, Verily, verily, I say unto thee, Except a man be born again, he cannot see the kingdom of God. Nicodemus saith unto him, How can a man be born when he is old? can he enter the second time into his mother's womb, and be born? Jesus answered, Verily, verily, I say unto thee, Except a man be born of water and of the Spirit, he cannot enter into the kingdom of God. That which is born of the flesh is flesh; and that which is born of the Spirit is spirit. Marvel not that I said unto thee, Ye must be born again. The wind bloweth where it listeth, and thou hearest the sound thereof, but canst not tell whence it cometh, and whither it goeth: so is every one that is born of the Spirit. Nicodemus answered and said unto him, How can these things be? Jesus answered and said unto him, Art thou a master of Israel, and knowest not these things? Verily, verily, I say unto thee, We speak that we do know, and testify that we have seen; and ye receive not our witness.
>
> —JOHN 3:1–11

Wrong belief or understandings regarding this topic is more dangerous than any other topic. This new birth will not take place without personal decision involvement. Others cannot do this for us. The apostle Peter said that water baptism is the answer of a clean conscience before God. We cannot answer for someone else's conscience. God does not have grandchildren, only children (John 1:12). I believe it to be a wonderful and godly praise offering and response to the Lord to acknowledge His giving by dedicating our children. We thereby seek God's blessing, to raise them up with godly wisdom.

If I believed that one can baptize another human being with the result being that they would receive the Holy Spirit and commensurately become part of the body of Christ, I would change my ministry habits. I would train myself and others in wrestling and martial arts. I would then manhandle people by baptizing them in a mobile water tank to increase the believer population. Once they were baptized, they would instantly become a dramatically changed people, due to the supposed Holy Spirit–renewal. They would respond with thanking me and others involved in pursuit of like habit for this experience. They would not be fighting and swinging mad for us getting them wet.

No! That is not how it works. I believe what the apostle Paul taught: "For in Christ Jesus neither circumcision availeth anything, nor uncircumcision, but a new creature. And as many as walk according to this rule, peace be on them, and mercy, and upon the Israel of God" (Gal. 6:15–16).

The same statements can be said regarding the truth of water baptism. Being or not being water baptized will not avail anything, but only being a new creature. A new creature is the result of a personal Christ confrontation, with faith in Him, His works, and Lordship. Paul taught that if any man be in Christ, he is a new creature with old things passing away (2 Cor. 5:17). Those who are baptized and are not discerned to be "new creatures" simply got wet. We all have and can discern sprinkled kids, including preachers' kids, who definitely do not portray a new creature in Christ. Any person "in Christ" is and will present a new creature. "Therefore if any man be in Christ, he is a new creature: old things are passed away; behold, all things are become new" (2 Cor. 5:17).

Those who practice this erroneous church rite make a farce out of this scripture. Infant baptism destroys and denies 1 Peter 3:21, where Peter taught this is an act resulting from a pure conscience toward God. Infant baptism either claims the infant can answer God or that adults can answer for their conscience. Bible scriptures do not annul one another.

Infant baptism is wrong and achieves nothing. I as an infant-baptized child was far from a new creature. I became a new creature in my late twenties, after seeking and prayer, after repenting and turning from sin, while placing my faith in Christ as my newfound Lord. I respect my parents and their good intentions, according to their understandings. Being raised in a Christian religious home that had a respect for the Bible and prayer certainly did do much good. This affected my thinking. Godly parents are a great testimony; however, I was a lost, unsaved, religious heathen sinner until I heard and believed.

I was blessed to have two parents who were an anomaly, due to both of them being saved in a church where few are. They were just limited by being under the influence of wrong doctrine. Both of them, while visiting me in their eighties, shared their personal testimony with me as to how they got saved. Neither one was in church attendance when this happened.

My fervent seeking and finding Christ resulted in an instant change to my person. This affected my choices, conversation, and time pursuits due to being born of and sealed by the Holy Spirit. A child can receive Christ at a young age. I know of some. There are needed factors to be considered to have this happen. Paul describes the needed factors of repentance and believing leading to salvation as described with these scriptures:

> This only would I learn of you, Received ye the Spirit by the works of the law, or by the hearing of faith?
> —Galatians 3:2

> Then Peter said unto them, Repent, and be baptized every one of you in the name of Jesus Christ for the remission of sins, and ye shall receive the gift of the Holy Ghost.
> —Acts 2:38

Peter was referring to the baptism of the Holy Spirit rather than water baptism. This gift was the promise of the Father, which would give them power.

And, behold, I send the promise of my Father upon you: but tarry ye
in the city of Jerusalem, until ye be endued with power from on high.
—Luke 24:49

In whom also we have obtained an inheritance, being predestinated
according to the purpose of him who worketh all things after the
counsel of his own will: That we should be to the praise of his glory,
who first trusted in Christ. In whom ye also trusted, after that ye
heard the word of truth, the gospel of your salvation: in whom also
after that ye believed, ye were sealed with that holy Spirit of promise.
—Ephesians 1:11–13

We cannot trust for another person.

How then shall they call on him in whom they have not believed?
and how shall they believe in him of whom they have not heard?
and how shall they hear without a preacher? And how shall they
preach, except they be sent? as it is written, How beautiful are the
feet of them that preach the gospel of peace, and bring glad tidings
of good things! But they have not all obeyed the gospel. For Esaias
said, Lord, who hath believed our report? So then faith cometh by
hearing, and hearing by the word of God.
—Romans 10:14–17

Faith and trusting always involve a response to hearing and
understanding.

The New Testament is quite different from the Old Testament covenant, including circumcision law. Circumcision was a demanded act God
required in order to participate in God's covenant. "And the uncircumcised male child whose flesh of his foreskin is not circumcised, that soul
shall be cut off from his people; he hath broken my covenant" (Gen.
17:14). Being circumcised was never intended to demonstrate an automatic salvation standing. Consider Korah and his family with their possessions, who were instantly buried when the ground opened under them,
swallowing them up due to their not recognizing God's authority (Num.
16:32). Only a remnant of the circumcised Jews received salvation. "Esaias

also crieth concerning Israel, Though the number of the children of Israel be as the sand of the sea, a remnant shall be saved" (Rom. 9:27).

Then consider the nation of Israel, who left off from serving God a few generations after Joshua died. These circumcised descendants caused their children to be sacrificed to Moloch, and God no longer spoke to them. "For when ye offer your gifts, when ye make your sons to pass through the fire, ye pollute yourselves with all your idols, even unto this day: and shall I be enquired of by you, O house of Israel? As I live, saith the Lord God, I will not be enquired of by you" (Ezek. 20:31). Does God have people in heaven whom He does not speak to?

Circumcision was a daily reminder and sermon of uncloaked transparency in sowing and works, what we produce. Baptism is a one-time testimony. This is an answer to God subsequent to accepting Christ. The Bible does not contradict itself. Those who administer infant baptism dent the truths reflected in all of these scriptures referred to. The worst tragic result is that they limit many from seeking and finding an experience born of the Spirit reality. They miss the result of them due to having been taught by "God's representatives" that they have already received this. The result is some ethereal mystic past receiving, which no one can explain anyway, and we need not understand. This is so different from the genuine experiential new birth. I have dealt with many who can identify with this truth.

Yes, the children of believers are holy in the sight of God, without any religious rite being performed on them. This truth applies even if only one parent is a born-of-the-Spirit believer.

> For the unbelieving husband is sanctified by the wife, and the unbelieving wife is sanctified by the husband: else were your children unclean; but now are they holy.
>
> —1 Corinthians 7:14

We must know the truth of Romans 10:1–3:

> Brethren, my heart's desire and prayer to God for Israel is, that they might be saved. For I bear them record that they have a zeal of God,

but not according to knowledge. For they being ignorant of God's righteousness, and going about to establish their own righteousness, have not submitted themselves unto the righteousness of God.

This same truth applies to infant sprinkling. What is so needed is the rest of this scriptural passage:

> That if thou shalt confess with thy mouth the Lord Jesus, and shalt believe in thine heart that God hath raised him from the dead, thou shalt be saved. For with the heart man believeth unto righteousness; and with the mouth confession is made unto salvation. For the scripture saith, Whosoever believeth on him shall not be shamed. For there is no difference between the Jew and the Greek: for the same Lord over all is rich unto all that call upon him. For whosoever shall call upon the name of the Lord shall be saved. How then shall they call on him in whom they have not believed? and how shall they believe in him of whom they have not heard? and how shall they hear without a preacher?
>
> —Romans 10:9–14

Many mentally "wimp out" and will not face this factual biblical truth. All people must hear, believe, and accept the gospel in order to be "sealed" by the Holy Spirit (Eph. 1:13). When one accepts Christ, he inherits eternal life, and the blessing effect comes upon their children as well, but not an automatic salvation. Our God will graciously deal with them and do His all to draw them.

Pray and intercede. Raise them up with a holy God fear. May they not be as an Esau. Upon an age of accountability these children still need to hear, believe, and accept Christ, followed by answering Him from their clean conscience. This is only possible by those who are born of the Spirit (1 Pet. 3:21). These weak-kneed and limp-wristed "preachers" never face a clear line regarding salvation. The following textual truth is often disregarded and avoided in their preaching, which is a selective sin.

And the Lord descended in the cloud, and stood with him there, and proclaimed the name of the Lord. And the Lord passed by before him, and proclaimed, The Lord, The Lord God, merciful and gracious, longsuffering, and abundant in goodness and truth, keeping mercy for thousands, forgiving iniquity and transgression and sin, and that will by no means clear the guilty; visiting the iniquity of the fathers upon the children, and upon the children's children, unto the third and to the fourth generation.

—Exodus 34:5–7

God deals with us as individuals in sin and salvation matters. Our lives do have an effect upon our descendants and heritage, but God judges individuals by their choices, as He did with Isaac's children, Esau whom He hated and Jacob whom He loved. "As it is written, Jacob have I loved, but Esau have I hated" (Rom. 9:13). Esau's circumcision did nothing for him! His heart's pursuits in life were not sown in uncloaked transparency and righteousness. The intended symbolism was lost. This is also true in infant baptism, which leads to a wrong understanding. Every child must hear and personally receive, and then answer our God (1 Pet. 3:21). However, should a Christian baby or young child have a premature death, I have no doubt they will be in heaven since God declares them holy.

Those who ignore these truths will always struggle with God's judgments and the intent thereof. They never internally come to terms with the fact that our just and merciful God demanded the killing of all men, women, and children—the commanded death and killing of the heritage of an idol-worshipping nation, when Israel entered and were taking their land. When this directive was not followed due to disobedience, within a couple of generations the inhabitants of the Promised Land brought death to most of Israel.

These idol-worshipping children became young men and women who enticed and intermarried with Israel. Their intermarriage turned Israelite hearts from the living God. "And they took their daughters to be their wives, and gave their daughters to their sons, and served their gods. And the children of Israel did evil in the sight of the Lord, and forgot the Lord their God, and served Baalim and the groves" (Judg. 3:6–7).

The same applies to us and our land (our person, heart, mind, and soul). Godliness requires radical decisions. When we allow ungodly remnants to remain, these remnants will eventually bring death to us as well.

Israel left Egypt's bondage and endured their desert journey testing. Likewise we and our children come from our unsaved Egypt bondage status. We also travel through our desert of life, constantly being tested as to our true heart values and God focus. We must also put to death whatever is bound in ungodliness, because if we do not, it will bring death to us. "And thou shalt remember all the way which the Lord thy God led thee these forty years in the wilderness, in order to humble thee, and to prove thee, to know what is in thine heart, whether thou wouldest keep his commandments, or no" (Deut. 8:2).

These preachers will not come to terms with the holy truth why God honored Phinehas for spearing a leader of the Simeonites along with a woman through the belly. "And when Phinehas, the son of Eleazar, the son of Aaron the priest, saw it, he rose up from among the congregation, and took a javelin in his hand; and he went after the man of Israel into the tent, and thrust both of them through, the man of Israel, and the woman through her belly. So the plague was stayed from the children of Israel" (Num. 25:7–8). Twenty-four thousand Israelites died in the plague that the Lord brought upon them. God's firm judgments are His love to us and them to preserve the nation from sin and death.

Eventually the nation went into idolatry, serving the gods of the nations they did not kill, and departed from the living God. This was because of two factors. They did not completely destroy the nations they were commanded to upon entering the Promised Land. Then they gave their sons and daughters in marriage to the godless idol-worshipping people of these nations. Our holy God gave this strong judgment to prevent this very thing. His ways are higher and wiser than ours.

The belly spearing is a prophetic picture of death to their fruitfulness.

This seemingly hard truth of killing an Israelite leader with an idol-worshipping woman is somewhat softened by the righteous Christ teachings regarding the difference applicable to all mankind in eternal judgment. Our holy and righteous God will differentiate in judgment for both the saved and unsaved. This is shown by the following Bible textual truths, where man's actions will be weighed, resulting in differing eternal judgment assessment.

To the saved, Jesus said, "And that servant, which knew his lord's will, and prepared not himself, neither did according to his will, shall be beaten with many stripes. But he that knew not, and did commit things worthy of stripes, shall be beaten with few stripes. For unto whomsoever much is given, of him shall be much required: and to whom men have committed much, of him they will ask the more" (Luke 12:47–48).

> And many of them that sleep in the dust of the earth shall awake, some to everlasting life, and some to shame and everlasting contempt. And they that be wise shall shine as the brightness of the firmament; and they that turn many to righteousness as the stars forever and ever.
>
> —Daniel 12:2–3

> Every man's work shall be made manifest: for the day shall declare it, because it shall be revealed by fire; and the fire shall try every man's work of what sort it is. If any man's work abide which he hath built thereupon, he shall receive a reward.
>
> —1 Corinthians 3:13–14

All who are not named in the Book of Life are eternally condemned in the second resurrection judgment. Yet their judgment will also vary, which is according to their works (Rev. 20:12). This verifies the fairness and righteousness of our holy God's judgment of all (Gen. 18:25). When we consider eternal judgment and the consequences, there will be a difference made between one person and another even among the unsaved, who are not part of the first resurrection. Yet all at the second resurrection judgment are destined for an eternal hell and separation from God.

Only the names of the saved are in this holy Book of Life, which is in the heavenly Zion. The new believer has come there and belongs to this city, upon his receiving salvation. "But ye are come unto mount Sion, and unto the city of the living God, the heavenly Jerusalem, and to an innumerable company of angels, to the general assembly and church of the firstborn, which are written in heaven" (Heb. 12:22–23).

The saved are judged at Christ's judgment seat prior to the wedding banquet. These believers are the blessed who rise in the first resurrection (Rev. 20:6). "Every man's work shall be made manifest: for the day shall declare it, because it shall be revealed by fire; and the fire shall try every man's work as to what sort it is. If any man's work abide which he hath built thereupon, he shall receive a reward. If any man's work shall be burned, he shall suffer loss: but he himself shall be saved; yet so as by fire" (1 Cor. 3:13–15).

Christ speaks of a greater condemnation for those who wrongfully misuse and abuse people financially. "Which devour widows' houses, and for a shew make long prayers: the same shall receive greater damnation" (Luke 20:47).

Again we observe the difference in judgment from one person to another. To avoid a negative eternal judgment, both for us the saved and for the unsaved, we must share the gospel with the unsaved. May they find the only way, truth, and life, our God revealed in the person of Jesus (John 14:6; 10:30–33; Isa. 9:6).

One cannot enter the kingdom without personally receiving Christ. Those who do not teach how this is to take place have never personally experienced this needed event. This is no different than in Christ's day when the Pharisees and Sadducees were the ruling ministry. Israel looked up to these leaders as God's representatives, but they did not know Christ and blocked the door for others to know Him, never personally having experienced this.

Likewise today many spiritual leaders claim ministry titles but do not personally know the Christ they speak of. The Pharisees and elders rejected Christ, crucifying Him. They, like many today, were imposters. Their anger for being confronted with their sin, along with their jealousy due to Christ drawing crowds they wished were theirs, was the root cause for crucifying Him. They still manifest the problem of the original sin in wanting to be honored as religious mini gods. The same is true today. The mystery of the wind and where it comes from and where it goes to remains an unknown fact to these leaders, never having experienced the new birth (John 3:8).

## LET'S STOP BEING "POLITICALLY CORRECT"

Our Lord Jesus was never "politically correct." Being politically correct can be the basis of sustaining a lie and the disease of untruth. Truth is confronting! In our presentation of truth we will require wisdom, but presenting truth is the wisdom of God. Our Lord Jesus answered His disciples with straightforward answers. He did so when the topic of unsaved religious preachers was being questioned: "Then came his disciples, and said unto him, Knowest thou that the Pharisees were offended, after they heard this saying? But he answered and said, Every plant, which my heavenly Father hath not planted, shall be rooted up. Let them alone: they be blind leaders of the blind. And if the blind lead the blind, both shall fall into the ditch" (Matt. 15:12–14).

Holy and godly ministry will always experience a measure of confrontation. They will attempt to get along with all men as much as lies within them, but a certain amount of standard-bearing confrontation will exist. "If it be possible, as much as lieth in you, live peaceably with all men" (Rom. 12:18). However, we need to understand the holy and anointed understanding and words the angel spoke to Peter and fellow apostles after being imprisoned for testifying of Christ when ordered not to by the high priest and the Sanhedrin. "Go, stand and speak in the temple to the people all the words of this life" (Acts 5:20). We attempt to get along but never deny Christ and witnessing to and for Him.

Those who claim a ministry standing, without having experienced a revelation of God's glory, are hirelings, religious bigots, and the blind leading the blind, not knowing the God and Christ they speak of. Why be so confronting?

David, upon hearing Goliath challenging Israel, spoke up with, "Who is this uncircumcised Philistine, that he should defy the armies of the living God"? (1 Sam. 17:26). His brothers ridiculed David for speaking up and saying this. David answered them with a strong question. "Is there not a cause?" Because many are perishing, due to no confronted untruth, should we like David in this day not equally state, "Is there not a cause?" The prophet Hosea spoke God's heart: "My people are destroyed for lack of knowledge" (Hosea 4:6). Because many are perishing, we must confront untruth and sin with truth and declared knowledge.

The painful truth is, many unsaved religious leaders hold masses of people in blindness, as they lead the blind who follow them. Christ confronted these blind leaders when He said, "Thou blind Pharisee, cleanse first that which is within the cup and platter, that the outside of them may be clean also. Woe unto you, scribes and Pharisees, hypocrites! for ye are like whited sepulchres, which indeed appear beautiful outward, but are within full of dead men's bones, and of all uncleanness. Even so ye also outwardly appear righteous unto men, but within ye are full of hypocrisy and iniquity.... Ye serpents, ye generation of vipers, how can ye escape the damnation of hell?" (Matt. 23:26–28, 33). Confrontation, when this exposes a lie by presenting truth, is love in action. People actually get saved due to such confrontation. Paul often went to synagogues to dispute righteous truth with the ministry leaders of his day.

These were confronting no-nonsense words by our Savior. These love statements were meant to get their attention. They were not polite or politically correct. To call these ministry and respected leaders of His day snakes and whitewashed tombs full of death was hard confronting language.

It was a tough confrontation. Pharisee ministry was a financial career of seeking religious visibility and status (Matt. 23:14, 27, 33). They believed in salvation by their good religious works and prayers. Our salvation is by faith in Christ, trusting in His person, love, forgiveness, and what He did for us. Faith is similar to the trust a child holds in their mother. Faith is made available by God's grace, which brings salvation (Eph. 2:8–9).

May we know when to confront with truth in love, yet not shirk from confrontation. Confrontation must always be with an appropriate heart and spirit. What would make one think this type of Pharisee ministry is nonexistent today? Most simply do not discern what exists today and what Christ constantly discerned and dealt with. What is the motive for one's ministry? This will determine our speaking. This is a key question that needs to be answered by any ministry candidates after a truthful self-examination.

## CHAPTER NINE

# FIVE CHRIST "GIFT" CALLINGS

*Fivefold Ministry Callings*

*A*LLOW ME TO fire a cannonball across the pirate ship's bow from the battleship named "truth."

Most within the church need to be taught and to understand scriptural truth about church government and ministry callings. The scriptures state that upon Christ ascending, He gave five different and unique ministry callings to the church. Most believers and churches, including charismatic, full gospel, and Pentecostal churches, have inglorious holes in their understanding and application of this topic. Our Lord ascended and gave to men (or mankind) and the church five differing ministry callings.

We perpetrate a terrible sin of wrong in our theology when we presumptuously determine and say that some of these callings no longer are given or exist. We bring great destruction to the kingdom of God by doing this. Sadly, this is done by presumptive reasoning with no scriptural basis. Most churches eliminate several of the Christ-given callings by their erroneous unbelief of Holy Writ.

Full gospel churches who uphold a separate baptism of the Holy Spirit doctrine chide evangelical churches who deny this experiential baptism. Yet these same full gospel churches turn a blind eye to those who strive for the recognition of a scriptural multiple-calling ministry structure. In part this recognition of differing ministries is made possible and as a result of this baptism of the Holy Spirit.

Christ did not give the gift ministries to some of men or some of the church, as many blindly read this. He gave five differing ministries, which our risen Lord called "gifts to men." "Wherefore he saith, When he ascended up on high, he led captivity captive, and gave gifts unto men" (Eph. 4:8). Christ said all five of these are needed to bring the church to maturity. "And he gave some, apostles; and some, prophets; and some, evangelists; and some, pastors and teachers; for the perfecting of the saints, for the work of the ministry, for the edifying of the body of Christ: Till we all come in the unity of the faith, and of the knowledge of the Son of God, unto a perfect man, unto the measure of the stature of the fullness of Christ" (Eph. 4:11–13).

Due to ignorance, some of these five Christ-given ministry callings, by presumptive conclusions, are eliminated and not recognized by many. Our Lord Jesus Christ has not eliminated them! Man has decided to eliminate some ministries from the risen Savior's giving by not discerning these ministry callings. They blindly do not accept and see the purpose of or need for the callings they do not recognize.

We must learn how to discern these callings. The church is not mature and is still continuously being established worldwide. The commonly unrecognized callings of apostle and prophet are foundation-laying ministries: "And are built upon the foundation of the apostles and prophets, Jesus Christ himself being the chief corner stone" (Eph. 2:20).

This unscriptural sin of unbelief is due to a denial of God's Word. How dare man apply their "unbelief" scissors and dissect this giving to "men" with no scriptural reference for doing so? How can many make a determination that some of the giving was for an early and not a latter church? Our Lord pours out the Spirit as the early and latter rain. The Holy Spirit on earth does not change. Christ gave to all of mankind what was needed for the entire church. He is Lord. May we refrain from sinning against Him by toying with His giving or what He says that we need.

The Lord of the church in the Book of Acts is still the same Lord who gives to men today. We the church must have a clear biblical understanding of who Christ is and what He has done in giving five differing ministry callings. Much of this problem is due to the same unbelief scissors having been applied to a separate and necessary "baptism of the Holy Spirit." Apostles and prophets are much more difficult to discern when they do not operate in the supernatural spiritual gifts, such as healing and miracles and the prophetic revelation gifts. These come by the experiential baptism of the Holy Spirit.

Unbelief scissors have erroneously redefined prophecy to mean expository preaching. This supernatural gifting always reveals matters that would normally be unknown by the Holy Spirit's revealing. Those armed with these scissors of unbelief cut out numerous scriptures applicable to you and I. Unbelief scissors read God's Word and then apply a different meaning to it by adding or deleting with humanistic rational. Often they just deny the Word with no relevant basis for doing so.

The first apostles were told to wait in Jerusalem. This was not to receive salvation but power. "And, behold, I send the promise of my Father upon you: but tarry ye in the city of Jerusalem, until ye be endued with power from on high" (Luke 24:49). Evangelicals tend to redefine this power to being born of the Spirit, ignoring the effect of Christ blowing on His disciples fifty days prior to Pentecost. "Then said Jesus to them again, Peace be unto you: as my Father hath sent me, even so send I you. And when he had said this, he breathed on them, and saith unto them, Receive ye the Holy Ghost" (John 20:21–22).

Fifty days later those waiting received this promised power, which was evidenced by the supernatural gifts. This power was first received by the one hundred twenty as they spoke in tongues and prophesied. Peter afterward stated to a repentant crowd who had observed this, "For the promise is unto you, and to your children, and to all that are afar off, even as many as the Lord our God shall call" (Acts 2:39). This gift of being baptized in the Holy Spirit is promised to "as many as are afar off." This is experiential. The receiving of this is evidenced by experiential tongues and prophecy.

Our Lord also stated that these Christian believers would go into all of the world, speaking in tongues, casting out devils, and healing people. "And these signs shall follow them that believe; In my name shall they cast out devils; they shall speak with new tongues" (Mark 16:17). This was written to the church. The first-century church did not reach the whole world, and the gospel is still going into all of the world. When that is completed, Christ will return. "And this gospel of the kingdom shall be preached in all the world for a witness unto all nations; and then shall the end come" (Matt. 24:14).

Unbelieving scissor-minded people disregard these truths. Often they reason that since they are born of the Spirit and since this tongues-evidenced profound experience has not happened to them, this must not be for today. These rely on no experience and not God's Word. The opposite is true. Faith in God's Word will produce experience. Destroy these scissors and believe the Word and promises of God. Wait upon the Lord in your Jerusalem, your place of worship, your bedroom, shower, or quiet place. Seek out the scriptures and believe them rather than accepting unbelief and the traditions of unbelieving elders.

Many discard this promised experience due to their questioning of "tongues." They have no understanding that tongues is man's spirit praying and not their mind. They debate that since the mind has no understanding of this, what is its value. Faith tells us that God gives and places value on this. Whatever God gives is good, and I want it. "For if I pray in an unknown tongue, my spirit prayeth, but my understanding is unfruitful. What is it then? I will pray with the spirit, and I will pray with the understanding also" (1 Cor. 14:14–15).

The result will be that many scriptures now read over and disregarded will become obvious and alive. Suddenly one will believe that the initial twelve apostles were just the beginning of many more. We will believe and understand the continual additional apostles and prophets being given by Christ the Lord as a gift to the church. No one has ever found scriptures where our Lord said that He would limit this giving after a brief time. Review these scriptures of called apostles:

> Which when the apostles, Barnabas and Paul, heard of, they rent their clothes, and ran in among the people, crying out...
> —Acts 14:14

Paul, and Silvanus, and Timotheus, unto the church of the Thessalonians…Nor of men sought we glory, neither of you, nor yet of others, when we might have been burdensome, as the apostles of Christ.

—1 THESSALONIANS 1:1; 2:6

But other of the apostles saw I none, save James the Lord's brother.

—GALATIANS 1:19

Our Lord is still the gracious Lord of heaven and earth and the church. He has never changed His giving. Men armed with unbelief have brought change from His Word! May we understand that Christ is Lord. Paul spoke of the Lordship of Christ, the glorious mystery: "And without controversy great is the mystery of godliness: God was manifest in the flesh, justified in the Spirit, seen of angels, preached unto the Gentiles, believed on in the world, received up into glory" (1 Tim. 3:16). Christ is the Lord and Lord of the church.

After the crucifixion and resurrection of Christ, His prayer to the Father was answered, "And now, O Father, glorify thou me with thy own self with the glory which I had with thee before the world was" (John 17:5). The apostle Peter advised the crowd at Pentecost, fifty days after Christ's glorification, "that God hath made that same Jesus, whom ye have crucified, both Lord and Christ" (Acts 2:36).

Paul when writing to the Colossian church explained, "And he is the head of the body, the church: who is the beginning, the firstborn from the dead; that in all things he might have the preeminence" (Col. 1:18). Our Lord Jesus Christ is Lord of all. We have denied His Lordship in the church by disregarding His giving. We deny this by denying the need and discernment of what He gave and why He gave these.

## UNHOLY WRONG DOING

It is painfully wrong that we and most of the church have denied Christ His headship, Lordship, and preeminence. The Scriptures are very clear as to this topic, as found in Ephesians 4:8, 11: "Wherefore he saith,

When he ascended up on high, he led captivity captive, and gave gifts unto men. . . . And he gave some, apostles; and some, prophets; and some, evangelists; and some, pastors and teachers." Who are we to gainsay His giving and need for same? Who are we to presume that we only need pastors and evangelists and have the right to delete teachers, prophets, and apostles? We have not prayerfully studied or sought out discernment. Most have not sought out understanding regarding the identification of these. We need to identify these differing callings from the commonly accepted pastors or evangelists. We have not searched out who they are and why these people are different and how this giving works.

Most churches have little or no understanding of our Lord's giving. This fact is evidenced by denial in their theology and practice, denial with no scriptural justification by the Word of God. This giving has not stopped from the first century until now. Much of this wrong is caused due to a limited knowledge of how the Holy Spirit works within the differing ministry callings.

Since the scriptures state the risen Christ gave five differing callings to men or mankind, we must repent of taking our unbelief scissors and denying this truth. This is regardless of whether they understand it or not. This is simply because He said so. Then we must work at understanding how this giving works.

## Error in Doctrinal Understanding

Much of this error can readily be proven by the wrong teaching that there were only twelve apostles and no more. This wrong teaching is a clearly evidenced and an easily proven fact. The easy-to-research facts of this truth, should cause the more than 90 percent of all Bible seminaries and schools who teach this wrong theology to humbly reexamine their teachings and repent.

There is no debate that the initial giving by Christ was twelve called and appointed apostles. However, the New Testament records a minimum of twenty and possibly twenty-four apostles. There is no textual evidence of this giving ever having stopped. We must consider that these additionally identified apostles lived and ministered at the same time as the originally chosen twelve. Many more were and are required as the church expands and continues to go into all of the world.

Rather than throwing out the scripturally attested examples of more apostles than the original twelve, we should carefully weigh how to identify who is an apostle and what makes them so. Of course this becomes very difficult in churches that deny the experiential baptism of the Holy Spirit with tongues and prophecy gifts. Only those who believe the scriptures that this is a God-given promise to all flesh and not limited to some flesh will potentially be capable of this discernment: "And it shall come to pass in the last days, saith God, I will pour out of my Spirit upon all flesh: and your sons and your daughters shall prophesy, and your young men shall see visions, and your old men shall dream dreams" (Acts 2:17).

Faith in God's Word where it states "*all flesh*," instead of what it does not say and many erroneously conclude, will cause a higher discernment potential. Believing in God's Word and promises is always the key to understanding and seeking this awesome experience. This experience greatly changes a believer's walk in the Holy Ghost (Joel 2:28).

The Bible evidence of many apostles continuously being given is a matter of record. This giving has never quit. We read that it was the apostle James, the Lord's brother, who authored the Book of James, not the first apostle James who was the brother of the apostle John. That apostle was the first apostle to be martyred by Herod: "And he killed James the brother of John with the sword" (Acts 12:2).

We seem to have upheld some of the callings given, like pastors or evangelists, but bring unspeakable damage to the church by not having recognized but deleted the teacher, apostle, and prophet callings. We only accept pastors and priests in traditional and Roman Catholic churches, where the pope is a supposed apostle. They interject mini-god titles and nonscriptural names for their non-servant elite ministry status personages.

Unfortunately, the apostle, prophet, and teacher ministries usually hide under the naming of evangelists or pastors. This is due to this naming being more acceptable and readily received by the masses. When these ministries do not stand with the correct naming of or are not focusing on their true calling, the church and believers are robbed of understanding Christ's intended gift giving.

Then we have the erroneous identification by some that a prophet such as Benny Hinn of today is an apostle. More confusion is ministered to the body of Christ.

When these callings are not freed to operate in what they are wired to be, they limit their intended ministry. Often this reduces a two-ton truck to being used as a taxicab. Often the result is similar to the janitor running IBM, or the groundskeeper managing Boeing. Should we understand the damage done to the church, believers, and worldwide ministry due to our disregard of this giving, we should weep. I do.

Disregarding Christ's church government due to not understanding how and why these differing callings and offices should function is criminal. May we repent of our wrong disregard of Christ's desired giving and the resulting damage to church ministry government, which should be discerned and in place. Even when we do not understand the application of this truth, may we at least acknowledge this giving by the written Word and then pray for and seek understanding. "And God hath set some in the church, first apostles, secondarily prophets, thirdly teachers, after that miracles..." (1 Cor. 12:28).

It is not rocket science to see the progression in the path of doubt and destruction that exists. Throw out the miracles, prophecy, and the supernatural gifts of the Spirit by denying the genuine and separate from the spiritual birth baptism of the Holy Spirit, and we will also throw out the prophet and apostle. These spiritual gifts should operate in these ministries.

This is repetitious but so important. Consider that the early church received the Holy Spirit long before Pentecost—immediately subsequent to Christ's blood being applied to heaven's mercy seat, on the same day the believers became born of the Spirit when Christ blew on them. The baptism of the Holy Spirit with the promise of receiving power, administered by our Lord Jesus, took place some fifty days after (John 1:33; 20:22; Luke 24:49; Acts 1:4–5, 8).

## Scriptural Government

We must allow the scriptures to speak to this subject. The balanced scriptural presentation regarding this topic will destroy the traditions of men, as taught by many. Wherever the Word of God is distorted or denied, death prevails. Our God has always established a ministry government among His people. Governmental order was in place in Israel before Christ and in the early New Testament church as well. Some scriptures that support these observations are: "And God hath set some in the church, first apostles, secondarily prophets, thirdly teachers, after that miracles, then gifts of healings, helps, governments, diversities of tongues" (1 Cor. 12:28). To teach that this was only written for the first-century starting church only is an absurdity and foolishness. One cannot find a church in the Bible that did not have a multiple ministry and eldership!

"For this cause left I thee in Crete, that thou shouldest set in order the things that are wanting, and ordain elders in every city, as I had appointed thee" (Titus 1:5). Paul said that any churches that do not have a multiple eldership are "out of order." Most traditional and many of the last-century churches, including the born-again or full gospel churches, ignore the reality of this text. Some will say that does not apply to us since we have a board of elders. In most cases, they are about of equal value when compared to a wooden board, because those given this title do not meet the New Testament definition of functioning elders. Most carry the name but are unqualified for this office. We MUST understand what constitutes scriptural eldership.

True scriptural elders have a maturity and function within the church, because they have been molded by the Holy Spirit to meet this function. Unless those persons named "elders" are functioning in feeding and overseeing the flock, they are not qualified for such. "And from Miletus he sent to Ephesus, and called the elders of the church. And when they were come to him, he said unto them…Take heed therefore unto yourselves, and to all the flock, over the which the Holy Ghost hath made you overseers, to feed the church of God" (Acts 20:17–18, 28).

Biblical elders are not a Board of Directors who give opinions, like a

Board to a CEO of a corporation in financial and business matters. Deacons should be looking after these financial needs, with elder oversight. Biblical elders are those who share in teaching, counseling, and pulpit ministry. They minister in spiritual matters. All elders should be released to minister the Word, teach, and oversee the flock. The average church control group should be named a board of deacons, since they mostly deal with financial, maintenance, and business matters. Elders minister to spiritual needs.

The fivefold-called ministers should attain unto an elder's status and function when they reach a level of maturity. Besides these five callings, any man with a right heart and maturity due to the Holy Spirit working in his life may be ordained as an elder. "This is a true saying, If a man desire the office of a bishop, he desireth a good work" (1 Tim. 3:1). Elder standards immediately follow this "any man" topic in this chapter, just as a deacon candidate can be any qualified person whose qualifications are and must be "men full of the Holy Ghost" (Acts 6:3).

## HOLY GHOST MADE ELDERS

All elder candidates must have a burden for the flock, desiring to minister the Word and spiritual truths to the church. They must be heart burdened and never be ordained due to being good business people. Acts 20:28 contains a great truth spotlight. Any genuine right-hearted elder will be a product of the Holy Spirit working within him. The Holy Spirit will draw elders into godly understandings of the Word. They will seek wisdom, knowledge, and maturity along with the fruit of the Spirit. He is the one who places a burden within elders to take care of the flock with a desire to teach and preach holy truth. We are not to ordain novices: "Not a novice, lest being lifted up with pride he fall into the condemnation of the devil" (1 Tim. 3:6). When someone has the desire to take this office upon themselves with the responsibilities involved, may the existing mature elders discern their maturity and motive for their expressed desire. Thereby they protect the flock as well as the elder candidate.

Some get hung up on the terms *elder, bishop*, or *overseer*. Basically these are one and the same. The elders whom Paul called to meet with him in Acts 20:17 are called overseers in verse 28. The elders Titus was sent to ordain in Titus 1:5 were called bishops in verse 7. "For this cause left I thee in Crete, that you should set in order the things that are wanting, and ordain elders in every city, as I had appointed thee: If any be blameless, the husband of one wife, having faithful children not accused of riot or unruly. For a bishop must be blameless, as the steward of God; not selfwilled, not soon angry, not given to wine, no striker, not given to filthy lucre" (vv. 5–7). These are similar and interchangeable titles for the same office function.

These titles of bishop, elder, or overseer are a correct naming of all mature called ministry. However, the elder position should not delete or replace the proper callings of apostle or other of the five callings when applicable. This is commonly done.

Many of the five callings use an elder or bishop title, because this is less confronting to those who do not understand these apostle and prophet callings for today. This may seem smart, but they thereby deny bringing forth what Christ gave. They thereby administer a shadowed picture of the church government and callings. To my observation and forty years of ministry, less than 1 percent of all churches accept the apostle calling. If they do acknowledge their existence, most still do not have them placed in a functional relational capacity. This problem has many facets to it, causing much confusion due to doctrinal error and lack of knowledge and a limited presentation by those who carry these calling.

Another factor worsening this wrong and confusion is that many who claim some of these callings do so in error out of ignorance. Some blindly claim they are apostles as well as prophets or some combination of multiple callings. These sow further confusion and error. Mostly this is due by ministries who are functioning in a different office from their Christ-given calling. They then lay claim to that calling as well, along with what they genuinely are (Rom. 1:1). More confusion is spread when some who are genuinely called to these offices destroy the correct example of character and demeanor. Often the wrong example is seen by having a wrong spirit as to godly authority and financial matters. They do so by not esteeming their brethren and fellow elders. Lord Jesus, help us to get things right.

## CHRIST HONORING

Consider the praise our risen Savior gave the church of Ephesus, one of the seven churches Christ addressed in the Book of Revelation. Please remember that these churches are examples to us and representative of all churches until Christ comes again. "I know thy works, and thy labour, and thy patience, and how thou canst not bear them which are evil: and thou hast tried them which say they are apostles, and are not, and hast found them liars" (Rev. 2:2). When we believe the truths written there are applicable to all churches today, why is this an ignored scripture? Why do we not attain unto having this knowledge and discernment regarding the genuine attributes of an apostle today? This testing is relevant now.

Our Lord speaks of an authority structure in the church which is apostle led. "And God hath set some in the church, first apostles, secondarily prophets, thirdly teachers, after that miracles, then gifts of healings, helps, governments, diversities of tongues" (1 Cor. 12:28). Those who deny apostles and prophets add to this text. They add the nonexistent words "for a limited time."

This is our Lord's expressed directive and intent! Only by obedient believing in and accepting His Word with repentance will this be corrected. We must study and believe God's Word, thereby seeking to understand what is presented. Since most preachers teach the seven letters to these churches are applicable to all churches now, why then ignore this praise to Ephesus for aggressively and correctly judging ministry callings?

Christ gave and continues to give five differing ministry callings to men, to all of mankind and the church. All are robbed when this truth is not understood and not functional. I will explain why and how this robbing exists; however, just because our Lord said He gave them should be enough for us to believe and pray for understanding of this Christ giving. "And he gave some, apostles; and some, prophets; and some, evangelists; and some, pastors and teachers; for the perfecting of the saints, for the work of the ministry, for the edifying of the body of Christ" (Eph. 4:11–12). Only churches and ministers in rebellion to Christ will ignore this scripture by taking away from the Word of God!

Equally important, vast numbers of believers are in rebellion to Christ by disregarding ministry authority, with no genuine submission to leadership over them. "Obey them that have the rule over you, and submit yourselves: for they watch for your souls, as they that must give account, that they may do it with joy, and not with grief: for that is unprofitable for you" (Heb. 13:17).

Perhaps the largest reason for believers not obeying those over them is that we do not have the God-designed and intended leadership government. The lack in ministry structure does not allow for the personal and knowledgeable interrelationship the elders and believers are to enjoy.

"And the apostles and elders came together for to consider of this matter" (Acts 15:6). Here we read about multiple apostles, elders, and believers submitted one to another. This is a holy example of what we should have as godly church ministry government. Acts 15 demonstrates a Christ-pleasing and Holy Ghost–attending leadership, who with love and humility were submitting one to another. The fault lies with the ministry in charge for not taking responsibility to develop a functional multiple ministry. Mostly this is due to a one-man eldership with a few limited dysfunctional elders who have no genuine placement of authority or ministry responsibility. This is a readily discerned reality, proven by the lack of a scriptural functioning multiple eldership demonstrated in most churches. Too strongly stated? Why? The proof of this reality is seen by:

- How many attendees have an intimate sharing with an elder several times a year, discussing where they are at with the Lord? Or a pastoral visit by an elder, a visit where they can share their hearts, cares, and problems as well as joys—and not just work, politics, and sports.

- How many attendees in large churches can miss one or several Sundays and never be noticed or contacted to see if they are in good spiritual and natural health?

- How many leaders know their people in a personal way, with their leadership having a good knowledge of their spiritual status and the difficulties they face? How many believers have an elder in their lives from whom they can receive leadership and heartfelt direction? Where they have a trust relationship where they can discuss their personal issues of life considering God, His pursuit, and ministry? Hello?

The need of this presented truth is great. The church, believers, and the kingdom suffers when less than a scriptural ministry structure with a multiple elders is established and received! When the church sees a multiple eldership ministry submitted one to another, a greater respect for God and godly authority will result. The believers are limited due to the nonexistent ministry structure per the New Testament example.

## Paul, a Separated Unto the Gospel Minister

The differing five ministry callings need to be received and functioning in their callings by the church. "Paul, a servant of Jesus Christ, called to be an apostle, separated unto the gospel of God...by whom we have received grace and apostleship, for obedience to the faith among all nations, for his name" (Rom. 1:1, 5). Paul knew who he was. He knew he was separated due to his calling and ministry to the nations. Genuine apostles are still reaching out and establishing churches in the nations of the world. They are still mentoring leadership and laying foundations of church government and doctrine. "But when it pleased God, who separated me from my mother's womb, and called me by his grace, to reveal his Son in me, that I might preach him among the heathen" (Gal. 1:15–16).

Paul knew what his single specific calling was. We today who are called ministry should likewise know what our calling is by having discerned our BURDEN AND VISION. Should the church today not have a mature ministry calling discernment? Paul and other ministries are readily identified by their burden and vision.

## CHAPTER TEN

# HOLY SPIRIT WORK
# WITHIN CALLED

*The Holy Spirit at Work Within the Called*

T HE HOLY SPIRIT is God the Holy Spirit, the great teacher of holy truth: "But the Comforter, which is the Holy Ghost, whom the Father will send in my name, he shall teach you all things, and bring all things to your remembrance, whatsoever I have said unto you" (John 14:26). The Holy Spirit has come to reside within the believer and has joined Himself to the spirit of man. "The Spirit itself beareth witness with our spirit, that we are the children of God" (Rom. 8:16).

The apostle Paul understood how the Holy Spirit works within the believer and subsequently how this worked within the called of God ministry. "For it is God which worketh in you both to will and to do of his good pleasure" (Phil. 2:13). To understand this, we must understand the spirit of man as part of our tripartite being. Man has a conscience, which theologically is termed the spirit of man. One's conscience is a separate being or part of us that can and will differ with the mind of man: "Which shew the work of the law written in their hearts, their conscience also bearing witness, and their thoughts the mean while accusing or else excusing one another" (Rom. 2:15).

Our spirit of man is a moral referee. In Proverbs we read, "The spirit of man is the candle of the Lord, searching all the inward parts of the belly" (Prov. 20:27).

Our conscience gets amplified because of the Holy Spirit's presence due to being born of the Holy Spirit. As we prayerfully walk before the Lord, we will receive direction, His voice and thoughts, by His still small voice within. Few hear an audible voice such as Paul heard on the road to Damascus. Many hear a still small inner voice. This voice brings thoughts, words, and songs from our spirit man to our minds. It takes patient listening and waiting on the Lord to hear this speaking with our minds uncluttered with personal thoughts. The Holy Spirit unceasingly works within the called, "The Lord will perfect that which concerneth me: thy mercy, O Lord, endureth for ever" (Ps. 138:8). By His mercy He does not quit unless we do. We quit when we ignore and transgress our spirit conscience.

Only those who mature to learn the nudging voice and promptings of the Holy Spirit within will fully enter into a Holy Spirit–led ministry. The Holy Spirit places a prompting and burden upon the believer's heart to fulfill a ministry task. The devil will never produce a burden within a godly woman to pray for a sick neighbor and bring flowers to express the love of God.

Only the Holy Spirit will place a specific Word burden within the heart of a preacher to give a word in season. I will never forget ministering in Ilocus Sur, north of Manila, in the northern Philippines. Prior to going there I had received a great anointing come over my mind, as the Holy Spirit witnessed to me that I was to go to this rebel-infested territory in 1986. While I was walking through a suburb of Santa Maria, the Holy Spirit spoke to me, pressing on my thoughts to preach about, "Whoso eateth my flesh, and drinketh my blood, hath eternal life; and I will raise him up at the last day" (John 6:54). I had not read that for some time or ever directly spoken on this.

After finding it in my Bible, I then spent several hours meditating on this scripture. That night after speaking on this truth, I saw a tremendous response with a huge salvation crowd with hundreds of healings and miracles. A huge line came up to testify starting at 8:30 p.m. We cut this off at midnight, with an increased crowd attending as many ran and brought others. Had I not listened, heard, and acted on this hearing, I believe I would have missed that holy move of God. This grew and continued for two more nights and became numerous church works. When

I first received this still small impression and voice, I argued within myself. I debated whether this would not be more suitable for a mature crowd. Praise God that by His grace I relinquished to the hearing and saw God move mightily.

The born of the Spirit ministries who have not learned how this holy living Word works within will minister, but they will miss the perfect will and Word of God. This hearing increases dramatically for those who have an experiential baptism in the Holy Spirit. They who do not hear will lack the matured accurate holy guidance God desires to give: "And the Lord said, Who then is that faithful and wise steward, whom his lord shall make ruler over his household, to give them their portion of meat in due season?" (Luke 12:42). Food, a word in season, takes a discerning and hearing ear.

The mature man or women of God will understand how the Holy Spirit works within our spirit. He will convict us of sin and righteousness. He will give us a "check" in our spirit to limit us from proceeding in a wrong conversation or direction. He will prompt us to speak and act, with a knowing within when we have failed Him by not obeying these nudges. He will interrupt our normal thoughts and bring out a Word or song, which we know did not just come from our minds, since this usually has no part of or history in our recent thought life.

I always stand amazed at the work of the Holy Spirit within. He speaks in our normal life's walk when we are striving for a Holy Spirit–led life. Our God knows all things and all of our thoughts moment by moment. He is wired into a billion people at once. I stand in awe of Him! If this is not your experience, just prayerfully wait on Him, and soon it will be, as He is not a respecter of persons. He will do for all what He will do for one.

The mature-minded servant of the Lord will seek to hear His voice within. Opportunity and invitations for ministry may be exciting. Unfortunately for some, due to a wrong-hearted focus, ego, or financial reward potential, they will pursue any invitation. Opportunity may not be Holy Ghost direction. The Holy Spirit–led ministry will experience what the apostle Paul experienced. Paul listened and wrote half of the

New Testament due to this holy hearing. Due to listening he experienced knowledge, direction, and timing in ministry. He heard the Holy Spirit, who sees and directs all.

> Now when they had gone throughout Phrygia and the region of Galatia, and were forbidden of the Holy Ghost to preach the word in Asia, after they were come to Mysia, they assayed [determined] to go into Bithynia: but the Spirit suffered them not. And they passing by Mysia came down to Troas. And a vision appeared to Paul in the night; There stood a man of Macedonia, and prayed him, saying, Come over into Macedonia, and help us. And after he had seen the vision, immediately we endeavored to go into Macedonia, assuredly gathering that the Lord had called us for to preach the gospel unto them.
>
> —ACTS 16:6–10

Hearing this "forbidding to go" to Asia was key to Paul's ministry direction. Our Lord had no lack of love or desire for converts in Asia, that the gospel should not be preached there. Later Paul spent much effort by the Holy Spirit's direction to minister in Asia (Acts 19:10). The Lord of the church knows the need and timing. God the Holy Spirit knows what priorities are. Had Paul not listened to this "check" in his spirit, he would have missed the call to Macedonia and that harvest. The burden for Asia just had to wait for God's timing to minister to that need. The Holy Spirit knows when people are prepared to hear the gospel and receive ministry. He knows the prayers of the oppressed prisoners and the seeking.

Many evangelical Christians are wonderfully saved family in the Lord, but they do not understand the voice of the anointing. This is usually experienced by those who have spent a deep time in waiting on the Lord in prayer and worship, or especially by those who have experienced the baptism of the Holy Spirit, as those at Pentecost did. Therefore when discussing this terminology, many do not relate to or even get fearful due to not understanding. The experiential anointing manifests in differing ways. Some sense the Holy Spirit's presence by what we term "goose bumps," similar to our skin being cold and wet, but in a pleasant sense with no discomfort. Others sense a light tingling sensation come over their being or mind. Mostly this happens when the Holy Spirit confirms a spoken truth or testimony of a Holy Spirit word or work, such as sharing about a miracle or healing. We must learn to discern the source of this voice just as with any other heard voice. Those who deny this voice have a limited understanding of the witness of the Spirit. "The Spirit itself beareth witness with our spirit, that we are the children of God" (Rom. 8:16).

The first time I experienced this, it scared me, since I had never heard anyone speaking of Holy Spirit experience due to my limited church background. Theologically consider what Paul said: "I say the truth in Christ, I lie not, my conscience also bearing me witness in the Holy Ghost" (Rom. 9:1). These scriptures are vague gibberish to those who have not experienced the manifested Holy Spirit presence, which is usually termed as the witness of the Holy Spirit or the anointing. This is available to all in Christ who humbly seek and worship Him. He is the baptizer in the Holy Spirit, while man can only baptize in water. "And I knew him not: but he that sent me to baptize with water, the same said unto me, Upon whom thou shalt see the Spirit descending, and remaining on him, the same is he which baptizeth with the Holy Ghost" (John 1:33).

Obedience to the voice and burden of the Holy Spirit is essential when serving our Lord in ministry. Whether involved in a pulpit ministry or a kitchen and friendship ministry, we must quietly listen to hear.

The call of God to ministry should always be motivated by a burden of the heart. He shares His heart and ministry desires for us to act upon as we relinquish ourselves to fulfill His purposes. "Faithful is he that calleth you, who also will do it" (1 Thess. 5:24). God who calls us to ministry will do His gospel work through us. He uses people just like you and me to perform His ministry to the church and world. What an honor above all honors!

> How then shall they call on him in whom they have not believed?
> and how shall they believe in him of whom they have not heard?

and how shall they hear without a preacher? And how shall they
preach, except they be sent? as it is written, How beautiful are the
feet of them that preach the gospel of peace, and bring glad tidings
of good things!

—Romans 10:14–15

## Burden and Vision Constitute the Call of God

The calling of God to us in ministry will cause two things to be experienced within the called. Much like a statue that stands on two legs,
these legs can be named BURDEN and VISION. They are a direct
result of the Holy Spirit working within.

The experiential result of the Holy Spirit working within the believer
is the development of a holy kingdom desire. This holy desire focuses
us to minister to the needs of others. The experiential first leg of this
ministry walk will always be a burden of the heart. This burden is due
to seeing people's needs and desiring to provide God's answers. This
holy burden is the key evidence of a Christ-given, Holy Spirit–led ministry. God-given ministry will always be in response to having seen need,
both spiritually and in the natural realm. All people we deal with will
be measured by our spiritual eyes. Due to having on our "God glasses"
when we see our fellow man, the question of their receiving eternal salvation versus heading for an eternal hell will be foremost in our minds.
We desire to show the world that Christ is the answer to all needs. We
will see man's brokenness and wounding, the result of sin and the death
affecting all of our lives and theirs, now and eternally.

Vision is seeing God's plan for us, then seeing how to minister to
these needs. Vision is seeing a plan much like a blueprint for building a
house. The plan will become clearer in time as we weigh how we may
be most effective in ministering to the needs we see. Seeing this plan
will result in action from the believer due to a burdened heart. We will
wholeheartedly want to maximize our effectiveness, to preach and teach
and minister to the needs we see in Christ's stead. All Holy Spirit–led
ministries will be burdened for the souls of mankind. They know that

all needs are met by knowing the God of Abraham, Isaac, and Jacob through our God and Savior Jesus Christ. Those who respond to the Holy Spirit–imparted burden will receive a vision in due time of how to minister their burden most effectively.

## Holy Spirit burden

God's burden works like this. At salvation, when the Holy Spirit immersed the believer into the body of Christ, the first baptism (1 Cor. 12:13), God's Holy Spirit joined Himself to our spirit man. The result will be an experiential new life. We will be drawn to a different walk. We will see life and moral issues in ourselves and others in a brand-new way. We will hunger for understanding and knowledge. Sadly some who receive the gospel, genuinely experiencing this, will turn away due to trials or ridicule by others or the love of this world and things thereof: "They on the rock are they, which, when they hear, receive the word with joy; and these have no root, which for a while believe, and in time of temptation fall away" (Luke 8:13).

> For it is impossible for those who were once enlightened, and have tasted of the heavenly gift, and were made partakers of the Holy Ghost, and have tasted the good word of God, and the powers of the world to come, if they shall fall away, to renew them again unto repentance.
>
> —Hebrews 6:4–6

> For if after they have escaped the pollutions of the world through the knowledge of the Lord and Savior Jesus Christ, they are again entangled therein, and overcome, the latter end is worse with them than the beginning. For it had been better for them not to have known the way of righteousness, than, after they have known it, to turn from the holy commandment delivered unto them.
>
> —2 Peter 2:20–21

Following our initial salvation experience we grow in faith by the holy Word. We prayerfully seek His presence. The voice of the Holy Spirit becomes louder within us as we seek and wait on Him. GOD WORKS IN YOU (Phil. 2:13). God the Holy Spirit speaks to us by continually placing burdens of heart on the called as we are prayerfully open to the Lord.

Stay in a prayerful waiting mode until we receive burden. Pray for the lost souls of friends, family, and your city. Pray for the Lord's salvation and the Holy Spirit's work throughout the nations. Pray for ministries, churches, missions, and gospel workers (Luke 10:2). Pray, "Thy kingdom come. Thy will be done," that righteousness and holiness may prevail.

This waiting on Him will include taking time to read His Word and meditating on Him. The resulting burden may lead us to witness by writing to family, visiting the sick, or minister by providing help in a physical manner. When we in obedience do what we were burdened to accomplish, we will know if this in fact was the Lord by the burden being lifted.

We may experience a longer-term burden, perhaps while reaching out to a particular soul for salvation. I continually pray for some from time to time whom I have not seen for the last twenty years. However, the initial weight is lifted and should be accompanied with a sense of well-being due to knowing we completed the task of our ministry burden efforts.

Another scripture that reveals part of this truth is found in 1 Thessalonians 5:23–24: "And the very God of peace sanctify you wholly; and I pray God your whole spirit and soul and body be preserved blameless unto the coming of our Lord Jesus Christ. Faithful is he that calleth you, who also will do it." How does God "do it" when we are doing it? He calls us by the inner work of the Holy Spirit by placing the burden on our hearts, thereby directing us. "I will instruct thee and teach thee in the way which thou shall go: I will guide thee with mine eye" (Ps. 32:8).

Our God always searches our hearts and thoughts, our motives and desires. "The spirit of man is the candle of the Lord, searching all the inward parts of the belly" (Prov. 20:27). Our spirit man seeks out the moral issues of right and wrong within our soul. Our spirit man can and will differ with the soul man (mind and will) when wrong is being entered into. We are capable of ignoring and overriding our conscience by denying this voice. We are denying the voice of the Holy Spirit when we deny our conscience. Paul said in 1 Timothy 4:2 that we can burn and harden our conscience: "Speaking lies in hypocrisy; having their conscience seared with a hot iron [immorality, pornography, gossip, sin actions etc.]"

## Vision

In time, as we respond to holy ministry nudgings, a burden will mature resulting in the birthing of a ministry vision. The ministering one will strive to fulfill this vision as a priority in their life pursuits. Ministry vision only comes and grows within those who are obedient to the voice of the Holy Spirit in little things. "His lord said unto him, Well done, good and faithful servant; thou hast been faithful over a few things, I will make thee ruler over many things" (Matt. 25:23). The many things referred to in this passage follow faithfulness in small things. An enlarged ministry vision follows faithfulness in ministry and obedience to the Holy Spirit promptings. Vision is different from bright ideas. An idea may stir some momentary action. A vision is a long-term heart pursuit that we work toward over years of our lives.

Vision brings a heartfelt dream, a ministry desire, a picture, and longing for what the ministry-minded person believes for and would like to see in the future. A holy vision always focuses on touching people in the name of the Lord. A carnal vision believes for their personal image, grandeur, and stature. Carnal vision includes personal achievements such as numbers, accolades, buildings, and stature of person—our spirituality and visibility. This carnal vision is what we call an "empire vision." An empire vision pleases the visibility of our person and ministry success. We bask in the sunshine of applause and accolades for our knowledge and gifts.

A kingdom vision wants to see Christ as Lord and all mankind know and worship Him. This holy vision wants God's kingdom to come on earth, as it is in heaven. This vision enters into Christ's vision of "I will build My church." We His servants build as He directs us.

Those who have this heart will spend time preparing for this vision, knowing "the just shall live by faith." They believe that if they wait upon the God-given vision, in time it will come to pass (Hab. 2:4). The Lord will bless and cause us to bring His given vision to fruitfulness.

## COMPASSION BURDENED MINISTRY

True ministry is birthed by having a compassion for people. Our Savior constantly ministered from compassion, and the mature called ministry will minister from this same fountain of motivation. "But when he saw the multitudes, he was moved with compassion on them, because they fainted, and were scattered abroad, as sheep having no shepherd" (Matt. 9:36). Holy Spirit–led ministry will always see what others do not see, having a ministry and shepherding heart for the needy and hurting, whether believers or unsaved. Our Lord stated this and continually acted this out. He fed the hungry, healed the sick, raised the dead, preached, and taught while attempting to reach humanity in the city of Jerusalem (Matt. 14:14; 15:32; 23:37; John 11:35). Jesus hugged and loved little children (Mark 9:36).

We minister out of Christ's compassion and in His stead. When the five called and Christ-appointed ministries minister to the needs of others, the motive must not be clouded with personal ambitions such as selfish financial pursuits or the idolizing of our ministry, which many pursue. Spiritual matured ministers look beyond their personal needs. Their ministering Christ to others will take priority over their personal carnal desires. Humble called ministry will always esteem the value of and uphold other fellow called ministers. They are equally Christ called. We see the greatest act of compassion the world has ever seen when Christ in humility came as a babe in the manger, heading toward His planned crucifixion, because He saw our need. The godly called ministry with a right spirit will likewise talk, walk, and act out of a burdened heart, seeing humanity's needs that are ultimately met in Christ alone.

This ministry and burden must always be balanced with equitable reality dealings in other normal life responsibilities. Marriage, home, and children are part of our husbands-love-wives and wives-honor-husbands covenant. Financial responsibility also needs to be balanced in our time and heart focus. "But if any provide not for his own, and specially for those of his own house, he hath denied the faith, and is worse than an infidel" (1 Tim. 5:8). Rest and coming aside is a need for the entire family so we will not "come apart." To balance church, ministry, home, and financial matters is a great juggling act. This needs to be balanced and conquered by any ministry. Another consideration is that the spouse and children must also understand and honor the Lord in upholding the called ministry in their responsibilities. We must establish and set this in order. I sometimes wonder how the apostle Peter did this while following Christ and how he managed his marriage (Matt. 8:14).

## LOSING THE BURDEN, ONLY HAVING VISION

When we idolize our ministry and lose a genuine heartfelt burden for people and their needs, we only have ministry vision left. Having a truth ministry but having lost compassion brings death. The ministry will still see a vision of preaching and being "the ministry," but it may lose a burden and a love for the people. The result of this is written in the Holy Bible: "Though I speak with the tongues of men and of angels, and have not charity, I am become as sounding brass, or a tinkling cymbal. And though I have the gift of prophecy, and understand all mysteries, and all knowledge; and though I have all faith, so that I could remove mountains, and have not charity, I am nothing" (1 Cor. 13:1–2). "Am become" states that the person was not always this way. This state arrived at of operating in spiritual gifts yet being loveless is a sad beyond tears reality. When a knowledgeable ministry loses compassionate love for the people they minister to, an ugly selfishness becomes visible. A failing pride of self emerges due to a mind-set of "look at who I am and what I have attained."

Financial goals and ministry success become the thorns our Lord spoke of as much as the gods of possessions and pleasures, which choked true fruitfulness. Rather, may healing of the broken become the overshadowing burden and vision of our ministry thrust. Some think it is not possible for a tongue-speaking prophesying ministry to lose a genuine love for people. These Bible scriptures were written to prove this is a very real possibility. They tell us that these people described had spiritual gifts but "am become" a deteriorated love-lacking ministry. We now please the god of self, our image, and well-being. We now flaunt the idol of our ministry, who we are and our accomplishments. We always need to examine if our first love for Christ is alive (Rev. 2:4). Jesus wept over Lazarus and Jerusalem (John 11:35). May we weep with those who weep (Rom. 12:15).

When the burden and compassion for people are left behind, only a vision for ministry success and prominence remains. The ministry then becomes comparable to what the prophet Ezekiel said about the shepherds in his day:

> And the word of the LORD came unto me, saying, Son of man, prophesy against the shepherds of Israel, prophesy, and say unto them, Thus says the Lord GOD unto the shepherds; Woe be to the shepherds of Israel that do feed themselves! should not the shepherds feed the flocks? Ye eat the fat, and ye clothe you with the wool, ye kill them that are fed: but ye feed not the flock. The diseased have ye not strengthened, neither have ye healed that which was sick, neither have ye bound up that which was broken, neither have ye brought again that which was driven away, neither have ye sought that which was lost; but with force and with cruelty have ye ruled them. And they were scattered, because there is no shepherd: and they became meat to all the beasts of the field, when they were scattered. My sheep wandered through all the mountains, and upon every high hill: yea, my flock was scattered upon all the face of the earth, and none did search or seek after them.
>
> —EZEKIEL 34:1–6

They preached Bible truth but did not personally touch the people. They stayed at arm's length, just as many do today.

These called ministries continually buried the people under mounds of truth but did not embrace them with love. They, like many today, saw them as financial potentials instead of beloved needy souls. I remember for a short season working with a certain ministry. Twice I observed the instant attention both he and his wife smothered two different business owners with following their first attending of our church service. Within two weeks they had visited both of their business establishments with "ministry and prophetic" talk. I compared that to the obvious disregard for some poor people who attended our church. To understand how many get to this state of wrong mindedness, one must understand genuine eldership.

## Three Ministry Expressions

There are differing ministry gifts and expressions. Some walk in few, and some function in all of them. In my personal experience I was greatly disturbed by my ministry experience with a ministry relationship I no longer walk with. The person had a great Word knowledge, preached a great message, and was definitely called to an Ephesians 4:11 calling as a fivefold prophet minister. He preached the importance of submitting one to another, that we should esteem each other better than ourselves (Phil. 2:3). This in part is what caused me to initially draw into this relationship.

One day a middle-aged lady attended our church service. It was obvious that she had a rough life and background. She looked rough with missing teeth but wore a great smile and was so happy to be accepted. She made herself at home in our service. After a couple of services she came forward upon an invitation directed to her alone and joyfully accepted Christ. I was blessed by sensing a cloud of the anointing at that divinely orchestrated moment.

The minister and his wife with insensitivity interfered with my priority ministry time. Immediately after the amen of closing the service, they diffused my ability to personally minister to this new babe in Christ by demanding attention to trivial and secondary matters. The thought of them welcoming this new babe into the family of God and ministering love and attention had not entered their minds. The wife immediately confronted me with a carnal demand to address the removal of some church possessions in their vehicle, as to being their top priority. He determined to leave in a rush to get to his television football game. I struggled with the failed priority of this. There is nothing wrong with football or liking sports. I felt the grieving of the Holy Spirit. There was no care demonstrated for this new lamb. Where was the compassionate elder's heart for the newly saved person?

The rest was made obvious a week later when taking them for a dinner. I asked what they thought about this lady accepting Christ. The response was, "She sure looks rough, doesn't she, with those missing teeth. I would not want to dig into her past." The following Sunday the new believer testified in amazement as to God's revealed intervention in her life. Within days of accepting Christ, God's mercy and love were demonstrated. A dentist "just happened" to come along and offered to fix her teeth free of charge. One would think that upon hearing this testimony, this ministry would have repented. I prayerfully weighed how to respond to this for several days.

I had mistakenly disregarded the need to discuss several matters for the sake of peace. What peace? It was a storm deferred. Many times avoidance of communication and confronting topics needing discussion simply brews an eventual storm.

The Holy Spirit directed me to not discuss this issue or several other things that I had erroneously not confronted, but simply to ask him to meet to discuss one simple question. I was to ask him if he was willing to take some time by appointment to discuss some needed ministry and eldership principles to avoid damage to our relationship.

Upon my request he accepted to meet, insisting his wife accompany him for their reasons. (Therein lay much of the problem.) Upon meeting and politely stating the need for discussion to communicate regarding eldership principles, they asked for one example, which was provided. He said they would make time. We shook hands and parted on that note.

Without my knowledge, the same evening they notified our church members that they were asked to leave the church. This was done with a complete deletion of discussion or of any submission one to another with a complete disregard for any common esteeming. His preaching of Philippians 2:3 was still ringing in my ears: "Let nothing be done through strife or vainglory; but in lowliness of mind let each esteem other better than themselves." The preaching of this message was great, but the inability to act on that which he preached spoke so much louder.

Their clanging cymbals spoke loudly. Hello! The real truth is they trumpeted out their lack of love for my wife and me and our eternal souls by this action. They confirmed their Pharisee hearts. Even if they had disagreed with us, a heart of love for us would have had concern for us. This genuine love would have been demonstrated by a deep desire to have heartfelt communication.

Our Lord described the Pharisees of His day:

> Then spake Jesus to the crowd, and to his disciples, saying, The scribes and the Pharisees sit in Moses' seat: All therefore whatsoever they bid you observe, that observe and do; but do not ye after their works: for they say, and do not. For they bind heavy burdens and grievous to be borne, and lay them on men's shoulders; but they themselves will not move them with one of their fingers. But all their works they do for to be seen of men: they make broad their phylacteries, and enlarge the borders of their garments, and love the uppermost rooms at feasts, and the chief seats in the synagogues.
> —Matthew 23:1–6

If they thought we were in error, their love for us would have constrained them to speak to us. Those who jump ship with no desire to communicate speak out their lack of true love for the brethren. Their actions trumpet out their pride and ungodly loveless hearts.

## An Elder's Heart

The ministry in example lacked an elder's heart. While living a short distance away from a needy family in our small congregation, neither this minister nor his wife had ever reached out to help a single dad within our church family. Over time it was made clear that this minister's wife was comfortable in being critical of the two boys and their dad. They saw no need for extending personal ministry to them. They claimed they were too busy to reach out to them, while having mega time for attending numerous social events and ministry dinners, always with financial supporters or other ministries.

They lacked a compassionate elder's heart, with no demonstrated love and care for this type of struggling people. All Pharisaical ministries who minister without compassion will miss Christ's heart for the broken and downtrodden. All balanced and mature fivefold ministers must have an elder's heart of compassion for the flock. Much can be observed by their testimony when returning from ministry outings. They cite offerings received, statistics of healings, and those baptized in the Holy Spirit as ministry wall trophies. They rarely speak of their heart of love for nor the beauty of the saints they ministered to. They are known to say, "We only minister in places where we are celebrated." As to their responsibility to their "Jerusalem," the place of their spiritual allegiance to their home church, which all should have, they will demonstrate their lack of personal ministry to the broken.

Even though they may have read the Bible through many times, they are unaware and blind to the writings of the apostle Paul: "Though I speak with the tongues of men and of angels, and have not charity, I am become as sounding brass, or a tinkling cymbal. And though I have the gift of prophecy, and understand all mysteries, and all knowledge; and though I have all faith, so that I could remove mountains, and have not charity, I am nothing" (1 Cor. 13:1). It is possible to have great mountain-moving faith and gifts, which they received while starting out with a right heart of humility, repentance, and a love for Christ and His people. They now demonstrate their loss of love for the people. These scriptures address this very topic. They now are separated from and place themselves above the people. Seeing and loving babes needing diaper changing is now beneath them. Subsequent to having attained unto growth in gifts, faith, and knowledge, they now preach "you" instead of "we."

They now no longer have a love for others, having forgotten the pit they were hewn from: "Hearken to me, ye that follow after righteousness, ye that seek the Lord: look unto the rock whence ye are hewn, and to the hole of the pit whence ye are dug" (Isa. 51:1).

They have entered into and aligned with the Moses problem. After spending forty days with the Lord in the mountain and receiving the Ten Commandment, Moses broke them upon seeing the people's sin. By doing so he judged them unworthy of these holy oracles. He no longer related to or identified with the people. He no longer related to the fact that he also was of similar sin material. This change came about due to his wrong response after having experienced God's presence, anointing, and grace in this mountain height experience.

In time the Lord taught Moses by His awesome and patient wisdom and love. The lesson resulted in a changed heart, where he was willing to place his life on the line to protect these very people. After this lesson Moses said, "Yet now, if thou wilt forgive their sin—; and if not, blot me, I pray thee, out of thy book which thou hast written" (Exod. 32:32). Splitting rock to get some writable slabs took real sweat and energy. Carrying them up a mountain will always remind us of our humanity (Exod. 34:1). When we believe that we have a close walk with God and due to this no longer identify with people, the broken and those of a weak spirit, we are on dangerous ground (Gal. 6:1). We are always to consider ourselves as to our own potential for failure, just like others.

I fearfully wonder how many of these ministries were the very ones our Lord Jesus spoke of when He said, "Many will say to me in that day, Lord, Lord, have we not prophesied in thy name? and in thy name have cast out devils? and in thy name done many wonderful works? And then will I profess unto them, I never knew you: depart from me, ye that work iniquity" (Matt. 7:22–23). Our Lord did not refute their claims of works done in His name. Rather He said, "I have erased all knowledge of you." Never forget: "But when the righteous turneth away from his righteousness, and committeth iniquity, and doeth according to all the abominations that the wicked man doeth, shall he live? All his righteousness that he hath done shall not be mentioned: in his trespass that he hath trespassed, and in his sin that he hath sinned, in them shall he die" (Ezek. 18:24).

Notice God's answer to Moses as to the removal of his name or any name out of His Book of Life: "And the Lord said unto Moses, Whosoever hath sinned against me, him will I blot out of my book" (Exod. 32:33). Our God does blot names out of His Book, names that were in there. The unsaved were never in this book. Please be cautioned as to a right heart toward God and man.

A ministry who no longer seeks out the broken and wounded usually becomes a professional "merchandiser" of God's people and purveyor of their ministry anointing and knowledge.

The ones Christ spoke of ministered under the anointing at one point. Think and weigh this truth, clean animal, as you chew the cud. Upon salvation being experienced, we do not lose our will and ability of choice. Our God holds us accountable for our actions and decisions because we have this free will ability.

I learned much by these events as to differing levels of ministry functions. This is irrelevant of any fivefold ministry anointing. Some operate in only one of these levels, as a gift ministry, but all called fivefold elders should operate in all of these.

**A gift ministry**

One may have a gift ministry, such as singing, musical abilities, or gifts of the Spirit that edify and bless the church body. This includes the prophetic and healing gifts. These minister inspiration and faith as well as comfort to the body of Christ. These gifts may flow in those who may or may not be elders (1 Cor. 12:11).

**A pulpit ministry**

All called fivefold ministries, when mature, should to be capable of functioning in a pulpit ministry. This ministry involves teaching, preaching, and expounding holy God truths, by which the body of believers grows. This should always include depth and revelation of holy Word principles.

**An elder's ministry**

A genuine elder ministry ministers to the personal needs in people—whether they are in fellowship meetings, at a café get together, or in their homes. The elder must be hospitable, with a love for people. They see people's needs and always want to bring help to these needs. The "Holy Ghost made" mature and spirituality balanced elder, Paul said in

Acts 20:28, will seek out and fellowship with the believers and not just fellowship with ministries and fellow elders. They will not just "visit" the believers of the flock. Upon visiting they will discern in a gentle and wise loving fashion what the needs are. They will discern growth needs. Then with holy hearts they will minister knowledge and understanding to these needs. All fivefold ministry should involve mature eldership ministry.

Also, all elders who are not of the Ephesians 4:11 fivefold ministries must mature with burden and compassion for the flock, for the young and the mature saints.

To those who desire to walk in this office, we find written guidelines of maturity conduct: "This is a true saying, If a man desire the office of a bishop, he desireth a good work. A bishop then must be blameless, the husband of one wife, vigilant, sober, of good behaviour, given to hospitality, apt to teach; not given to wine, no striker, not greedy of filthy lucre; but patient, not a brawler, not covetous; one that ruleth well his own house, having his children in subjection with all gravity" (1 Tim. 3:1–4). Any believer maturing to fill this elder ministry office may become an ordained elder. They must allow the Holy Spirit to mold them to maturity to fulfill this office (Acts 20:28).

Some wonderful eldership minded people unfortunately have mature children who are rebellious. May all elder potentials learn how to deal with the rebellious by teaching them responsibility with accountability. We must demonstrate the strength to teach the rebellious that they will bear the results of their rebellion and unaccountability. How else can these potential elders guide the church? May the husbands and wives be in unity about this matter, upholding each other with appropriate love and honor, as required in a godly marriage. Also we must not hold elders responsible for rebellious children who are of age. Young adults need to make their choices. God honored Isaac, knowing full well he had Esau for a son.

## Women in Ministry

Consider God's writing of Deborah, a powerful woman minister. Also remember a number of prophetesses, such as Anna at Christ's birth (Luke 2:36). These women heard and acted in ministry upon God's voice to them. May we not eliminate spiritually mature women from potentially being elders as many wrongfully do. "And Deborah, a prophetess, the wife of Lapidoth, she judged Israel at that time" (Judg. 4:4). This married and anointed prophetess minister ruled Israel, resulting in godly victory and peace in the nation for twenty years.

This holy biblical fact confuses the understanding of people opposed to women in ministry. This is because they struggle with scriptures such as, "But I suffer not a woman to teach, nor to usurp authority over the man, but to be in silence" (1 Tim. 2:12). They have not studied the Greek, where it is clear this scripture is to be applied to a woman in a marital context. Paul was considering and honoring the headship of a husband, upholding the correct marital authority structure. This statement applies to a husband and wife in a marriage relationship. The wife should honor and uphold her husband. This is not written to limit women in ministry. Lapidoth both recognized and was quite content with God's appointment of his wife to ministry. He respected God, His calling upon his wife, and God dealings.

According to Strong's concordance, the Greek word for "a woman" in this text is *gune*, which is interpreted as "specifically a wife." An unmarried woman would have been referred to as a maid, maiden, or virgin. The Greek for these entities is very different from *gune*. In the Greek, "maid" is paidiske, and "virgin" is parthenos.

We have examples of women ministries who are mature in Christ. Some minister in a tremendous way under Holy Spirit anointing. For example, consider Joyce Meyer, who affects hundreds of thousands of people, building faith with wisdom. Her husband upholds and honors her as Deborah's husband did. Likewise Beth Moore is an unusually anointed teacher of the Word with a great depth of Holy Word revelation, thereby teaching many. Few pastors possess her depth of Word knowledge.

The most anointed ministry I have ever experienced is a woman now deceased, Kathryn Kuhlman. As a young assistant pastor I was assigned to look after an upper section of the stadium in Vancouver, British Columbia, when she ministered there. I will never forget when she walked on stage from behind the curtained backstage area. A wave of the anointing hit me. Her Christ and Holy Spirit teachings and the tremendous miracles she called out were verified. She always spoke of the Holy Spirit as her friend. Hundreds of thousands came to Christ through her ministry in tents, stadiums, radio, and television outreaches. Knowing this caused me to study God's Word regarding women in ministry. I was opposed to this back then.

The largest church in the world, having brought salvation to millions in Korea and elsewhere due to the outflow, has had hundreds of ministering women elders under Dr. Yonggi Cho.

Women as well as men receive gifts and anointing. Consider Mary the mother of Christ and other women who were in attendance in the Upper Room on the Day of Pentecost. The Holy Spirit came as tongues of fire. He rested on and anointed these women as well as on the apostles and men. The Bible tells us that God is no respecter of person. This applies to women as well as men. Those who deeply seek the Lord will receive from Him. There are numerous prophetesses mentioned in both the Old and New Testaments.

Those who reject women in ministry seem to be lost for an answer to Philip's daughters: "And the next day we that were of Paul's company departed, and came unto Caesarea: and we entered into the house of Philip the evangelist, which was one of the seven; and abode with him. And the same man had four daughters, virgins, which did prophesy" (Acts 21:8–9).

Now this prophetic speaking was a Holy Spirit–involved communication. These ladies did not prophesy over kitchen dishes: "Oh, dishes, hear the Word of the Lord." They prophesied over and to people and the church. "But he that prophesieth speaketh unto men to edification, and exhortation, and comfort. He that speaketh in an unknown tongue edifieth himself; but he that prophesieth edifieth the church" (1 Cor. 14:3–4). These women edified the church with their prophetic gifting.

We must discern the work of God in women as well as men. May we also discern the Jezebel spirit, which demands a wrongful place of authority. The Jezebel spirit is not limited to women and can be seen in many ministries. They always have a pretense of humility and coming under authority, but never do so in reality. They will always be very giving to gain acceptance, as they come alongside authority figures to control them. They have a wrong authority control motive. They breach the scripture of, "Likewise, ye younger, submit yourselves unto the elder. Yea, all of you be subject one to another, and be clothed with humility" (1 Pet. 5:5). They will come alongside true authority figures and demand to become the neck that turns the head. They are difficult to discern since they will usually be super helpful and be gracious in giving, just as some dear saints with a right heart are.

They will be recognized by their strong negative response when genuine God-given leadership says no to their pressing them into a direction they are not comfortable with. When they are withstood and leave, they usually confirm their Jezebel spirit by an obvious work of attempting to vilify and destroy genuine God-placed spiritual ministry and their authority.

A right spirited people will always want to communicate with love and patience. They will strive for a cooperative team work spirit, esteeming others and desiring a team ministry approach. With love, grace, and patience they will have a heart of humility. They will have no problem being "subject one to another." They will demonstrate great tolerance and patience when others do not see their direction or point of view. They allow the Holy Spirit to work in others and rejoice in the accomplishments of others. They honor the Holy Spirit and His deposit in fellow ministry.

With love and striving for unity, may we uphold and honor the works of the Holy Spirit in all fellow believers. Our Lord prayed, "That they all may be one; as thou, Father, art in me, and I in thee, that they also may be one in us: that the world may believe that thou hast sent me" (John 17:21).

## Genuine Elders

The genuine Holy Ghost made elder must be apt to teach, feed, and oversee the flock (Acts 20:28). A genuine right-hearted elder oversees the flock with a heart for the struggling the weak and the wounded. He is not satisfied with simply being a gift or a pulpit ministry. A genuine mature elder will have compassion on all with an elder's heart. He will seek out the discouraged and the struggling, unlike the Pharisees our Lord Jesus described.

Genuine elders will never be satisfied with being an advisory board to a pastor or just dealing with business matters. They will only feel fulfilled when they are released to touch and personally minister to the flock. They will understand why our Lord, with holy insight, cried out with a broken heart. "And Jesus, when he came out, saw much people, and was moved with compassion toward them, because they were as sheep not having a shepherd" (Mark 6:34). Our Savior well knew that there were many who were named elders, Pharisees, and Sadducees present in His day. The titles did not match their functioning. We must have compassion for the weak and weary. (For more information see my book and manual *Fivefold Ministry Churches*.)

## The Believer's Ministry, Holy Spirit Burden

Our risen Lord in the evening of the resurrection day met with His initial twelve apostles. This was subsequent to ascending into heaven, where He applied His blood to the heavenly mercy seat in the temple which was "made without hands" (Heb. 9:11–12). Upon meeting with them in the evening of the resurrection day, He "breathed on them" and said, "Receive ye the Holy Ghost" (John 20:22). This was days before Pentecost, when they were baptized in the Holy Ghost. When Christ blew on them and said "receive ye the Holy Ghost," they were born of the Spirit (*genao*).

Today we as well as all believers in those days should be baptized (*baptism*) in the Holy Spirit and not just born of the Spirit. We need to be *genao* and *baptismo*. These two baptisms will mostly occur on different occasions. The baptism of the Holy Spirit usually occurs as a result of anointed ministry laying hands on the recipients. We do not lay hands on people to receive salvation.

The experiential new birth our Lord Jesus spoke of is the most valued experience that exists. This is needed to receive eternal life. "For ye have not received the spirit of bondage again to fear; but ye have received the Spirit of adoption, whereby we cry, Abba, Father. The Spirit itself beareth witness with our spirit, that we are the children of God" (Rom. 8:15–16). Unfortunately many will attend church and live "good" lives, never experiencing what this scripture speaks of. I once was one of them. The new birth of the Spirit is experiential and not just theological. Being a dead religious person, I changed when I was in my late twenties. I was personally confronted of my sin before a loving Christ and heavenly Father. Believing in His love brought about my changed life.

Many have their fear of death and the judgment to come allayed by professional and unsaved religious clergy. They are advised that this is normal to humanity. They disregard Revelation 21:8, which states, "But the fearful, and unbelieving, and the abominable, and murderers, and whoremongers, and sorcerers, and idolaters, and all liars, shall have their part in the lake which burneth with fire and brimstone: which is the second death." They do not know how to bring relief to the fears within the unsaved by bringing them into a relationship with Christ, thereby dispelling those fears. "There is no fear in love; but perfect love casteth out fear: because fear hath torment. He that feareth is not made perfect in love" (1 John 4:18). This is more common and applicable to those who relate to traditional churches. They are wrongly taught a religious non-experiential, unscriptural falsehood.

My mom and dad visited me while in their early eighties. Shortly after that Dad wrote me a letter asking for advice. His sister in Holland had written him a sincere question and my father asked me how he should answer her. She wrote that she had faithfully attended her denominational Calvinistic church and had always lived a good and strong moral life. However, she had a strong fear of dying and no peace in meeting God. Her question was, "How can this be?" People were not taught how to become born again in that church.

## True Christian Ministry

"For if ye live after the flesh, ye shall die: but if ye through the Spirit do mortify the deeds of the body, ye shall live. For as many as are led by the Spirit of God, they are the sons of God" (Rom. 8:13–14). True Christian ministry emanates from being led by the Spirit of God. One cannot be led until they have the Spirit of God joined to their spirit man, abiding within and working within him.

"For God is my witness, whom I serve with my spirit in the gospel of his Son" (Rom. 1:9). Paul served God with his spirit as he was moved upon by the Holy Spirit, working within his conscience: "I say the truth in Christ, I lie not, my conscience also bearing me witness in the Holy Ghost" (Rom. 9:1). We all have a conscience, albeit some are greatly damaged. However, not all have a conscience "in the Holy Ghost," but only those who are born of the Spirit.

"And now, behold, I go bound in the spirit unto Jerusalem, not knowing the things that shall befall me there" (Acts 20:22). This is a key statement of understanding written by this apostle. The call of God places a sure knowledge and burden upon the hearing of the mature ministry. They know it would be a sin not to answer this holy burden. This is given due to the Holy Spirit working within them. Should one ignore this given burden, it will cost us, but the result of obediently following this holy leading will lead us into ministry paths and attainments that we will not be capable of foreseeing at the beginning of our faith journey.

## Covenant Ministry Promise

Notice God's preservation and sealing of all who take His burden upon themselves: "And the LORD said unto him, Go through the midst of the city, through the midst of Jerusalem, and set a mark upon the foreheads of the men that sigh and that cry for all the abominations that be done in the midst thereof" (Ezek. 9:4). Note what verses 5–6 say:

> And to the others he said in mine hearing, Go ye after him through the city, and smite: let not your eye spare, neither have ye pity: Slay utterly old and young, both maids, and little children, and women: but come not near any man upon whom is the mark; and begin at my sanctuary. Then they began at the ancient men which were before the house.

The mature men were held more accountable for their lack than others. Those who know truth and disregard the same will receive a greater judgment. These men should have been an example by leading to a godly focus. I heard one foolish man say, "Then it may be better to not know truth." I replied, "By not knowing truth, you make a covenant with death." Death is upon all who do not seek the truth. Jesus is the truth (John 14:6; 3:36).

Our Lord has a marked and sealed people. They sighed and cried out to God due to seeing and struggling with wrongdoing. Sin burdened their hearts. They spoke out and acted against wrongdoing. Others simply did not see or act; they turned a blind eye. "A good man out of the good treasure of his heart bringeth forth that which is good; and an evil man out of the evil treasure of his heart bringeth forth that which is evil: for of the abundance of the heart his mouth speaketh" (Luke 6:45). Those who do not speak out demonstrate their lack of burden. They are of those whom Christ shall be ashamed of in His future kingdom at the judgment (Mark 8:38).

Our God has not changed! The sealed and marked withstand evil. All of these are walking standards of holiness. All speak forth from the contents of our hearts. "But those things which proceed out of the mouth come forth from the heart; and they defile the man. For out of the heart proceed evil thoughts, murders, adulteries, fornications, thefts, false witness, blasphemies" (Matt. 15:18–19). Likewise today some people of the

Lord cry out for the wrongs of abortion, homosexuality, and the sinful wrongs of life and the world. These wrongs will be spoken against by fervent believers, more than their fellow pew warmers. It is a sad truth that many do not stand or speak out. They are the salt which has lost its savor. "Salt is good: but if the salt have lost his savor, wherewith shall it be seasoned? It is neither fit for the land, nor yet for the dunghill; but men cast it out. He that hath ears to hear, let him hear" (Luke 14:34–35). Christ said that salt can lose its savor.

When moved upon, the prophet prayed, crying out to God. He rang the bells of intercession, reaching heaven (Hab. 1:2). As the Lord moved on the prophet, he acted in response. This led to his crying out with a heart of love for both God and man. Similarly some will cry out to God in intercession today. They desire to turn man from sin and evil in this hour. In verse 3 the prophet Habakkuk realized it was the Lord Himself who had shown His prophet sin, grievance, and wrong doing.

This shown burden caused Habakkuk a great burden of heart. He struggled with what he saw. He realized God was sharing His heart and what the Lord constantly sees, things that are burdening our God's heart. This is why several prophets started their writings with "the burden of the Lord."

The burden of the Lord comes in many forms. This is understood by those who have received spiritual eyes and ears. Those who have an ear to hear will hear what the Spirit says to the churches. "He that hath an ear, let him hear what the Spirit says unto the churches" (Rev. 2:7). This is one of the repetitious statements made seven times in all of the letters to the seven churches our Lord addressed, along with the "to him that overcomes" promises. Not all church-attending people see or hear, due to only having natural eyes and ears.

Their spiritual eyes are closed because they do not seek the Lord. They are satisfied with a Sunday morning relationship, doing their dutiful religious act of attending a church service. Many are "fire insurance" Christians. God reveals Himself, but only to the hungry and seeking.

## CHAPTER ELEVEN

# CHRIST'S VISION, OUR VISION

*Christ's Vision*

*A*LL MINISTRY SHOULD stem from having seen and entered into Christ our Lord's vision. His vision is salvation for a bride company with eyes of eternity. These eyes see this earth with a temporal perspective. We His ministry servants enter into the building of His kingdom and His church. We see His love for us and humanity. We act due to this.

Jesus said, "I will build My church." (See Matthew 16.) We see this unchanging passion and purpose in Christ our Lord. By His omniscience He foresaw the result of salvation's plan: "Who verily was foreordained before the foundation of the world, but was manifest in these last times for you" (1 Pet. 1:20). Our Lord's vision was in place before the world was founded. Our Alpha and Omega, beginning and end, eternal God created time, but only for us His created, until "time shall be no more." He is God and omniscient, knowing all from eternity past and future. This existing world ends when the church is complete (Rev. 10:6).

The new world begins with the New Jerusalem coming down "as a bride adorned for her husband" (Rev. 21:2). The ministry of God must have eyes of eternity—the seeing of the prize and Christ's glorious eternal kingdom.

This determination of having our eyes focused on eternity will sustain us as we endure the battles that accompany ministry. It takes effort to hold this focus in place, but this will greatly help as we focus on an overcoming in our battles. Every day wake up with the determined first thoughts of:

- I am a child of the King!

- Lord Jesus, I am Your servant.

- I am progressing toward the heavenly Jerusalem as I journey through today.

- Come, Holy Spirit; I love and need You.

- Holy Spirit, reveal Yourself in a greater way, and draw me closer.

- Guide me and use me in touching others as I project the cross and salvation.

The apostle Paul shared with us the church, the focus we need. He pointed to Christ and His vision: "Looking unto Jesus the author and finisher of our faith; who for the joy that was set before him endured the cross, despising the shame, and is set down at the right hand of the throne of God. For consider him that endured such contradiction of sinners against himself, lest ye be wearied and faint in your minds" (Heb. 12:2–3).

We must see Christ's vision from His High Priestly prayer. Our Lord Jesus spoke of our eternal glory with Him and in eternity future, just prior to the cross: "Father, I will that they also, whom thou hast given me, be with me where I am; that they may behold my glory, which thou hast given me: for thou lovest me before the foundation of the world" (John 17:24). We must see Our Lord's heart desire. He longs for all of the redeemed to be with Him for eternity in perfect union with Him.

We as His ambassadors are to reach as many souls as possible (2 Cor 5:20). He appeals to us to be His messengers, so all will hear and know. Our greatest expression of love, besides personal worship, is demonstrated by sharing His love and reaching out to others. "How then shall they call on him in whom they have not believed? and how shall they believe in him of whom they have not heard? and how shall they hear without a preacher? And how shall they preach, except they be sent? as it is written, How beautiful are the feet of them that preach the gospel of peace, and bring glad tidings of good things!" (Rom. 10:14–15). Our God declares our travels and ministry as beautiful since we are bringing life into death. If we are not physically raising the dead, we certainly are raising the spiritually dead.

## CHRIST'S AND OUR EARTHLY MINISTRY

Our Lord summarized His ministry purpose near the end of His earthly mission: "*I have glorified thee* on the earth: I have finished the work which you gave me to do....For I have given unto them the words which thou gavest me; and they have received them, and have known surely that I came out from thee, and they have believed that thou didst send me....And I have declared unto them thy name, and will declare it: that the love wherewith thou hast loved me may be in them, and I in them" (John 17:4, 8, 26, emphasis added).

Here we have the recipe for a Christlike right-hearted ministry.

- Jesus glorified the Father and not Himself. May we likewise glorify Him and not us.

- Jesus completed the work His Father desired Him to do. May we in like manner see and do Christ's work, not our own. We must have our understanding saturated with the unspeakable worth of our Father's salvation for many.

- Jesus gave mankind the Father's words and not His own. This is possible and must be for those who prayerfully wait upon our Lord, seeking His face. This means daily prayerfully speaking and acting out how the Lord impresses us, the result of a prayer-without-ceasing experiential walk. Without this we may well be doing our thing (1 Thess. 5:17).

- Jesus declared the Father's name while revealing the Father's identity and heart. May we also know His name (Exod. 33:19). We must know Him intimately and proclaim Him.

The success of Christ's ministry was in denying self-glory. He demonstrated and ministered a revelation of the Father's glory. He showed the Father's love, message, and works in His earthly ministry. We must show Christ's glory. He is seated on the right hand of the Father, with the Holy Spirit. The Father sends the Holy Spirit in Christ's name. "Howbeit when he, the Spirit of truth, is come, he will guide you into all truth: for he shall not speak of himself; but whatsoever he shall hear, that shall he speak: and he will shew you things to come. He shall *glorify me*: for he shall receive of mine, and shall shew it unto you. All things that the Father hath are mine: therefore said I, that he shall take of mine, and shall shew it unto you" (John 16:13–15, emphasis added).

During Christ's earthly ministry He glorified the Father in a perfection of walk, talk, prayer, people ministry, and time expenditures.

This divinely embodied ministry included holy demonstrations of love, which only the holy understand. Christ expressed holy anger shown by a whip, overthrowing the tables of the moneymakers. Likewise today we also have our temple moneymakers and merchandisers of God's people. The ministries that sell what Christ and the Holy Spirit has given them need to consider the God-given truth of, "Buy the truth, and sell it not; also wisdom, and instruction, and understanding" (Prov. 23:23). Christ's temple whip and scathing words to Pharisee ministry about their wrong financial focus is a caution to you and I: "…which devour widows' houses, and for a shew make long prayers: the same shall receive greater condemnation" (Luke 20:47). There is good reason for this statement to be repeated in three of the Gospels.

Some do rightfully share great truths to cover their costs, such as books and tapes. However, others produce materials with the heart of selling them to make a living. The motive is the real issue. Are we fighting to bless, equip, and minister to the purchasers because of our love for them, or are we sustaining a living? Many seem to be guilty of what Christ said of Pharisee ministry.

Jesus never made merchandise out of people. Many cannot deny guilt of being party to what our Lord cautioned us not to be: "And many shall follow their pernicious ways; by reason of whom the way of truth shall be evil spoken of. And through covetousness shall they with feigned words make merchandise of you: whose judgment now of a long time lingereth not, and their damnation slumbereth not" (2 Pet. 2:2–3). Since Peter said this with Holy Ghost–anointing as a caution to us, we need to discern those who use well-turned words due to covetousness. We know that many speak evil of the gospel truth today because of money dealings.

Due to this covetousness and making merchandise of God's people, huge damage is done to many souls and the gospel is critically and ill spoken of. May we prayerfully proceed when dealing with this sensitive topic of kingdom finances.

We must be holy and wise when raising legitimate finances for world outreach and church planting or mercy projects. The question is, how carefully are we when expending these sacrificially given dollars? Are we ministering due to having a burden for souls and their welfare, or are we making a living from preaching while posturing our gloriously feathered peacock tails—tails made up of our wisdom, knowledge, gifts, or wit?

Do we minister from a deep burden for the hearers with hearts of wisdom and compassion? This must be the overflowing thrust of our well and what we draw from in our ministry. Our Lord always ministered with genuine mercy, void of pretense or legalism. He always dealt with the reality in front of Him, with a presentation of salvation and righteousness being portrayed. He spoke out his disdain for a Pharisaical ministry and a lack of mercy demonstrated by their hypocrisy at the question of, "Shall we stone this woman?" Where is the man?

He completed teachings of coming events, a hell to be shunned and a heaven to gain, for those who brought forth works of righteousness. He had fully disclosed God's love for the world and redemption for those who brought forth works worthy of repentance. He spoke of the believer's future and God's heart toward them.

Here we see Christ's heart and the vision all ministries should continually walk with: the heavenly Jerusalem coming down as a bride adorned for her husband. Seeing life and people through the filter of this vision will always cause one to uphold the glory of our God and Savior, while we will simultaneously have less focus on us and who we are. John the Baptist was named the greatest prophet by our Lord. No doubt a part of this standing was achieved by John's vision even while being threatened by an imminent death. John said, "He must increase and I must decrease." After a fashion John was already dead, due to how he viewed his self-image. Now that is worship.

## "I WILL BUILD MY CHURCH": OUR MINISTRY VISION

The matured and sanctified ministry sees holy purpose in Christ's building. "And I say also unto thee, That thou art Peter, and upon this rock I will build my church; and the gates of hell shall not prevail against it" (Matt. 16:18). Our God uses apostles and prophets who know from the depths of their hearts that Christ is the Son of the living God. They lay foundation stones of doctrine and truth. Then they build His church on these foundation stones. "And are built upon the foundation of the apostles and prophets, Jesus Christ himself being the chief corner stone" (Eph. 2:20).

The nonrecognition and identification of these ministry callings has and is doing great damage to church building. This church is the fruit of the earth (James 5:7). Our eternal, Alpha and Omega, omniscient God's vision and purpose is to redeem and bring home His church, as we see in Matthew 25:34: "Then shall the King say unto them on his right hand, Come, ye blessed of my Father, inherit the kingdom prepared for you from the foundation of the world." Peter was one of many apostles among the herein named foundation stones. Apostles still lay, repair, and establish church foundations.

Our vision should always be a furthering of and uniting with Christ's vision. We as His servants build His church. We must treasure and respect God's people, His little ones. "And whosoever shall offend one of these little ones that believe in me, it is better for him that a millstone were hanged about his neck, and he were cast into the sea" (Mark 9:42). Respect the least in stature and education when they are redeemed. They are God's kings and priests (Rev. 1:6).

May we respect the truth that any of us are only one part of His called ministry callings and His desired church government. May the church come to the place where we will be operating under what has been destroyed for centuries. Christ desires the government He speaks of—an apostle-led church with a multiple eldership. This will be a functional reality when all of the five Christ-given callings and elder-ship are recognized instead of the common onefold leadership. May the "foundation" ministries of the apostle and prophet come to a maturity with knowledge. This must be demonstrated by their heart, vision, and humility so that "the church" can receive them. "And God hath set some in the church, first apostles, secondarily prophets, thirdly teachers, after that miracles, then gifts of healings, helps, governments, diversities of tongues" (1 Cor. 12:28). When we deny this scripture, we are denying Christ His place of Lordship.

Then again we have the many "glory seekers" who claim to have a multiple calling such as an apostle and prophet, or some other combina-tion, which destroys the identification of callings. No doubt scriptural ignorance is involved on the part of those who are guilty of doing this. They lack understanding of what constitutes the call of God and their personal calling. May they in humility be corrected.

To rebel and ignore the Bible truth of Christ giving all five of these multiple ministry callings is a sin and a crime. His church is constantly less and achieving less than what it should be due to this nonrecognition of His intended giving. Bringing this into order and allowing all of these their place and functionality will produce what the Book of Acts portrayed.

This is not happening due to preachers and believers saying, "I am wiser than God." This is due to ignoring the many New Testament writings about the multiple Christ-given ministries. This is due to most ministries erroneously being comfortable with a pastor-led, non-genuine multiple eldership structure and ministry government. "For as the heavens are higher than the earth, so are my ways higher than your ways, and my thoughts than your thoughts" (Isa. 55:9).

May we come to the place where our Lord will bless our humility. "For all those things hath mine hand made, and all those things have been, saith the Lord: but to this man will I look, even to him that is humble and of a contrite spirit, and trembleth at my word" (Isa. 66:2). Those who in humility tremble at God's Word will with humility worship Him. They desire what He desires. This humble and obedient people will strive to establish His church and kingdom, loving and pleasing Him. Our God will bless these because they sought His kingdom as a priority of life.

## Author's Prophetic Word

We are going to experience two things affecting the worldwide church. The living church shall be restored to what we see in the Book of Acts. Then, prior to Christ's return, there will be a worldwide revival that will pale Pentecost.

Read the second and third chapters of Joel describing "the day of the Lord" when Christ comes for His bride company, the church. We will see a mighty unparalleled ministry coming forth in the future church. Joel prophesied that this future ministry will not break rank or thrust one another through.

This end-time army will be different from anything we have seen so far. They will not be as what Paul in disappointment lamented about when speaking to the church of Philippi. "But I trust in the Lord Jesus to send Timotheus shortly unto you, that I also may be of good comfort, when I know your state. For I have no man likeminded, who will naturally care for your state. For *all seek their own*, not the things which are Jesus Christ's. But ye know the proof of him, that, as a son with the father, he hath served with me in the gospel" (Phil. 2:19–22, emphasis added). A servant of Christ will bless and love their fellow elders and ministry. They will seek their Lord's kingdom and glory and not "their own."

The Holy Bible–exampled church is not happening because of many seeking their own group, power, and visibility: "For all seek their own, not the things which are Jesus Christ's" (v. 21). All ministry plans will be laid at Christ's feet, recognizing His Lordship. This church will discern, respect, and function with all of the called ministries flowing together.

## Unholy Wrong and Lack

This lack is seen in the numerous churches that predominantly have a one-man pulpit ministry. This is totally unscriptural. This common onefold ministry versus the intended fivefold ministry impoverishes the banquet table intended for believers. This can readily be observed everywhere. Most demonstrate a disrespectful disregard of what our Lord gave to the church (Eph. 4:8, 11).

Most demonstrate a spiritual self-sufficiency by disregarding the need of the other callings.

Most demonstrate an inability to submit to fellow called minister. Meanwhile in hypocrisy they demand and teach their people to recognize their personal ministry authority.

Most do not seek for a multiple eldership. In a correct church structure ministry will both have a place of authority and submission to fellow elders. What a great demonstration this will be to those whom we are responsible for, should ministry demonstrate submission with unity. But this is not easy to achieve. I have several failed efforts of this in my past. I always have to search my heart with, "Was there wrongful pride involved on my part in this failure?" Pride is a root problem in limiting the reality of unity and a multiple eldership. "Only by pride cometh contention: but with the well advised is wisdom" (Prov. 13:10).

Unholy pride is demonstrated by not esteeming others.

> Let nothing be done through strife or vainglory; but in lowliness of mind let each esteem other better than themselves. Look not every man on his own things, but every man also on the things of others. Let this mind be in you, which was also in Christ Jesus: Who, being in the form of God, thought it not robbery to be equal with

God: But made himself of no reputation, and took upon him the form of a servant, and was made in the likeness of men:

—PHILIPPIANS 2:3–7

All of these wrongful authority accusations are canceled when ministries and churches seek out and recognize the acceptance of the multiple callings Christ gave. We must strive to fulfill His Word. All of these five gift callings should function. This is not happening as long as the one in charge protects their position, authority, and power terrain, further fueled by the root of evil, their income money from the flock. We have numerous Diotrephes ministries everywhere today,

Beloved, thou doest faithfully whatsoever thou doest to the brethren, and to strangers; which have borne witness of thy charity before the church: whom if thou bring forward on their journey after a godly sort, thou shalt do well: Because that for his name's sake they went forth, taking nothing of the Gentiles. We therefore ought to receive such, that we might be fellowhelpers to the truth. I wrote unto the church: but Diotrephes, who loves to have the preeminence among them, receiveth us not.

—3 JOHN 5–9

Holy God, have mercy on us. May we by Your grace and strength correct our recognition of our fellow servants and those whom You call!

We the New Testament churches must discern the work of the Holy Spirit in the people of God. We must discern those who have a holy calling, raising them up and encouraging multiple eldership. We must nurture the Holy Spirit–motivated believer ministry. All should seek out and find genuinely called apostles and destroy our man-made church government sustained by ignorance.

## LOVE MINISTRY

The Lord asked a disillusioned Peter a difficult question. Peter had returned to fishing, after Christ's death. He had returned to his familiar comfort zone. In a post-resurrection appearance our Lord confronted

Peter with a questioning of Peter's love commitment to Him: "So when they had dined, Jesus said to Simon Peter, Simon, son of Jonas, lovest thou me more than these?" (John 21:15).

"Do you love Me?" was the first part of a two-part question. Twice Jesus asked Peter, "Do you love Me with a godly love [*agape*]?" And then the third time our Lord asked Peter, "Do you love [*phileo*] Me?", which means, "Do you love Me with the kind of love brothers-in-arms share, as soldiers in a common battle? Peter, do we have the same heart and goals as we confront this battle for the souls of man?"

The second part of this question was a comparison. "Do you love Me more than these? Do you love Me more than your fishing and your familiar personal past self-life?" After our experience of seeing the risen Christ, the believer and called ministry are also asked this question. Should we with integrity yield an answer of "Yes, Lord," His words to us will likewise be, "Feed My lambs and sheep."

Our Lord asked Peter this love question three times. We may also be asked this question three times or fifty times, until we really hear and deeply weigh the question. We will continuously be asked this question until we answer with a heartfelt determined response. We will eventually become hot or cold, as Christ is never satisfied with lukewarm. He will spit those out of His mouth (Rev. 3:16). Our answer must be fervent with zeal and purpose. This must be an answer of surrender to His love and given purposes, which is the redemption of the beloved. The called must answer and mean it, "I love You, Lord, and I will feed Your lambs and sheep."

How often do we not hear the casual meaningless words in life of "I love you." Usually this is attached to being politically correct in communications to retain a friendly neutral relationship. I once had a nearby neighbor family with children. They would always say "I love you." Yet for several years they would rarely interact. When they did, conversation would always be about the weather and meaningless things, never entering into meaningful fellowship. Many in Christ are just like that.

Our God demands a total genuine yielding and priority status...real love with a depth of heart...a heart that longs to be understood and that will communicate on genuine heart issues. This heart is never satisfied with a casual relationship. Love demands a heart that cares for the thoughts of others, always striving for meaningful unity in relationships with those they love.

Demas could not answer this question with a truthful heart, as his love lay in a personal care for this world (2 Tim. 4:10). Our Lord said that no man can serve two masters. Christ also taught of the ruined seed: "And some fell among thorns, and the thorns grew up, and choked it, and it yielded no fruit. And other fell on good ground, and did yield fruit that sprang up and increased; and brought forth, some thirty, and some sixty, and some an hundred" (Mark 4:7–8). Demas exemplified the healthy seed that sprang up among the thorns in Christ's parable of the sower. We must recognize and deal with the thorns in our lives. If we love Him, we will serve Him by loving His people, building His vision, and ministering in the building of His church.

## God's Highway Building

Isaiah said much truth about this topic. He gave holy direction for us, the consecrated ministry to follow. "Go through, go through the gates; prepare ye the way of the people; cast up, *cast up the highway; gather out the stones*; lift up a standard for the people. Behold, the LORD hath proclaimed unto the end of the world, Say ye to the daughter of Zion, Behold, thy salvation cometh; behold, his reward is with him, and his work before him" (Isa. 62:10–11, emphasis added).

First, a ministry cannot give out what it does not possess. The prepared ministry obtains knowledge and wisdom by seeking and experience. We must always first enter through the gates of that city ourselves, before touching the lost and redeemed. Anointed and life-giving ministry follows as a fruit from an experiential and personal God relationship.

Second, we are called to cast up a highway that is easy for the lost to travel on. Casting up a highway in gospel pursuits is comparable to building our modern paved high-speed highways. A highway makes travel easy and is a comparison of modern paved travels to what the early American settlers faced while settling western America. Most of us have seen the rutted wagon wheel trails in pioneering films. The settlers were fortunate if some days they mastered a distance of one mile. They crossed rocky terrain, swamps, and rivers. A wrongful presentation by the church in doctrine or a lack of Christ's truth and love is comparable to causing people to travel through swamps and impassable trails while attempting to reach Christ and salvation.

The gospel highway is constructed by called men and women of understanding, those whom the Holy Spirit has prepared with knowledge and grace to communicate the redeeming love of Christ by Calvary's cross. They present the gospel by making sin, separation, and faith matters easy to be understood. They remove the stumbling stones of wrong doctrine and loveless behavior. Their highway building makes gospel truth easy for the seeking to receive.

**Stones**

The taking out of stones is the removing of obstacles that people trip over, stones that make the gospel journey and seeking difficult. Many ministries place stones instead of removing them in their highway construction. These impede the progress of the seeking instead of making their finding and travel easier. There are many disturbing stones and craters placed as impediments, stones and hindering holes that rightful ministries strive to correct.

Millions are seeking. Good highways will greatly aid those struggling to enter the gospel highway. Foremost some of these stones are:

*Cult doctrine and wrong theology*

Holy ministry will prioritize the exposing of wrong doctrine and those who deny the truth of two of the several foundational doctrines the true church stands on. The first foundational doctrine is the deity of Christ, and the second is eternal judgment. All cults deny these two doctrines. If they say that is not true, it is because they are applying "term switching." The way to deal with term switching is to question them as to what these doctrines mean to them.

This wrong doctrine is followed by Jehovah's Witnesses, Mormons, Christian Scientists, and many more. They always deny these two foundational church doctrines, which limit salvation knowledge. This is why true churches label them as cults.

Many seeking people are captured by their web of deceit. May we know how to teach our people the light of truth. Darkness does not bring to light. Light always exposes darkness. Teach them sound doctrine.

All cults deny the deity of Christ, that Christ was very God in the flesh, Immanuel, God with us (Matt. 1:23). Christ is denied by them as to being the "I AM" who was and is and is to come (Rev. 4:8; 1:17–18). The Pharisees in Christ's day wanted to stone our Savior for saying He was the "I AM" (John 8:58). Be aware that to attain unto salvation, one must know who Christ is (vv. 24–28).

Cults deny the doctrine of eternal judgment and an everlasting hell where the flame is not quenched and the worm does not die (Rev. 14:11; Mark 9:44).

Sound doctrine involves the understanding of man being lost and dead in sin… man being separated from our Creator and living God. This involves the teachings of the gospel, which is the good news. Christ who is Emmanuel, or God with us, is the only way (Matt. 1:23). He came in love and mercy as the sin bearer. Only He—no other person or church organization—died on the cross for the sins of all who will believe in Him. Preach the ugliness of sin. Preach faith in what He has done. Preach that He alone is the truth and the way, that only faith in His person will bring us forgiveness of sin and eternal life. We will never be accepted by Him due to our works and religious homage (Eph. 2:8–9).

*Personal decision*

Teach what the apostate church does not teach. Only after hearing the gospel and making a personal decision does one receive Christ and salvation. No one can obtain salvation for others. "That we should be to the praise of his glory, who first trusted in Christ. In whom ye also trusted, after that ye heard the word of truth, the gospel of your salvation: in whom also after that ye believed, ye were sealed with that holy Spirit of promise" (Eph. 1:12–13). Even when one parent is a believer,

God considers the children holy, but they in time must make their own decisions whether to seek Christ or not (1 Cor. 7:14).

Wrong preaching leaves their followers trapped in a box canyon due to wrong theology. They produce followers who always wonder if they are saved. When they are asked if they know for sure whether they would be in heaven if a bomb destroyed their lives today, they usually say "I hope so" as opposed to "I know so." Often they will say, "If I can just have a place in a back row or in a corner of heaven, I would be satisfied." There is no assurance of salvation. If you wonder about your salvation, you probably are not saved. This horrible wrong involves most of the old-time denominations. Consider both of the circumcised sons of Isaac. Esau was hated while his brother Jacob was loved. This judgment decision by God was based on observing their life choices (Heb. 12:16–17; Rom. 9:13; Mal. 1:2–3). Esau's circumcision was of no avail. Isaac's choices brought a relationship with God. Isaac treasured birthright, promises, and blessings due to his growing respect for God and His person. Studying Jacob and Esau, we see that one sought the Lord and the other despised holy things.

We cannot answer for someone else's conscience. A child is a different person from us and has their own conscience. "…baptism doth also now save us (not the putting away of the filth of the flesh, but the answer of a good conscience toward God,) by the resurrection of Jesus Christ" (1 Pet. 3:21).

### *Legal non-grace salvation*

Wrongly focused legalistic works and law teachings as opposed to the truth of the law of sin and death balanced with grace leading to salvation by faith bring much death to the seeking. They in their doctrine attach works to salvation, such as the correct worship day, foods, etc. They ignore Romans 14:2–6 (emphasis added):

> For one believeth that he may eat all things: another, who is weak, eats herbs. Let not him that eateth despise him that eateth not; and *let not him which eateth not judge him that eateth*: for God hath received him. Who art thou that judges another man's servant? to his own master he standeth or falleth. Yea, he shall be holden up:

for God is able to make him stand. *One man esteemeth one day above another: another esteemeth every day alike.* Let every man be fully persuaded in his own mind. He that regardeth the day, regardeth it unto the Lord; and he that regardeth not the day, to the Lord he doth not regard it. He that eateth, eateth to the Lord, for he giveth God thanks; and he that eateth not, to the Lord he eateth not, and giveth God thanks.

Those who press these issues of food and the exact right day of worship wind up preaching a different gospel. Their gospel often causes people to focus on works instead of faith. They usually hammer the issues of right foods, the exact day of worship (Saturday verses Sunday), and end-time theology. Their focus on these issues defers from the primary issues of repentance from sin and faith in Christ. Usually these people are limited in their understanding of the mandatory new birth, which is required in salvation. They do not apply an altar call to allow people to express a personal acceptance of Christ by confronted sin.

They will have other rites, the ritual of expressing faith in their church and what they teach, expected of them at an appropriate age. Been there and done that. In this rite there is no depth of personal sin being confronted and repented of. There is an expression of believing what they have been taught to be truth as far as they know it. The religious and unsaved will be incapable of sharing about an experiential point of salvation. It is a rare individual who by means of these rites confronts sin with faith in the Savior that leads to salvation.

They often press for followers, making them comparable to what our Lord described of the Pharisee captives: "Woe unto you, scribes and Pharisees, hypocrites! for ye compass sea and land to make one proselyte, and when he is made, ye make him twofold more the child of hell than yourselves" (Matt. 23:15). They often become enmeshed with a Christian web of religiosity but no saving relationship with Christ. Does the confessed believer have a faith assurance accompanied with joy? That is the key question and test of being saved.

*Grace preachers*

The opposite scenario also applies to many by responding to the "grace" preachers. They preach love and grace without the balancing demand for holiness, "...without which no man shall see the Lord" (Heb. 12:14). True salvation comes when personal sin is confronted and repented of on a one-to-one basis with Christ. This will bring an experiential peace and joy due to the work of the Holy Spirit within. The result will be demonstrated by the fruit of a holy seeking and walk before the Lord. Many ignore what Paul clearly states. Those who are involved with pornography (fornicators) and effeminate (homosexuals), along with drunkards, shall not inherit the kingdom of God (1 Cor. 6:9).

Born-again believers are capable of indulging in all of these sins. In James 4:7 we are taught that we are to resist the devil, but some will not. Why be told this if this resisting is not a needed act of our will? Upon conviction of failure and sin, the backslider may repent and be forgiven (1 John 1:9). "If we confess our sins, he is faithful and just to forgive us our sins, and to cleanse us from all unrighteousness. If we say that we have not sinned, we make him a liar, and his word is not in us" (1 John 1:9–10).

However, one must be aware of the dangers of walking too close to the edge of the sin cliff. "But the Spirit of the Lord departed from Saul" (1 Sam. 16:14). Some will foolishly argue that Saul prophesied and had walked in spiritual experience, so regardless of all he will be in heaven. I severely doubt that. If the Spirit of God departed from Saul, who had killed many of God's prophets (God's voice), that departure stood in life and death.

Also, "The dog is turned to his own vomit again; and the sow that was washed to her wallowing in the mire" (2 Pet. 2:22).

I am a grace preacher who balances this message with the truth of God's holy judgments in life and death resulting from our decisions and actions. "Be not deceived; God is not mocked: for whatsoever a man soweth, that shall he also reap" (Gal. 6:7).

> Oh that my people had hearkened unto me, and Israel had walked
> in my ways! I should soon have subdued their enemies, and turned
> my hand against their adversaries.
>
> —PSALM 81:13–14

I recognize the admonition warnings of scripture to the backslider. "For if after they have escaped the pollutions of the world through the knowledge of the Lord and Saviour Jesus Christ, they are again entangled therein, and overcome, the latter end is worse with them than the beginning" (2 Pet. 2:20). One who escaped by salvation in Christ can lose this. "Worse with them than the beginning" is clear when one understands that the beginning was prior to salvation being entered into. They "had escaped by the knowledge of Christ" but are again overcome by the entanglements of this world. Our Lord Jesus said, "But if thine eye be evil, thy whole body shall be full of darkness. If therefore the light that is in thee be darkness, how great is that darkness!" (Matt. 6:23).

God holds us accountable for our free will choices. To receive salvation and to maintain our salvation with a continued repentance of sin is our responsibility. Salvation and accepting Christ is not a momentary issue of repentance and believing. This is why 1 John 1:9–10 was written to the believer. "If we confess our sins, he is faithful and just to forgive us our sins, and to cleanse us from all unrighteousness. If we say that we have not sinned, we make Him a liar, and his word is not in us." We continually resist temptations of many kinds, whether in our thoughts or to commit sinful actions.

There must be a believing and maintaining until we perish or are taken up. "Take heed, brethren, lest there be in any of you an evil heart of unbelief, in departing from the living God. But exhort one another daily, while it is called To day; lest any of you be hardened through the deceitfulness of sin. For we are made partakers of Christ, if we hold the beginning of our confidence stedfast unto the end" (Heb. 3:12–14). Note this potential of departing is in "any of you brethren," my faith family of God. You will not be a partaker of Christ if you do not hold your confidence steadfastly.

How can we say we are servants of Christ when we do not preach, "For if we sin wilfully after that we have received the knowledge of the truth, there remaineth no more sacrifice for sins, but a certain fearful looking for of judgment and fiery indignation, which shall devour the adversaries. He that despised Moses' law died without mercy under two or three witnesses: Of how much sorer punishment, suppose ye, shall he be thought worthy, who hath trodden under foot the Son of God, and hath counted the blood of the covenant, *where with he was sanctified*, an unholy thing, and hath done despite unto the Spirit of grace?" (Heb. 10:26–29, emphasis added). Note the past tense of "was sanctified."

To preach and teach about these scriptures and their exhortations is not a popular pulpit topic. If we love our people as Christ does, we will include these scriptures as He has said they are needed manna for all believers. Counting Christ's blood as an unholy thing is by continuing in a life for self and of sin. We constantly make choices. How important is the blood and the cross to us. This will be seen by our life choices, conversation, and our ministry or lack of same to others.

*Money pushers*

Then we have those who incessantly press for money. This wrongful priority focus has done huge damage to the gospel. Presenting a gospel need is acceptable. Paul spoke of the needs of other churches. He only spoke of his personal needs and supply of same when he was in new terrain and planting new works. Paul never took financial support from the new works he was building up while with them. We today are so far from what Paul and the ministries he raised up were like when we consider finances. "Behold, the third time I am ready to come to you; and I will not be burdensome to you: for I seek not yours, but you: for the children ought not to lay up for the parents, but the parents for the children. And I will very gladly spend and be spent for you; though the more abundantly I love you, the less I be loved. But be it so, I did not burden you: nevertheless, being crafty, I caught you with guile. Did I make a gain of you by any of them whom I sent unto you? I desired Titus, and with him I sent a brother. Did Titus make a gain of you? walked we not in the same spirit? walked we not in the same steps?" (2 Cor. 12:14–18).

Paul and the young ministries he raised up did not burden the people financially.

When financial offerings and appeals take up more than a brief time within a service or program, we become unspiritual beggars or manipulators. How many people are "tuned out" from the true gospel road by this wrongful pressured soliciting for money. Those ministries would do well to read, "But we were gentle among you, even as a nurse cherisheth her children: So being affectionately desirous of you, we were willing to have imparted unto you, not the gospel of God only, but also our own souls, because ye were dear unto us. For ye remember, brethren, our labour and travail: for labouring night and day, because we would not be chargeable unto any of you, we preached unto you the gospel of God" (1 Thess. 2:7–9).

I was very troubled by a known ministry. The minister sent out a financial appeal using scriptures to manipulate recipients. This manipulation was in leading a person as a test of "faith," to send and give $1,000 to him. Had he taught on the blessings of giving or taught people to prayerfully give to the gospel with prayerful holy direction, or had he shared a gospel need, it would have been scriptural and correct. He tied a test of sowing in faith to giving to him. Watch out for these immoral purveyors who make merchandise of the church.

### Failed morality in clergy

Another huge stone of offense is the failed morality in clergy—whether by involvement in immoral affairs or homosexual acceptance by some churches. Many seekers are deterred. These examples are stones of bad Christian conduct. Yes, we walk by grace; however, we must consider our great responsibility. We the ministry, above all Christians, are to be an example. "Let no man despise thy youth; but be thou an example of the believers, in word, in conversation, in charity, in spirit, in faith, in purity" (1 Tim. 4:12). The failure will always bear consequences, as David experienced, "Thus saith the Lord, Behold, I will raise up evil against thee out of your own house.... Howbeit, because by this deed thou hast given great occasion to the enemies of the Lord to blaspheme, the child also that is born unto thee shall surely die" (2 Sam. 12:11, 14). Notwithstanding, may God's grace minister to those who have stumbled and repented as David did. David rose from failures, ultimately becoming a man after God's heart following sincere repentance. It was not simply a moment of repentance, but a life of God seeking.

## Lift Up a Standard

Isaiah instructed us to raise a standard, which applies in two ways, both toward God and toward man. The first part of this standard is our personal relationship walk with the Lord. The second part is what we depict to others and what they see in us. We must consider the responsibility we carry as a ministry. We always affect many others. Do our personal lives away from pulpit ministry reflect Christ—His person, holiness, and grace—twenty-four hours a day, seven days a week? Our attitude speaks when dealing with others on life's common road.

On occasion I have enjoyed watching Joyce Meyer. I respect her ministry, operating in a calling different from mine. I remember her sharing one day how an all-thumbs, nervous, and fumbling waitress spilled food on her good ministry dress after a service. She remembered to be kind and considerate in her conversation, when tired and worn out and relaxing with a couple of personal friends. The waitress apologized and said that besides having a "bad hair day," she was nervous due to recognizing Joyce with a quasi celebrity ministry status. Joyce shared how she said a big "Thank You, Lord" for not responding according to the flesh, thereby possibly damaging a soul and the gospel.

May we raise a godly banner without creating stumbling stones for others who observe us. This applies to our financial dealings, public and personal conversation as well.

I will always remember a minister I heard while attending a church in Maui, Hawaii. He preached a good message. Unintentionally I observed him later as he was heading into the airport where I was flying out of. He visibly treated his mature wife with impatience and a bad attitude.

This double life spoke to me as to my own walk with my wife. Lord Jesus, may we Your epistles be easy to read!

## GOD'S HIGHWAY STANDARD

God Almighty has a highway that He has constructed. May we learn from its construction properties and design. He has only one highway identified in His Holy Word, "the way of holiness." Isaiah spoke a holy God-anointed and appointed word when he described God's highway: "And *an highway* shall be there, and a way, and *it shall be called The way of holiness*; the unclean shall not pass over it; but it shall be for those: the wayfaring men, though fools, shall not err therein" (Isa. 35:8, emphasis added).

This highway is for those who are a unique people, the redeemed. Only the wise, due to seeking, will travel this highway, having found the approach ramp, the way, truth, and life, our Lord Jesus (John 14:6). Wayfaring men may not traverse thereon. The foolish who ignore salvation and God's ways (whether religious or not) and the unclean who have not confronted sin and wrong will not stumble onto this highway by chance. Only those who have made concerted effort to confront sin and wrong may traverse this highway. The unclean will not pass thereon. May defiled Christians know this. Do not read into this text that the born again are an exception to this "unclean statement." Holiness is the name given to this highway. Holiness must be in the hearts of these travelers and be applied by those who travel thereon.

We the ministry are to be God's highway builders. We direct people to the approach ramps and the door. We teach people the importance of guardrails to avoid sin when tempted in treacherous places. We teach people the profound privilege of traveling on this highway with the saints of all ages. We teach them about the eternal glory destination this highway brings them to.

Our God gave Jacob a dream at the beginning of his maturing journey, when he left his parental control. The dream showed Jacob a ladder reaching into heaven, marked by angels ascending and descending on this ladder (Gen. 28:12). Thereby the Lord showed there was a way that

He created for ascending into the heavens. We must preach and teach the swamp dwellers about the effects of sin and wrong that separate man from God. Show them the way, the truth, and Jacob's ladder. We build this highway on a sure foundation, Jesus Christ (Eph. 2:20). We teach them to maintain their salvation.

We proclaim one message: "Behold, the Lord hath proclaimed unto the end of the world, Say ye to the daughter of Zion, Behold, thy salvation cometh; behold, his reward is with him, and his work before him" (Isa. 62:11). May we fervently proclaim this while we are able. The night is coming when no man can labor or blow the warning trumpet (John 9:4; Joel 2:1).

## A KEY QUESTION

Many times from my early salvation on, while reading the New Testament and especially the Book of Acts, I have asked myself the question, Why are so many things different in the church today compared to Peter's and Paul's day? Why would our Lord portray a church that is so different from what we normally consider acceptable?

Most of the church does not see miracles or true prophetic utterances. Questions of theology are not being answered by an apostle-headed church. We see this by the difference of what the people of the world said: "And when they found them not, they drew Jason and certain brethren unto the rulers of the city, crying, These that have turned the world upside down are come hither also" (Acts 17:6). What does it take to turn our world upside down in one generation, our generation? The answer is found by the following truths.

*Miracles.* "And the people with one accord gave heed to those things which Philip spoke, hearing and seeing the miracles which he did" (Acts 8:6). Huge crowds turned to Christ throughout the Book of Acts due to seeing miracles. They are a testimony to the Lord.

I will always remember what it took to bring many Muslims to Christ in Alor Sotar, in northern Malaysia. The Lord had delivered and healed a deaf mute in a "Baptacostal" church. The Baptist leadership, while traveling on furlough, had received the baptism of the Holy Spirit. Believing for and the receiving of this is contrary to their denominational theology. Our team came by invitation as a result.

Due to the signs they had posted, which read "bring the sick, deaf, and dumb," a few Muslims attended. They brought in this born deaf mute man. The next night a beyond-building capacity of Muslims attended. Upon hearing the gospel for the first time, many received salvation.

We have lost this power due to denying the baptism of the Holy Spirit as an experiential New Testament church normal event. The gifts of the Spirit result from this. Those who teach a nonexperiential baptism of the Holy Spirit and only a supposed theological one, with no evidenced tongues or prophecy, will never experience these miracles (Acts 19:6). Without faith in God's Word and promises, this will not take place. This holy receiving was promised to all: "For the promise is unto you, and to your children, and to all that are afar off, even as many as the Lord our God shall call" (Acts 2:39). Tongues and prophesying are the evidence given in Acts chapters 2, 8, and 11. Simon the sorcerer saw people receiving. These gifts of the Spirit only come with the "baptism of the Holy Spirit." Many born-of-the-Spirit believers deny this promise to them.

*Apostles and prophets.* We have denied these ministries their rightful place. We have not worked at determining who they are and how we are to know they are appropriately titled. When we deny the baptism of the Holy Spirit, it becomes very difficult to discern these callings as they are part of the ministry people who commonly operate in the miracle gifts, along with the evangelists.

We are guilty of having accepted a completely different ministry government structure in the churches without a scriptural multiple ministry and multiple elders.

What we now commonly have is not portrayed by the scriptural New Testament examples given. We see the evidence of competition and a non-esteeming of each other in ministry. We rarely see a multiple eldership submitting one to another. This will be changed. We will see the time when none in the Lord's army will thrust one another through. They will walk in power! (Joel 2:2–10).

## CHAPTER TWELVE

# EXAMPLES OF GOD'S CHOOSING

## ABRAHAM

ABRAHAM IS THE giant of faith. He is named the father of all believers (Rom. 4:11). Abraham possessed tremendous insight. He saw the temporal status of life. He concluded that life in general and the affairs of man were not a lasting matter worthy to be consumed with. He saw the strength and glory of the everlasting and eternal works of our creator God. Abraham concluded that only the God of heaven and earth could build a dwelling place that had a sure foundation. Abraham had eliminated and discounted all earthly possibilities. This insight was responded to by his life choices and actions: "For he looked for a city which hath foundations, whose builder and maker is God" (Heb. 11:10).

This revelation insight affected his personal building pursuits, choosing to dwell in temporary quarters such as tents. "By faith he sojourned in the land of promise, as in a strange country, dwelling in tabernacles [tents] with Isaac and Jacob" (Heb. 11:9). No matter what man builds, it is all temporary. Only what God builds has true foundations and is eternal. This foundational insight orchestrated Abraham's actions.

The focused called ministry will act likewise, due to similar conclusions having been reached. May our glory cease and burn. May God's glory arise by our ministry, due to an eternal focus.

The Bible says little of Abraham's roots prior to the Lord communicating with him as recorded in Genesis 12. We do know that his father and heritage were active in idolatry. We also know much from Abraham and his response to God's directive, "Get thee out of thy country, and from thy kindred, and from thy father's house, unto a land that I will shew thee" (Gen. 12:1). Abraham had been seeking God and His ways for the Lord of all to speak to Him. Others did not hear or receive God's voice. Perhaps they were not listening.

This we do know. Our God is not a respecter of persons, and when we seek Him, He will reveal Himself to all. "Then Peter opened his mouth, and said, Of a truth I perceive that God is no respecter of persons" (Acts 10:34).

God spoke to our father of faith, knowing that Abraham had the heart to hear and obey. He trusted God and His voice enough to leave his roots and personal relationships. This trust was strong enough for Abraham to start on an unknown journey destination to follow this voice.

Herein we see the demonstrated material components our Lord is looking for within the called ministry. Our God progressively led Abraham through many trials and tests of faith. He was vulnerable to struggles due to the desirable beauty of Sarah, his beloved wife. Also we see the test of love in the question of, "Do I place my life and servants on the line for an unwise nephew, Lot?" This was with the knowledge of Lot's unwise decisions and choices, which included proximity to Sodom and Sodomites. The culminating trial was the request to offer his only miracle son, Isaac. Abraham knew that all of God's promises to him resided in Isaac. Abraham overcame with obedience in this most difficult request. The knife was only stopped due to God's last-minute voice. This overcoming resulted with a particular promise because of his faith, attested to by his actions.

> And said, By myself have I sworn, saith the LORD, for because thou hast done this thing, and hast not withheld thy son, thine only son: That in blessing I will bless thee, and in multiplying I will multiply thy seed as the stars of the heaven, and as the sand which is upon the sea shore; and thy seed shall possess the gate of his enemies; and in thy seed shall all the nations of the earth be blessed; because thou hast obeyed my voice.
>
> —GENESIS 22:16–18

This willingness and obedience to give his son brought about the basis for God's righteous atonement of man, when our God gave His only begotten Son. Consider this.

All of God's promises to Abraham were wrapped up in Isaac, who was Abraham's true offspring successor. Abraham fully carried out this sacrifice to the final moment when God said "withhold your knife." The rarely presented truth of what our God said in response to Abraham's obedience of faith is a statement beginning with the key word *because*.

*Because* is a cause-and-effect word. The cause of God blessing and multiplying and "all nations" being blessed due to Abraham's obedience in this giving up his only son is hugely important! This act of obedience was different from all of the other acts of Abraham's obedience with a different and tremendous result.

We understand why the gospel is going into all nations because of what Christ and His cross have done. Why would salvation go to bless all nations due to what Abraham did in his obedience to offer Isaac? Why would this promise not be associated with and be a result of the several other faith actions done by Abraham in obedience? This is made possible in righteousness because Abraham was willing to give up his only son. This is due to the holy principle of God doing all things in perfect righteousness. Consider the following statements about our God doing all things in perfect righteousness and judgment:

> The LORD is righteous in all his ways, and holy in all his works.
> —PSALM 145:17

> But the LORD of hosts shall be exalted in judgment, and God that is holy shall be sanctified in righteousness.
> —ISAIAH 5:16

> And I will betroth thee unto me for ever; yea, I will betroth thee unto me in righteousness, and in judgment, and in lovingkindness, and in mercies.
> —HOSEA 2:19

Our betrothal to the Lord is genuinely done by His mercy in righteousness. The righteous salvation, in part, is due to the "because" Abraham, a man of faith, was willing to give and not withhold his only son. Our God judged and established this as the righteous basis for Him giving His only Son. Note that this particular trial was never again asked of any giant of faith such as Elijah or Moses.

The devil or all enemies to the gospel in all of eternity future will never point at God and say, "Where is Your holy righteousness in that You could give Your Son for man's salvation?", because God will point to Abraham and his willing obedience to give his son. You and I are the innumerable number of children because of this. We are the innumerable sand of the seashores and stars in the heavens. We believe as our father Abraham has. We in righteousness benefit from the blessing to all nations.

We the saved are blessed due to Abraham's obedience. If he had not obeyed, the promise of having countless children of faith would have been withheld.

May the called ministry receive a glimpse of the potential and results of our obedience to God's voice. We must consider the many we will affect for eternity when we in obedience respond to our calling and His voice with a "Yes, Lord!" Mighty eternal holy and gracious Father, we determine to walk before You embraced with Your love in obedience!

## DAVID

In Psalm 19:1–6 David speaks of the earth and heavens being a glorious revelation of God's creation and perfection in works. Then in verses 7–9 David speaks about this equally grand revelation and comparable truth: "The law of the LORD is perfect, converting the soul: the testimony of the LORD is sure, making wise the simple. The statutes of the LORD are right, rejoicing the heart: the commandment of the LORD is pure, enlightening the eyes. The fear of the LORD is clean, enduring for ever: the judgments of the LORD are true and righteous altogether."

David saw the comparable two truths of perfection, observing both the natural creation and the holy moral laws of our eternal God. David observed this perfection while reveling in the glory of God's holy moral being. He used the perfection of creation as the telescope of insight to God's moral holiness.

May we the ministry see likewise and act from this revelation of moral glory. This revelation of God's holy order and moral perfection affected David's actions. As he thought about these truths, they became part of his life's motivational forces, affecting his decisions and life accomplishments.

David eventually set the singers, musicians, and Levites in order, bringing in holy worship. Furthermore, under God's hand David gathered the materials and all that was necessary for the building of the tabernacle. This brought in a mighty move of holiness, faith, and worship affecting all of Israel. Revelation insight when Holy Spirit inspired motivates us to godly pursuits.

The resulting actions by David due to his revelation insight of our God are still spoken of today. We read, "After this I will return, and will build again *the tabernacle of David, which is fallen down*; and I will build again the ruins thereof, and I will set it up: *That the residue of men might seek after the Lord, and all the Gentiles,* upon whom my name is called, saith the Lord, who doeth all these things" (Acts 15:16–17, emphasis added). We the worshipping church, mostly made up of Gentiles, are the temple of God and the tabernacle of David, a house of worship in God's order when we determine to have God's order there (1 Cor. 3:16). May His ministry dwell on, then be moved by and act due to holy revelation. May we in our ministry be party to the constructing of the tabernacle of David. We do so by bringing the Gentile believing end-time church into being a praising and worshipping body! We give Him praise!

## God's Destiny Purpose in the Called

We the "called to ministry" must see our God's eternal plan. Then we must see our destiny, how our ministry lives fit into God's plan. It is He who has called us and tells us, "But thou, Israel, art my servant, Jacob whom I have chosen, the seed of Abraham my friend. Thou whom I have taken from the ends of the earth, and called thee from the chief men thereof, and said unto thee, Thou art my servant; I have chosen thee, and not cast thee away" (Isa. 41:8–9).

*Know that our God has chosen us!* "Fear thou not; for I am with thee: be not dismayed; for I am thy God: I will strengthen thee; yea, I will help thee; yea, I will uphold thee with the right hand of my righteousness" (v. 10).

*Know that our God upholds us!* "For I the Lord thy God will hold thy right hand, saying unto thee, Fear not; I will help thee. Fear not, thou worm Jacob, and ye men of Israel; I will help thee, says the Lord, and thy redeemer, the Holy One of Israel" (vv. 13–14). We may know ourselves to be as a limited feeble worm. But our God says do not fear because He will help and defend us.

*Know that we the ministry will be made into overcoming tools in His hand!* "Behold, I will make thee a new sharp threshing instrument having teeth: you shall thresh the mountains, and beat them small, and shall make the hills as chaff" (v. 15).

*Know that we the called ministry must see what our God is doing while changing us from glory to glory.* "But we all, with open face beholding as in a glass the glory of the Lord, are changed into the same image from glory to glory, even as by the Spirit of the Lord" (2 Cor. 3:18).

*Know that we must keep looking to Him.* He continually changes us from weakness into strength. We become the man or woman of God who threshes the mountains of unbelief and beats the devil's fear tactics into chaff. "Behold, I have made thy face strong against their faces, and thy forehead strong against their foreheads. As an adamant harder than flint have I made thy forehead" (Ezek. 3:8–9). Trust the Lord, the potter who transforms us, the clay, through life's experiences to become a strong overcoming instrument in His hand. In our future we will not be as we are just now. Just keep looking to and seeking Christ Jesus our Lord.

*Know that we must know of His continued work in us as we seek His face and His presence!* "For I know the thoughts that I think toward you, says the Lord, thoughts of peace, and not of evil, to give you an expected end. Then shall ye call upon me, and ye shall go and pray unto me, and I will hearken unto you. And ye shall seek me, and find me, when ye shall search for me with all your heart" (Jer. 29:11–13).

*Know that the Lord is constantly working with and developing our person through life's trials, including the difficulties we endure.* "Thou hast caused men to ride over our heads; we went through fire and through water: but you brought us out into a wealthy place" (Ps. 66:12). "The Lord will perfect that which concerneth me: thy mercy, O Lord, endureth for ever" (Ps. 138:8). "But the path of the just is as the shining light, that shineth more and more unto the perfect day" (Prov. 4:18).

## PAUL

This apostle knew of his predestined calling from God. "But when it pleased God, who separated me from my mother's womb, and called me by his grace" (Gal. 1:15). The called ministry must know that the calling and purpose in our lives are of God. Receiving this knowledge steadies our steps! We see the roots of this calling within a zealous man who was on the wrong trail while pursuing what he believed to be correct. With holy revelation as to the correct, "the way, the truth, and the life," Paul simply continued with a holy zeal, now being zealous for right. May we likewise burn with a zealous passion for the only right.

Recently a young called minister, Jamie Jenicek, within my sphere of influence, an elder in Wellsprings of Life Christian Fellowship, voiced his dismay over people who quoted half-truth scriptures. Someone had just quoted a partial truth of "just love and seek the kingdom, and you will be doing all right" to a business gathering. This quotation was constantly made from the speaker, who kept stating to love all—God loves and everybody love everybody teachings, with no inclusion of righteousness. Elder Jamie was frustrated due to the rest of that scriptural quote, "and His righteousness," being left off. This struggle upon hearing an unclear and fallaciously loose scriptural quotation is a natural response from the genuinely called to ministry. The Holy Spirit will stir the heart to speech and act against such loose bastardized truth, much as Paul's spirit was stirred when he visited Athens. "Now while Paul waited for them at Athens, his spirit was stirred in him, when he saw the city wholly given to idolatry" (Acts 17:16). Holy stirring to oppose untruth and sin are and should be normal to the God-pursuing ministry!

## Jeremiah

This prophet was advised of the Lord as to his calling and the purpose for his life. "Before I formed thee in the belly *I knew thee*; and before thou camest forth out of the womb I sanctified thee, and I ordained thee a prophet unto the nations" (Jer. 1:5, emphasis added). God knows our being! This helps me tremendously. I know of my weakness and failures, but God knows them a thousand times more than I do. Yet He still chooses to call me and use me for His divine purposes. God knew of my failures as well as ministry works, with positive eternal consequences before I was even conceived. He dwells in eternity, and time has no bearing on His knowledge. The called ministry must know this grace!

## Many Called, Few Chosen

Many are called, not just to salvation but also to ministry as well, and few are chosen. The need is great. "Pray ye therefore the Lord of the harvest, that he will send forth labourers into his harvest" (Matt. 9:38). Many deny the calling: "Now when Jesus heard these things, he said unto him, Yet lackest thou one thing: sell all that thou hast, and distribute unto the poor, and thou shalt have treasure in heaven: and come, follow me. And when he heard this, he was very sorrowful: for he was very rich. And when Jesus saw that he was very sorrowful, he said, How hardly shall they that have riches enter into the kingdom of God!" (Luke 18:22–24). This rich young ruler denied the call of "follow Me." His riches and possessions were his god above God. Our Lord does not shrink at blessing His called, unless the blessings become "God." The rich young ruler denied the call of God due to a wrong-hearted priority. Perhaps we need to be willing to become poor before He can make us rich in several ways. The called of God must know this truth!

## JUDAS

This man who betrayed Christ, resulting in the crucifixion process, was called of God to the ministry. He was loved, empowered, and honored to be of the original twelve apostles.

> And when he had called unto him his *twelve disciples*, he gave them power against unclean spirits, to cast them out, and to heal all manner of sickness and all manner of disease. Now the names of the twelve apostles are these; The first, Simon, who is called Peter, and Andrew his brother; James the son of Zebedee, and John his brother; Philip, and Bartholomew; Thomas, and Matthew the publican; James the son of Alphaeus, and Lebbaeus, whose surname was Thaddaeus; Simon the Canaanite, *and Judas Iscariot, who also betrayed him.*
>
> —MATTHEW 10:1–4, EMPHASIS ADDED

We like Judas can be empowered for ministry, but we must know of our potential to err and betray Christ and our calling. Judas was "called": "For he *was numbered with us, and had obtained part of this ministry....*For it is written in the book of Psalms, Let his habitation be desolate, and let no man dwell therein: and *his bishoprick* [eldership], let another take" (Acts 1:17, 20, emphasis added). He "had obtained" part of this apostle ministry. He was a called to the office of an elder: "Let his days be few; and let another take *his office*" (Ps. 109:8, emphasis added). May the called know their fleshly vulnerability as Paul did: "But I keep under my body, and bring it into subjection: lest that by any means, when I have preached to others, I myself should be a castaway" (1 Cor. 9:27).

Recently I observed a television program with a famous gospel singer and preacher, who often ministers with piano. I was so blessed to see this man of God coming back to stand in ministry. This brother had led over a million souls to Christ but had fallen and backslidden by the immorality he preached against. I personally know of at least one person who burned all of his tapes and records they had acquired.

I had prayed for this brother ministry many times, interceding for his restoration. What a joy to see him embracing gospel pursuits and the cross, marching on after public failure. David did so and achieved tremendously. I also continually pray for a well-known piano worship minister who needs to get back on track. Some repent and make it through the failures, and some do not. They are overcome by their choice to continue with sin (2 Pet. 2:20). May we be an available and wise ministry who are capable and are of a heart to pursue and encourage the restoration of the fallen.

David made it to victory after failures. We must know this! Judas did not. "Woe unto that man by whom the Son of man is betrayed! it had been good for that man if he had not been born" (Matt. 26:24). And yet some believe he will be at the wedding table in heaven?

## All Will Not Be Saved

This is so discouraging, a burden of heart for both God and the preacher. God wants all to be saved (2 Pet. 3:9). Likewise the servant of the Lord wants all to be saved. We find the prophet Isaiah was greatly troubled by this particular revelation truth: "Esaias also crieth concerning Israel, Though the number of the children of *Israel be as the sand of the sea, a remnant shall be saved*: For he will finish the work, and cut it short in righteousness: because a short work will the Lord make upon the earth. And as Esaias said before, Except the Lord of Saboath [rest] had left us a seed, we had been as Sodom, and been made like unto Gomorrah" (Rom. 9:27–29, emphasis added).

Clearly a limited number of the Israel covenant people will be receiving salvation, whether circumcised (baptized) or not. We constantly read of their idolatry and drifting from the Lord. In Revelation 3:4 we find our Lord Jesus speaking about a New Testament church where a large number attended but few in comparison to the attendance would inherit eternal life: "Thou hast a few names even in Sardis which have not defiled their garments; and they shall walk with me in white: for they are worthy."

How come only a few would walk in white? Why were only a few members worthy?

To balance this truth, some preach an imbalanced "remnant salvation" theology, stating very few actually get saved. This "remnant" salvation of the Israelites, although true, must be balanced with Revelation 5:11: "And I beheld, and I heard the voice of many angels round about the throne and the beasts and the elders: and the number of them was ten thousand times ten thousand, and thousands of thousands." Many will be saved out of every kindred, tribe, and nation. Nevertheless, we must preach that only a few in some churches will walk with Christ in white. May we the church be aware.

The called ministry must know this truth and consider what will affect this truth, to change this so many more will join those numbers. In so doing we preserve as many souls as possible. The knowledge of the foregoing facts will improve the numbers of those who will be saved. "My people are destroyed for lack of knowledge" (Hosea 4:6).

## The Mature Ministry Must Know

We cannot save anybody. Salvation is of the Lord, Our obedience in the call to ministry is to preach the Word. "Preach the word; be instant in season, out of season; reprove, rebuke, exhort with all longsuffering and doctrine" (2 Tim. 4:2). Rest in this knowledge!

Salvation is a work of the Holy Spirit. We were convicted of sin by the grace of the Holy Spirit. "And when he is come, he will reprove the world of sin, and of righteousness, and of judgment" (John 16:8). The Holy Spirit convicts mankind as we with love and in obedience preach.

It is up to man to respond. "Therefore whosoever hears these sayings of mine, *and doeth them*, I will liken him unto a wise man, which built his house upon a rock" (Matt. 7:24, emphasis added). Only the hearer can decide to respond by their doing, believing, repenting, and commitment.

Our God continuously calls the unbeliever, hoping he will seek Him. We should and must enter into this labor, or be honest and face the reality that we either do not believe or we do not love Him. To love

Him we will be a lover of His. The non- witnessing Christian is headed for trouble: "Whosoever therefore shall be ashamed of me and of my words in this adulterous and sinful generation; of him also shall the Son of man be ashamed, when he cometh in the glory of his Father with the holy angels" (Mark 8:38). We must teach our people to witness. Christ-loving Christians will share Christ with others.

Consider: "Whosoever therefore shall confess me before men, him will I confess also before my Father which is in heaven. But whosoever shall deny me before men, him will I also deny before my Father which is in heaven. Think not that I am come to send peace on earth: I came not to send peace, but a sword" (Matt. 10:32–34). This sword cuts by distinguishing truth from ungodliness. Are you and I "sent swords," or are we a dull knife? "For whosoever will save his life shall lose it: and whosoever will lose his life for my sake shall find it" (Matt. 16:25). The called preacher must warn the people of these truths! We are salt and light.

We must inform our people of the need for a holy walk. "Follow peace with all men, and holiness, without which no man shall see the Lord" (Heb. 12:14). Preaching holiness is preaching a love message.

Have we ever assimilated and presented the truth of 1 Corinthians 6:9–10? "Know ye not that the unrighteous shall not inherit the kingdom of God? Be not deceived: neither fornicators, nor idolaters, nor adulterers, nor effeminate, nor abusers of themselves with mankind, nor thieves, nor covetous, nor drunkards, nor revilers, nor extortioners, shall inherit the kingdom of God" If not, why not? When we do not preach this, we are dull-knife preachers, common among many.

Notice that this text does not say there are exceptions made due to one being born again. Nor are there exceptions made due to our being baptized or owning a Bible. The Greek for "effeminate" is "homosexuality." Fornication includes pornography. I was grieved by a local church where the leadership, aware that a member with a long-term pornographic addiction, still used this person in a visible function. This was never confronted in a strong manner, and ultimately the couple left this church and got a divorce. The sin that needed to be strongly confronted and dealt with was the central root to their eventual divorce.

The ministry involved will say that they left their post. The truth is, the ministry failed to be a post.

Extortion ministry will twist finances out of beguiled souls using the Word for their devious manipulation. They coerce the believers to give using the Word of God deceitfully. They do so by coercing the giving and funneling of these finances to their benefit. These unworthy manipulators pose themselves to be the unworthy spiritual prayer power recipients. The appropriate communication to promote giving to a cause is to explain the need and then back off and allow the hearers to prayerfully respond. Do not manipulate. A prayer organization I belonged to and supported for some thirty-four years took in the largest offering ever at a gathering. As a board advisor I learned of the results. The person who was asked to present the needs and take the offering broke the normal appeal and protocol. This believing doctor simply said, "Please take home your offering envelopes and pray how the Lord would have you give." End of appeal. Compare this to the normal lengthy worded financial pulling.

Integrity in finances is key, affecting our eternal judgment. Wrong-minded ministry should consider the apostle Peter's words: "And through covetousness shall they with feigned words make merchandise of you: whose judgment now of a long time lingereth not, and their damnation slumbereth not. For if God spared not the angels that sinned, but cast them down to hell, and delivered them into chains of darkness, to be reserved unto judgment" (2 Pet. 2:3–4). We must teach an honest and correct doctrine about the fact that one's name can be taken out of the Book of Life. Our omniscient God does not waste time by placing Jebusites, Hittites, Amorites, and unbelievers in His holy Book of Life. As I have stated previously, a name has to be in the Book of Life in order to have it taken out. "*He that overcometh*, the same shall be clothed in white raiment; and *I will not blot out his name out of the book of life*, but I will confess his name before my Father, and before his angels" (Rev. 3:5, emphasis added). The called must teach the believer that we must overcome sin and temptation, or our names can be blotted out of the

Book of Life; if this is not true, then Christ lied. (See my book *Salvation Gained, Maintained or Lost.*)

Consider this: The souls judged at the second resurrection were judged by one criterion only: are their names in the Lamb's Book of Life (Rev. 20:15). Only believers' names are in this book, and only believers' names can be blotted out.

Moses interceded for Israel when they sinned. "And Moses returned unto the Lord, and said, Oh, this people have sinned a great sin, and have made them gods of gold. Yet now, if thou wilt forgive their sin—; and if not, blot me, I pray thee, out of thy book which thou hast written. And the Lord said unto Moses, *Whosoever hath sinned against me, him will I blot out of my book*" (Exod. 32:31–33, emphasis added). Yes, our God will take a name out of His book, circumcised Israelite and the New Testament born-again believer as well. The called ministry must preach this to focus the Christian away from a lukewarm coasting. Jesus told the church—not the world—"Because you are lukewarm, I will vomit you out of My mouth." (See Revelation 3:16.)

Paul also said how he viewed this subject: "And every man that striveth for the mastery is temperate in all things. Now they do it to obtain a corruptible crown; but we an incorruptible. I therefore so run, not as uncertainly; so fight I, not as one that beateth the air: But I keep under my body, and bring it into subjection: *lest that by any means, when I have preached to others, I myself should be a castaway*" (1 Cor. 9:25–27, emphasis added). Paul preached to win souls. However, he was well aware of the possibility that he himself was subject to temptation and failure, just as all believers are. He kept on constant guard against this possibility.

The possibility of being "cast away" applies to all. Deny this, and you are accusing Paul of stupid talk and the Holy Spirit, who inspired Paul, of doing so as well when Paul spoke of his potential to becoming a "castaway."

Those who deny this potential for being cast away always rationalize away David's words to Solomon as well. "And thou, Solomon my son, know thou the God of thy father, and serve him with a perfect heart and with a willing mind: for the Lord searcheth all hearts, and understandeth all the imaginations of the thoughts: if thou seek him, he will be found of thee; but if thou forsake him, he will cast thee off for ever" (1 Chron. 28:9).

Solomon was heir to David's throne and received a God-given blessed wisdom. It was Solomon who prayed at the dedication of the glorious first temple, when the priests could not stand for the presence of the Lord. Solomon was told by his loving father, David, "The potential is there, based on your life choices, son, because the Lord will judge and act based on your choices and doings, *but if you forsake Him, He will cast you off forever.*" Forever…Solomon, James, Marilyn, Kevin, and Frank. According to Webster's dictionary, eternally means forever, ceaselessly, and without end. My understanding of this forever word is eternally as well.

The called ministry must caution their converts, church, and believers. Let them know why only a remnant of Israel will be receiving salvation. There is an overcoming requirement to receive the promises of God for eternity. This is why our Lord Jesus seven times said to all seven of His churches in Revelation 2 and 3 that "*to him that overcomes*" Christ promises life and blessings. This is why Paul said to work out your own salvation with fear and trembling. (See Philippians 2:12.) We must lead people to a holy, God-fearing pursuit. When one is dedicated to this, the joy and love of God are experiential.

### Holy artifacts: the ark of the covenant

When we think of holy and God-ordered religious artifacts on earth, the ark of the covenant has to be at the top of the list. Israel and the Philistine army knew this. The Philistines as well cited the greatness of the God of Israel signified by the ark, but yet they refused to embrace Him. When Israel was confronted by the enemy, they brought the ark into the battle camp, thinking the ark would help them get the victory over their enemies.

This did not happen; instead they were greatly defeated, and the enemy took the ark captive. This was written that we might know that religious artifacts will not save us or be the source of any victory in our lives. Owning ten Bibles or prayer beads or any religious artifacts will not save us. Having our names engraved within church structures for giving or good works will not save us.

> And when the ark of the covenant of the Lord came into the camp, all Israel shouted with a great shout, so that the earth rang again....And the Philistines were afraid, for they said, God is come into the camp. And they said, Woe unto us! for there hath not been such a thing heretofore....And the Philistines fought, and Israel was smitten, and they fled every man into his tent: and there was a very great slaughter; for there fell of Israel thirty thousand footmen. And the ark of God was taken; and the two sons of Eli, Hophni and Phinehas, were slain.
>
> —1 Samuel 4:5, 7, 10–11

In truth, after a fashion Hophni and Phinehas were already dead. They were relying on the religious artifacts they were responsible for as priests. Eli should have removed them. They rested in taking the name and office of the priesthood while engaging in a life of sin. They thought their position had enough meaning to God to avert judgment. Scholarly standings will not withhold God's judgment on the wrong-hearted. "Judah hath dealt treacherously, and an abomination is committed in Israel and in Jerusalem; for Judah hath profaned the holiness of the Lord which he loved, and hath married the daughter of a strange god. The Lord will cut off the man that doeth this, the master and the scholar, out of the tabernacles of Jacob, and him that offereth an offering unto the Lord of hosts" (Mal. 2:11–12).

All God-called ministry must teach their people that only faith in the shed blood of Christ and a pure heart with a genuine love for God the Savior will save us. We must preach as Paul did: "I kept back nothing that was profitable unto you, but have shewed you, and have taught you publicly, and from house to house....Wherefore I take you to record this day, that I am pure from the blood of all men. For I have not shunned to declare unto you all the counsel of God" (Acts 20:20, 26–27).

**Preach the whole truth**

We must preach with a sure knowledge that our hands are clean from the blood of all men. This cleanliness is attended with joy and peace within the preacher. This belongs to those who have not failed to preach the entire message, the preaching of the whole counsel of God. This preaching includes a clear textual exposition about hell judgment and damnation, as well as the gospel of love, mercy, and grace for the overcoming believer!

Preaching these truths will save people, preserve people, and help direct people as they travel through life's desert while working out their salvation, journeying to our promised land.

May we read and know what the Lord spoke to Ezekiel. Our God has never recanted these statements or truths.

> Son of man, I have made you a watchman to the house of Israel: therefore hear the word of my mouth, and give them warning from me. When I say unto the wicked, Thou shalt surely die; and thou givest him not warning, nor speakest to warn the wicked from his wicked way, to save his life; the same wicked man shall die in his iniquity; but his blood will I require at thine hand. Yet if thou warn the wicked, and he turn not from his wickedness, nor from his wicked way, he shall die in his iniquity; but thou hast delivered thy soul. Again, When a righteous man doth turn from his righteousness, and commit iniquity, and I lay a stumblingblock before him, he shall die: because thou hast not given him warning, he shall die in his sin, and his righteousness which he hath done shall not be remembered; but his blood will I require at thine hand.
> —Ezekiel 3:17–20

When God says that a previously righteous man can turn from his righteousness and die in his sins, this is a holy truth. This is a fact to be reckoned with. Then when God says this previously attained righteousness position is now forever forgotten, may we be cautioned by this.

Preach this truth to the church since the righteous need to hear of this truth, along with God's mercy grace and love.

## CHAPTER THIRTEEN

# MIGHTY MINISTRY ATTAINMENTS

*Mighty Attainments by Faith*

O UR UNBELIEF WILL always put chains of limitation on our God. Faith removes these chains. Our God has not changed: "Jesus Christ the same yesterday, and today, and for ever" (Heb. 13:8).

Ten of the twelve spies sent out did not believe. The result was a forty-year desert journey instead of a trip of less than one month. The three hundred of Gideon's army, those who stayed after being offered a way out to go home, were overcomers. Thousands of the fearful left. These believing ones saw a tremendous victory under God. They were the constantly discerning army. Hebrews 11 contains a long list of believing giants under God. These saw the humanly impossible, due to having eyes that saw the spiritually possible. They saw the spiritual realm and the God of the impossible. This is so important!

Habakkuk in chapter 2 was told the "just shall live by faith." This statement referred to not taking his eyes from the ministry vision shown! It was a broader exhortation from heaven for all just ministry. Is our walk demonstrated by our living faith? Our sustained focus on the vision will prove this matter. Unbelievers drown while believers take Christ, their Noah's ark, to safety.

> By faith they passed through the Red sea as by dry land: which the Egyptians assaying to do were drowned. By faith the walls of Jericho fell down, after they were compassed about seven days. By faith the harlot Rahab perished not with them that believed not,

when she had received the spies with peace. And what shall I more say? for the time would fail me to tell of Gedeon, and of Barak, and of Samson, and of Jephthae; of David also, and Samuel, and of the prophets: Who through faith subdued kingdoms, wrought righteousness, obtained promises, stopped the mouths of lions, quenched the violence of fire, escaped the edge of the sword, out of weakness were made strong, waxed valiant in fight, turned to flight the armies of the aliens. Women received their dead raised to life again: and others were tortured, not accepting deliverance; that they might obtain a better resurrection.

—Hebrews 11:29–35

Do we believe? Our Lord said that all things are possible to them who believe. I desire to experience greater manifestations of His presence and glory. I long to see more of His miracle power manifested to this generation. Glory!

One thing most ministries desire to hear upon the completion of their ministry journey, which I am in agreement with, are the words, "Well done, thou good and faithful servant." Many preachers and saints upon reading these words personally desire to hear these words from their Lord at Christ's throne. "His lord said unto him, Well done, good and faithful servant; thou hast been faithful over a few things, I will make thee ruler over many things: enter thou into the joy of thy lord" (Matt. 25:23).

This parable presented by our Savior included some of the master's servants being thrown into outer darkness, where they experienced weeping and gnashing of teeth. May we weigh and hear these words, with their intended application. Some servants after having received talents from our Lord will ultimately experience this terrible judgment. May we be faithful and profitable to Him.

The Bible speaks of David's mighty men. They were honored as to their valiant prowess in battle.

These be the names of the mighty men whom David had: The Tachmonite that sat in the seat, chief among the captains; the same was Adino the Eznite: he lift up his spear against eight hundred, whom he slew at one time. And after him was Eleazar the son of Dodo the Ahohite, one of the three mighty men with David, when they defied the Philistines that were there gathered together to battle, and the men of Israel were gone away: He arose, and smote the Philistines until his hand was weary, and his hand clave unto the sword: and the LORD wrought a great victory that day; and the people returned after him only to spoil. And after him was Shammah the son of Agee the Hararite. And the Philistines were gathered together into a troop, where was a piece of ground full of lentiles: and the people fled from the Philistines. But he stood in the midst of the ground, and defended it, and slew the Philistines: and the LORD wrought a great victory.

—2 SAMUEL 23:8–12

These men were memorialized for their warrior achievements in the natural realm. However, notice that they are only spoken of here and David is spoken of throughout the Scriptures. God acknowledges the spiritual warriors who overcome in adversity with a much greater honor. God's Hall of Fame believers in Hebrews 11 do not include those with physical exploit ability. Ministry, by preaching and standing for righteousness, will build His church and kingdom. These are eternally God honored.

May the ministry of God know their ministry attainments are written in God's Book of Remembrance. This book is one of the three that will be opened and shown to all at the soon coming judgment, along with the Book of Life and the Holy Bible, God's written Word. Even if we bring one soul to salvation or simply encourage a number of believers in their heaven-bound walk, Christ blesses us now and eternally. For those who mentally limit the truth of this awareness, our Lord does not limit recognition of our small deeds. He said that the simple giving of a cup of cold water would not go unrecognized (Mark 9:41). Be encouraged!

They who minster to others in Christ's name have accomplished a greater feat than all of David's mighty men. Those mighty warriors dealt with flesh warfare. In comparison, what is the value of a soul participating with Christ, knowing the joy of life for eternity? May blood-bought souls be precious in our sight (1 Pet. 1:19).

## ZERUBBABEL ATTAINMENT

Zerubbabel stands out as a mighty overcomer under God. In Ezra 5:2 we read of his tremendous God accomplishments: "Then rose up Zerubbabel the son of Shealtiel, and Jeshua the son of Jozadak, and began to build the house of God which is at Jerusalem: and with them were the prophets of God helping them."

Zerubbabel's background and naming is of great interest and a holy revelation. In Bible times names were very relevant with specific meaning attached to circumstances, and so was Zerubbabel's naming.

Zerubbabel had profound roots. He was born in adversity while Israel was in the bondage of Babylonian captivity for seventy years. Jerusalem was in ruins. The temple had been destroyed, as God had foretold by Jeremiah and others—the results of a nation turning from God into idolatry with the evident judgment that followed.

Do not think that our God does not judge the nations today. We, like Israel of old, can also fall from our blessings. Once vibrant churches are now denying Bible absolutes and ordaining homosexuals to their pulpits in our generation. I personally never heard of such until after 1980. Previously sodomy was a criminal activity worthy of imprisonment in America.

Zerubbabel was the son of Shealtiel. Shealtiel was a man of prayer. Part of his prayer was to be delivered from the bondage of captivity. The Hebrew name of *Shealtiel* means "I have asked God". The birth of a son whom he named Zerubbabel was no doubt part of the Lord's answer.

The Hebrew name *Zerubbabel* means "sown in Babylon." This baby was specifically identified with being born in Babylon. The name *Babylon* means "confusion." One might remember the confusion of languages at the tower of Babel.

To summarize, Zerubbabel, the answer to prayer, was sown in Babylon, the place of confusion. Profound. This ministry warrior was the Lord's vessel used to head up His leadership team, which restored the altar sacrifices and building of the temple. This God-ordained ministry was central to bringing in worship and praise. This was true ministry. Zerubbabel turned the people back to a God focus and relationship.

This was much more than just religious buildings and attire. His ministry was to a renewed people returning from captivity…a repentant, grateful people desiring holy renewal…a God-fearing people. These newly refocused people eventually stood all day to hear the Word of God. This people wept as they praised. They were an entirely different remnant, compared to those who went into captivity seventy years previously. Chastening and trials should result in eternal values, faith that is more precious than gold.

How was this Zerubbabel ministry possible against such resistance and Sanballat-like enemies? How is this possible, and how does this speak to you and me? The answer is found in Zechariah: "And the angel that talked with me came again, and waked me, as a man that is wakened out of his sleep, and said unto me, What seest thou?" (Zech. 4:1–2). We the ministry must also be awakened from our slumber to see what our Lord would have us see. "And I said, I have looked, and behold a candlestick all of gold, with a bowl upon the top of it, and his seven lamps thereon, and seven pipes to the seven lamps, which are upon the top thereof: And two olive trees by it, one upon the right side of the bowl, and the other upon the left side thereof" (vv. 2–3).

Our God will show an awakened ministry His seven lamps and His holy sovereignty, the seven spirits of God. "And out of the throne proceeded lightnings and thunderings and voices: and there were seven lamps of fire burning before the throne, which are the Seven spirits of God" (Rev. 4:5). "And the spirit of the Lord shall rest on him, the spirit of wisdom and understanding, the spirit of counsel and might, the spirit of knowledge and of the fear of the Lord" (Isa. 11:2). Those who have eyes to see and ears to hear will see His majesty. God often speaks in dreams and visions.

> So I answered and spake to the angel that talked with me, saying, What are these, my lord? Then the angel that talked with me answered and said unto me, Knowest thou not what these be? And I said, No, my lord. Then he answered and spake unto me, saying,

> This is the word of the LORD unto Zerubbabel, saying, Not by
> might, nor by power, but by my spirit, saith the LORD of hosts.
> —ZECHARIAH 4:4–6

The man of God, Zerubbabel, was to know what we are also to know. We will also experience being sown into a sea of unbelief, rebellion, and rejection of the living God. We likewise will be sown into a world where confusion reigns with no mortal answers. Our God knows our circumstances and expects us to overcome in these very difficult settings. We must and will overcome by the Holy Spirit of God, His wisdom, counsel, knowledge, and power.

## OVERCOMING

To overcome we must know that IT IS NOT BY OUR MIGHT OR POWER, BUT BY THE SPIRIT OF THE LORD OF HOSTS!

We must know the greatness of our God and the power of the Holy Spirit. "Who art thou, O great mountain? before Zerubbabel thou shalt become a plain: and he shall bring forth the headstone thereof with shoutings, crying, Grace, grace unto it" (Zech. 4:7). The mountain of obstacles will be removed when we look to the stone that the builders rejected (Luke 20:17; Eph. 2:20). Preach Him and His mercy and grace to a dying world. All adversity has to bow at the name above all names— the name of Jesus!

We must know what David learned from his training under God while hidden, prior to his public ministry, that enabled him with resolution and power: "This day will the Lord deliver thee into mine hand; and I will smite thee, and take your head from thee; and I will give the carcasses of the host of the Philistines this day unto the fowls of the air, and to the wild beasts of the earth; that all the earth may know that there is a God in Israel. And all this assembly shall know that the Lord saves not with sword and spear: for the battle is the Lord's, and he will give you into our hands" (1 Sam. 17:46–47).

David overcame bears and lions before facing this giant. We must know that if our work is done in righteousness, our God will cause the overcoming fruit to be evidenced in time. "Moreover the word of the Lord came unto me, saying, The hands of Zerubbabel have laid the foundation of this house; his hands shall also finish it; and thou shalt know that the Lord of hosts hath sent me unto you" (Zech. 4:8–9).

Do not be discouraged when you initiate battle with "small beginnings." Just be sure of your calling, mission, and message. "For who hath despised the day of small things? for they shall rejoice, and shall see the plummet in the hand of Zerubbabel with those seven; they are the eyes of the Lord, which run to and fro through the whole earth" (Zech. 4:10). When the Lord directs our paths and we are holding God's plumb line, we shall be given the victory. We see by His seeing. We battle by His strength. We know by His knowing. He overcomes by you and me as we are His surrendered instruments. We see and wage war with Holy Spirit eyes and insight!

## GREAT MINISTRY SECRET

The plummet is a weighted string used in building for many centuries. This string with a weight on the bottom shows perfect vertical alignment due to the effect of gravity, regardless of what side one looks at. This plummet that Zerubbabel held was unique in that it had the seven (number of perfection and God) eyes of the Lord imbedded in what today we normally name a plumb bob. This plumb bob was the power to Zerubbabel's overcoming ministry. Holy eyes are strengthened by prayer and waiting on the Lord. The understanding of what Paul said will make all of the difference: "Pray without ceasing" (1 Thess. 5:7). This is comparable to a constant walking in the Spirit, having the communion of the Holy Spirit with us (Eph. 6:18; Gal. 5:16; 2 Cor. 13:14).

Zerubbabel tightly gripped this instrument of truth being guided by the Lord's eye and by hearing this inner voice: "And thine ears shall hear a word behind thee, saying, This is the way, walk ye in it, when ye turn to the right hand, and when ye turn to the left" (Isa. 30:21).

When we walk in perfect alignment with God's holy plumb bob, which is by His righteous alignment, we cannot fail. Zerubbabel relied on the Lord's sight and holy values. The Lord's eyes guided his eyes and thoughts. By Holy Spirit eyes he saw his people set free. Their return from captivity was to a renewed holy focus, to true worship.

## Elijah

Personally I tremble at the grandeur of ministry achievement this giant of faith accomplished. We see the progression of his faith challenges. He sat in obedience by a drying brook for a year, being fed by ravens and hid from humanity. Meanwhile the brook was observed to progressively be drying up. That alone is a challenge—to sit in obedience in a place where we are not visible, by the Lord's direction. No entertainment, television, or people accompaniment. Only God and what He sends. To have the source of sustenance progressively appear to be drying up while we hold still. That is a faith challenge. Faith and trust in God overcome in this trial.

Elijah manifested the resulting power from this waiting in the presence of the Lord. We are allowed to see the results of this obedient invisibility. Under the anointing Elijah outran the king's horses to get to Jezreel before the king arrived (1 Kings 18:45).

We see this power demonstrated by his anointed hearing, gifting, and faith when confronting and destroying Jezebel's 850 prophets, those of Baal and the prophets of the groves. With holy power Elijah withstood the ungodly forces of Jezebel. He faced this army of false prophets with the holy direction of "at Your word." This word was received in private prayer while waiting. He demonstrated an overcoming of the idolatry of self-visibility in ministry, which is one of the greatest enemies to God's servants.

Elijah is one of the greatest giants of faith our God portrayed for our edification. I esteem and tremble at the stature of his achieved faith. When I weigh Elijah's spiritual response to his circumstances in the natural, I stand in awe and honor him.

> And he said, Go forth, and stand upon the mount before the Lord.
> And, behold, the Lord passed by, and a great and strong wind rent
> the mountains, and brake in pieces the rocks before the Lord; but
> the Lord was not in the wind: and after the wind an earthquake;

but the LORD was not in the earthquake: And after the earthquake a fire; but the LORD was not in the fire: and after the fire a still small voice. And it was so, when Elijah heard it, that he wrapped his face in his mantle, and went out, and stood in the entering in of the cave. And, behold, there came a voice unto him, and said, What doest thou here, Elijah?

—1 KINGS 19:11–13

Elijah followed God's instructions with strict obedience, including when directed to climb and stand on a remote mountain ledge, and then to stand there immovable regardless of the natural phenomena he encountered. This was his unmoving response to the tornado wind that tore mountain rocks around him. Natural circumstances did not move this servant of the Lord. The earthquake that followed and shook the rock beneath his feet did not move him. The roaring mountain fire, which followed these holy orchestrated events, with the heat and roar of the flames surrounding him where he stood, did not cause him to move a footstep.

When Elijah heard the still small voice of God, that and ONLY THAT caused reaction! This holy voice was all that he responded to, having overcome the fear of the natural challenges. When I consider my inner man being vulnerable to the shakings of the small things in life, small financial challenges or people and relational issues, and compare myself to this giant of faith, I can only say, "O Lord, how great is Your mercy to me." With that I breathe a prayer of, "Change my life, O God. I determine to trust in the shadow of Your wings. May I arise beyond the natural challenges that we constantly confront, resisting fears. May my faith grow to achieve a mustard-seed size so that I can move mountains for Your glory and not mine."

May the winds of wrongful wagging tongues not shake us. May the natural issues of life that seem so impossible to overcome from time to time not hinder our faith walk. Things of the will and face of man will fall on their face, with their hands and head cut off when faith within us arises. The presence of our God and knowing Him will uphold us. Yes, we can picture the fiery chariot being pulled with fiery horses that

Elijah boarded, thus taking him into God's heavenly realm. It all makes sense when we understand that after a fashion, Elijah (with failures) was already there. O God! Help us, Your ministry, to achieve this stature! Holy God of mercy, by Your grace we stand.

## ELISHA

The Bible tells us very little of Elisha's background. However, there are three noteworthy things we are told in brief text that tell us so much. Elisha was a proven man of discipline and character. He conquered difficult tasks with strong determination. He was radically God focused, as seen by his instant response in leaving past relationships and accomplishments to follow the man of God with no hesitation, which he did with the twelve yoke of oxen when Elijah found him. There was no history of relationship with Elijah prior to God's changing Elisha's direction. The important part is, God saw and knew him. The Lord had prepared a vessel unto honor.

His character and determination are evidenced by his accomplishments. Like David, it was not in the temple or among the Levitical priesthood that Elisha grew in faith. Rather, it was by the normal masteries of life and his response to life's trials. This should be the case with us as well, due to overcoming in life's normal challenges. David faced his bear and lion, putting his life on the line defending sheep. This testing and training was in preparation for a more responsible task—the defending, leading, and feeding of God's sheep.

Elisha was busily involved with plowing fields when the Lord commissioned Elijah to minister a life-altering direction appointment with Elisha: "So he departed thence, and found Elisha the son of Shaphat, who was plowing with twelve yoke of oxen before him, and he with the twelfth" (1 Kings 19:19).

It is a mean feat to master several teams of oxen. It takes patience and wisdom to yoke one matched team of oxen. A wrongful placement causes friction, just like an unequally yoked marriage. Then to manage and graduate to mastering twelve yoked teams is an extremely huge accomplishment. Elisha mastered this feat with a focused perseverance in pursuit of the mastery of this accomplishment. We must employ a great single-minded determination to achieve difficult tasks, to overcome the challenges to achieve accomplishments. Paul tells us, "And every man that striveth for the mastery is temperate in all things" (1 Cor. 9:25). We must be single-minded to achieve any goal, which is a basic prerequisite for the man and woman of God.

James tells us the end of double-mindedness. "A double minded man is unstable in all his ways" (James 1:8). We cannot serve two masters: "No servant can serve two masters: for either he will hate the one, and love the other; or else he will hold to the one, and despise the other. Ye cannot serve God and mammon" (Luke 16:13). It takes dedication of a huge scale to master twelve yoke of oxen. Having traveled in countries where the people actually use oxen to plow their rice fields, I have never seen more than one yoke of oxen being used. I have personally seen as many as six teams of horses yoked for pulling, but never twelve.

This training and dedication in a natural realm of life was a preparation for readiness. Natural wisdom in life builds strengths of character and capacity. The Lord uses our honed strengths and abilities in His ministry government functions to lead His people. Twelve is the number of God's government. There are twelve tribes of Israel, and twelve initial apostles and twenty-four elders in heaven.

The twelve doubled speaks to the kingdom of our Lord and Christ being established. Joseph understood much in dreams and vision matters. He understood that since Pharaoh had seen the same dream twice, the second dream took it out of the conditional realm and into an established "thus will it be" realm (Gen. 41:32). We see a prophetic picture here in Elisha's calling as a prepared vessel. As he had conquered in the natural strengths, he would now conquer in the spiritual strengths. He would establish God's kingdom ways among His people.

Many short-circuit this preparation by running when they should be walking or holding steady. Paul taught, "Brethren, let every man, wherein he is called, therein abide with God" (1 Cor. 7:24). This simply says that when a person realizes the initial inner pulling of the "calling of God," the ministry tug upon their lives, do not run. Move only at God's clear direction. Allow the Lord to bring maturity. He will train us on the job. He will move us when He determines we are ready. We should ready ourselves by studying ourselves to be approved unto God and eating His holy roll, written within and without with lamentations, mournings, and woe (Ezek. 2:10; 2 Tim. 2:15). This holy mentoring to become a man of dedication was further embellished by Elijah's continued mentoring. May we mature to mentor those whom the Lord gives us.

Our God will have His appointment for an anointed garment to be cast over us. He will bring change to our direction and usher in a new day at His exact time. Elisha was simply pressing into his daily work with focus and determination. I doubt whether he expected Elijah's visit. Yet he was ready for it, as demonstrated by his response. The Lord can change our anointing with a new cloaking and a new day when we least expect, should we be faithful in the little we have.

God holds and knows our seasons. "And Elijah passed by him, and cast his mantle upon him" (1 Kings 19:19).

Again we see the virtue of Elisha. He was gracious to his family and friends. He slaughtered a yoke of oxen to provide for a departing party. His past involvement of working with teams of oxen was thereby severed. He pursued a higher calling, taking him from his family and past commercial endeavors. He readily responded to change. The new day for this man of achievement started with a required humility, to serve Elijah, the man of God. He in humility was teachable, as great men always are. Prior to coming into his own ministry, Elisha gleaned spiritual strength and many vitamins from the rich field called Elijah. Running ahead of God may seem to be a move of faith, when real faith may be evidenced by standing still, waiting, and preparing.

We see the same determination that was exemplified in the natural oxen mastery pursuits now demonstrated in Elisha's dedication to his spiritual desire. He now demonstrated a determined desire to experience Elijah's anointed walk with God. Elisha saw and desired what the anointed and matured ministry Elijah exemplified. He would not take no for an answer in pursuing this desire. In fact, with eyes of faith he saw the possibility of the doubling potential.

When Elijah advised him, "Stay here; the Lord has called me to Bethel, Jericho, and Jordan," Elisha said, "I will not leave thee. And they two went on" (2 Kings 2:6). When other prophet ministries spoke out of turn with potential discouragement, Elisha continued on, disregarding their negative words.

Others stood and watched while Elisha experienced in this battle of faith. "And fifty men of the sons of the prophets went, and stood to view afar off: and they two stood by Jordan. And Elijah took his mantle, and wrapped it together, and smote the waters, and they were divided hither and thither, so that they two went over on dry ground. And it came to pass, when they were gone over, that Elijah said unto Elisha, Ask what I shall do for thee, before I be taken away from thee. And Elisha said, I pray thee, let a double portion of thy spirit be upon me" (2 Kings 2:7–9).

May we, God's ministry, likewise desire God's anointing with a right-hearted motive. Our desire must be to see the God of Israel glorified by bringing His people to faith. May we desire anointing to defeat the prophets of Baal. May we desire anointing to defeat the Jezebel spirit. This spirit always opposes godly authority and those whom God anoints and authorizes to bring the genuine holy words of God. They oppose the genuine prophetic word and prophets.

Ministry will always face challenges needing to be overcome in order to receive and carry the anointing God desires to give. The Holy Spirit knows the areas of the flesh that need to be overcome within us. The challenges placed before Elisha and us must be faced and overcome. These are pictured in the travels to Bethel, Jericho, and Jordan.

These are destinations that test the endurance of one's heart and righteous ministry integrity. Failure in achieving these destinations will limit our receiving.

Bethel is named and initially was "the house of God," a holy house of revelation and prayer. But it became corrupted and a house of ivory, a religious relic of wealth and idolatry. The man of God is called to minister righteousness to this setting. We are never to become comfortable there unless this house has been changed to righteousness. Visit it. Minister righteousness to it. Never become comfortable with dwelling there until it again identifies with its naming, a godly house of prayer.

Jericho was the heathen city once destroyed by Joshua but rebuilt in time. Our Lord described the road to Jericho. It was infested with criminals and robbers in the parable of the good Samaritan. The test will be for ministry to leave Bethel, the house of prayer, and go into the world preaching salvation to these inhabitants of Jericho having a willingness to face the dangers of the Jericho road. Sleeping church attendees with no heart for Jericho thieves and murderers will not fulfill the Lord's commission. "Behold, I send you forth as sheep in the midst of wolves: be ye therefore wise as serpents, and harmless as doves. But beware of men: for they will deliver you up to the councils, and they will scourge you in their synagogues; and ye shall be brought before governors and kings for my sake, for a testimony against them and the Gentiles" (Matt. 10:16–18). This is our ministry, even if our ministry of Christ only deletes excuses by many on that last day.

Jordan is always scripturally revealed as the place of crossing over, a transition from the place of desert trials to a new plateau, always upward with new testings and trials. One must desire upward progression and blessings with faith to cross over. We must die to the things of this world in order to have a changed desire to possess the promised land. We must desire and travel to that city that has immovable foundations (Heb. 11:5). Demas, after traveling in ministry with Paul, left the gospel road ministry. "Demas hath forsaken me, having loved this present world, and is departed unto Thessalonica" (2 Tim. 4:10). Demas has a long heritage family of like genes.

We must become separated from this world and what it offers, yet minister life to it. "They are not of the world, even as I am not of the world. Sanctify them through thy truth: thy word is truth. As thou hast sent me into the world, even so have I also sent them into the world" (John 17:16–18).

Elisha followed this path with determination to win the prize, while many fail.

The new road of ministry for Elisha after Elijah ascended was marked by the statement "Where is the God of Elijah?" This was said to part the waters needing to be crossed. As my friend Ernesto Balili has said, may we ask, "Where are the Elijahs of God?"

## EZEKIEL

This mighty prophet received God's choosing with holy reverence. With obedience he ate the roll when God said, "Eat the roll written within and without." This is an absorbing of reality, the painful chronicled matter of man without God. "Moreover he said unto me, Son of man, eat that thou findest; eat this roll, and go speak unto the house of Israel. So I opened my mouth, and he caused me to eat that roll" (Ezek. 3:1–2).

The great and successful ministries of God have taken time to learn and absorb God's Word. We as Ezekiel and Timothy are likewise told, "Study to shew thyself approved unto God, a workman that needeth not to be ashamed, rightly dividing the word of truth" (2 Tim. 2:15). The called ministry who is limited in eating the Word will always be a limited person compared to what our God intended for them to be. "And he said unto me, Son of man, cause thy belly to eat, and fill thy bowels with this roll that I give thee. Then did I eat it; and it was in my mouth as honey for sweetness" (Ezek. 3:3). To those who love the Lord, His Word will be sweet, although the truths written therein will expose woe and bitter truth while being ingested.

The instruction to "fill thy bowels" is very specific and must not be overlooked. The stomach breaks down the food. The bowels absorb the food. This was written several thousand years ago before medical science had this understanding. The God-ordained ministry must break down and absorb God's food, the Word. This absorbing involves understanding the intent of the writings. This provides nourishment and strength. The Word always reveals and brings understanding of God's purposes and heart.

To those who eat the roll, a sending is sure to follow.

> And he said unto me, Son of man, go, get thee unto the house of Israel, and speak with my words unto them. For thou art not sent to a people of a strange speech and of an hard language, but to the house of Israel; not to many people of a strange speech and of an hard language, whose words thou canst not understand. Surely, had I sent thee to them, they would have hearkened unto thee. But the house of Israel will not hearken unto thee; for they will not hearken unto me: for all the house of Israel are impudent and hardhearted.
>
> —EZEKIEL 3:4–7

When the sending comes, it usually begins with the hardest people to face and reach, those whom we are personally acquainted with.

I recall when shortly after being saved and being very ministry minded, I was aware of my lack. I considered myself too immature to preach, knowing I lacked the ability. I did not have the faith to pray for people but was excited to share the faith I had. Shortly afterward I was introduced to gospel tracts and determined to give these out. They preached what I wanted to say. Living in a countryside town near Vancouver, Canada, I felt it would be easiest to reach out to the needy people. The neediest were in an area commonly called "skid row" along Hastings Street in Vancouver. This was a gathering place of drunks and burned-out men and women who obviously needed help. It was so much easier to face people I did not know, who were a distance from my home. However, the Lord who knows all had me meet businesspeople whom I was acquainted with in time. Like Job, I was confronted with that which I feared and needed to overcome (Job 3:25).

While giving out these tracts, over time I graduated from standing in a protective business front alcove to boldly standing on the corner of Granville and Broadway. Several hundred people traversed this intersection at every change of the traffic light. Suddenly I was confronted with dressed-up businesspeople whom I did business with. They were having an evening out in this entertainment district. Upon being asked, "What are you doing?", I simply responded with, "I am sharing my faith; have a gospel tract." One of them accepted Christ due to this. Shortly after this one-and-a-half-year ministry outreach of two evenings a week, the Lord brought changes to my ministry life. Remarkable changes came.

Strength and opportunity change. Training under God's hand takes obedience. The training always faces our weak areas to receive His strengths. "Behold, I have made thy face strong against their faces, and thy forehead strong against their foreheads. As an adamant harder than flint have I made thy forehead: fear them not, neither be dismayed at their looks, though they be a rebellious house" (Ezek. 3:8–9). The man and woman of God must grow. We gain needed strengths to withstand opposition. We will always face opposition when called of God, if we are being godly. We must be strong to give forth God's words. "Moreover he said unto me, Son of man, all my words that I shall speak unto thee receive in your heart, and hear with your ears" (v. 10). Our ears must be attuned to hearing His voice and His words. Then we must obey.

Again we hear a strong directive of knowledge all ministries should know: "And go, get thee to them of the captivity, unto the children of thy people, and speak unto them, and tell them, Thus says the Lord God; whether they will hear, or whether they will forbear" (Ezek. 3:11). We must speak forth His Word whether popular or not. That is what makes us a servant of the Lord and not of man!

Eventually this mighty man of God was shown great prophetic revelation and prophesied events that we have seen come to pass in the last century. (See Ezekiel 36:18–24.) We have witnessed the gathering of the Jews out of all countries and their return to their original homeland after being scattered. There are nearly nineteen hundred years separating these two events. Jeremiah spoke of this profound God dealing. He prophesied that the hunter would bring this gathering about (Jer. 16:15). I believe this was perfectly described and fulfilled by Hitler's Jew hunt during World War II. Hitler hunted Jews throughout Europe and as far away as Russia, exterminating more than six million. I personally have extended family who were sent to concentration death camps due to being born in Holland, people who did all they could to protect those who were being persecuted.

This event was the main thrust that brought the Jews en masse to their original land. The Jews did not heed the prophesied words of Jeremiah, when God said "first I will allure them" prior to sending the hunter. The British Balfour Treaty did not work.

The next event is contrary to what all of the natural evidence and circumstances currently show in 2012, but will happen. Again we also have Ezekiel's prophesied knowledge of the fact that Israel will come to a time of safety and peace, living in unwalled or undefended cities, prior to Christ's return. "And thou shalt say, I will go up to the land of unwalled villages; I will go to them that are at rest, that dwell safely, all of them dwelling without walls, and having neither bars nor gates, to take a spoil, and to take a prey; to turn your hand upon the desolate places that are now inhabited, and upon the people that are gathered out of the nations, which have gotten cattle and goods, that dwell in the midst of the land" (Ezek. 38:11–12). What an example to you and me of our awesome God by this servant Ezekiel.

## DANIEL

We often teach kids about the heroics of Daniel and his victory in the lions' den. In actuality we see a young Jewish captive rise from obscurity, through many trials with God's favor. "LORD, by thy favour thou hast made my mountain to stand strong" (Ps. 30:7).

The great lesson and learning in Daniel's life and history is the roots of seeing a nobody arise to prominence under God. Daniel's rising was in the face of impossible and difficult circumstances humanly speaking. He was made a eunuch by his captors, with little hope in life or any heritage after his passing. To know and understand the basis of his success, we need to see Daniel's decisions that affected his friends and nation. It all began with a decision with determination: "But Daniel purposed in his heart that he would not defile himself with the portion of the king's meat, nor with the wine which he drank: therefore he requested of the prince of the eunuchs that he might not defile himself" (Dan. 1:8). All of us make decisions. Not making a decision when faced with challenges *is* a decision.

Daniel purposed in his heart! The wise man Solomon said, "For as he thinketh in his heart, so is he" (Prov. 23:7). The genuine determination of one's heart will ultimately tell the end of the matter. This initial decision strengthened and prepared Daniel for growth to face tougher decisions. The devil will always look for ways to resist the ministry of God. He seeks to kill and destroy:

> Then said these men, We shall not find any occasion against this Daniel, except we find it against him concerning the law of his God. Then these presidents and princes assembled together to the king, and said thus unto him, King Darius, live for ever. All the presidents of the kingdom, the governors, and the princes, the counsellors, and the captains, have consulted together to establish a royal statute, and to make a firm decree, that whosoever shall ask a petition of any God or man for thirty days, save of thee, O king, he shall be cast into the den of lions. Now, O king, establish the decree, and sign the writing, that it be not changed, according to the law of the Medes and Persians, which altereth not. Wherefore king Darius signed the writing and the decree. Now when Daniel knew that the writing was signed, he went into his house; and his windows being open in his chamber toward Jerusalem, he kneeled upon his knees three times a day, and prayed, and gave thanks before his God, as he did aforetime.
>
> —Daniel 6:5–10

These scheming jealous leaders appealed to King Darius's ego. He fell into the trap. Daniel knew of the writing but determined to stand. He was observed in prayer honoring his God, regardless of the threat. Hereby we see that the God of Israel was his true God. Unlike many today, he spoke out, putting himself on the line regardless of persecution. Many today will not speak of unpopular subject matter (i.e., homosexuality) due to the threats of the world, thereby being unfaithful to the gospel. They are bowing down to the statues of political correctness due to potential persecution. Hereby they have denied Him before whom all statues will fall. (See 1 Samuel 5:3.) Daniel came through this trial with the Lord being his defense. His persecutors did not.

On an earlier occasion, Daniel's three friends faced the enemy's plans while refusing to bow to Nebuchadnezzar's statue. Daniel and these man gained stature and promotion from the Lord as a result: "For promotion cometh neither from the east, nor from the west, nor from the south. But God is the judge: he putteth down one, and setteth up another" (Ps. 75:6–7). We the ministry must learn this truth as we progress and mature.

## Ministry Challenges

Joshua was a trained minister under Moses. The secret to Joshua's success is found in this single decision: "And the Lord spoke unto Moses face to face, as a man speaketh unto his friend. And he turned again into the camp: but his servant Joshua, the son of Nun, a young man, departed not out of the tabernacle" (Exod. 33:11). Joshua overcame the challenge of pursuing life's demands in making focused time for the Lord. His determined decision of staying in the tabernacle to seek God's presence is the root to his lifelong ministry success.

This waiting on the Lord is to obtain faith and eyes to see our God and Him being larger than the giants in our lives. Joshua saw that with the help of the God of Israel, the giants and obstacles to possessing the Promised Land would be overcome. May we see our faith challenges conquered, having kneeled as a prostrated servant ministry. Staying in the tabernacle while waiting upon the Lord gives us strength. "He giveth power to the faint; and to them that have no might he increaseth strength. Even the youths shall faint and be weary, and the young men shall utterly fall: But they that wait upon the Lord shall renew their strength; they shall mount up with wings as eagles; they shall run, and not be weary; and they shall walk, and not faint" (Isa. 40:29–31).

Respecting God-provided authority is of key and great importance. Respecting God-provided authority is not always just an authority being over us. More commonly the problem is submitting to authority alongside of us. The matching truth is that authority figures need to always be respectful of others and not bristle when politely questioned. Bristling speaks of a prideful spirit linked to the Nicolaitans. Nicolaitans mastered the art of controlling the people versus leading the flock and building them up. Christ hates Nicolaitans (Rev. 2:6). Pride destroys the truth of a servant heart and the exhortation by the elder Peter: "Likewise, ye younger, submit yourselves unto the elder. Yea, all of you be subject one to another, and be clothed with humility: for God resisteth the proud, and giveth grace to the humble" (1 Pet. 5:5).

Unlike Joshua, who respected Moses, Aaron did not fare as well due to disrespect and a wrong jealousy spirit. Aaron came into agreement with his sister Miriam, the prophetess. They took a rebellious and critical stand against Moses. They disregarded his God-given placement and authority, becoming critical due to Moses marrying a black woman. They evidenced what was in their hearts by revealing their desire to be of the same authority placement as what the Lord gave Moses. Just because we may not like a ministry's personal choices does not allow us the right to become critical. "The Lord heard Aaron and Miriam, and He hears us as well.

We not only may but also must judge sin in others. We need to be careful not to become critical of their personal choice decisions (Gal. 6:1; 1 Cor. 5:1).

The Lord came down and manifested in the cloud, bringing judgment on both Miriam and Aaron. Miriam became leprous with an "unclean" judgment, demonstrating the inner unclean. Many when observing this judgment thought Aaron escaped from such. However, Aaron's escaped judgment was in fact a deferred judgment, a judgment of a greater weight than the short-lived leprosy Miriam endured. Aaron's ministry responsibilities were greater and likewise his deferred judgment. We see the result of this judgment when the Lord commanded Moses to remove the high priestly garments from his brother, the garments that had portrayed his priestly office. Upon removal of these garments, Aaron immediately died (Num. 20:26). Ministry and those who have received much were and are judged by a different standard than the standard for those who have received little. "But he that knew not, and did commit things worthy of stripes, shall be beaten with few stripes. For unto whomsoever much is given, of him shall be much required: and to whom men have committed much, of him they will ask the more" (Luke 12:48). The question of are we clean and ready to face our Savior, should this be our last day on earth, is fitting.

"Be not many masters" is a saying to be considered by ungodly ministry. Taking a place of authority and visibility without a right heart will result in a greater judgment (James 3:1).

Samson was a mighty judge and warrior of Israel. When the Holy Spirit anointing came upon him, he did great exploits under God. His fall in ministry was due to one of the big three temptations to man: wealth, sex, and power, and not necessarily in this order. Delilah was part of the enemy's territory. She was a forbidden fruit of temptation that orchestrated Samson's downfall. These temptations that capture ministry never have a genuine love for the ministry person. Daily these destroy ministry due to being the devil's tools. These temptations demand to become mini gods, causing blindness and death as their reward.

These tempters desire to kill. They expose and destroy our holy secrets, the source of our power.

> And it came to pass, when she pressed him daily with her words, and urged him, so that his soul was vexed unto death; that he told her all his heart, and said unto her, There hath not come a razor upon mine head; for I have been a Nazarite unto God from my mother's womb: if I be shaven, then my strength will go from me, and I shall become weak, and be like any other man. And when Delilah saw that he had told her all his heart, she sent and called for the lords of the Philistines.... But the Philistines took him, and put out his eyes, and brought him down to Gaza, and bound him with fetters of brass; and he did grind in the prison house.
> —JUDGES 16:16–18, 21

When temptations succeed, they always leave the ministry in bondage. Giving in to these temptations will always destroy our clear sight and replace it with blindness. This was the prophetic picture Samson depicted.

Delilah was long gone with her reward of silver, leaving the crippled

God-called warrior incapacitated. Lord, help us to discern people and the motives of those whom we meet and deal with. May "soul ties" and emotions not dissuade us from a holy worship and truth walk. May we continually walk with the wheels with eyes, discerning every part of our journey.

May those who have experienced chains of failure always remember this. When Samson was captured and enslaved, the hour came where faith arose. In time his hair grew back. At the end of the day and his ministry, by the grace and Spirit of God, he destroyed his enemies.

The Lord will give us the victory when confronting His and our enemies. Confronting the enemy and sin is always a minister's duty and message. Of course one always must balance this message with love and godly wisdom.

## Tough Message

We find this confronting of sin and speaking forth the judgments of our God to be a normal preaching by all of the prophets. When we read the first three chapters of Amos, these scriptures speak a continuous theme, the word of the Lord through this prophet. We hear a nonstop pronouncement of the judgments of the Lord upon the people in sin and wrong. These true words such as Amos spoke are common among all of the Bible prophets.

> Thus says the LORD; For three transgressions of Tyrus, and for four, I will not turn away the punishment thereof; because they delivered up the whole captivity to Edom, and remembered not the brotherly covenant: But I will send a fire on the wall of Tyrus, which shall devour the palaces thereof. Thus saith the LORD; For three transgressions of Edom, and for four, I will not turn away the punishment thereof; because he did pursue his brother with the sword, and did cast off all pity, and his anger did tear perpetually, and he kept his wrath for ever: But I will send a fire upon Teman, which shall devour the palaces of Bozrah. Thus saith the LORD; For three transgressions of the children of Ammon, and for four, I will not turn away the punishment thereof; because they have ripped

up the women with child of Gilead, that they might enlarge their border: But I will kindle a fire in the wall of Rabbah, and it shall devour the palaces thereof, with shouting in the day of battle, with a tempest in the day of the whirlwind: And their king shall go into captivity, he and his princes together, saith the LORD.

—Amos 1:9–15

No honey coated words here.

Why do so few speak of God's coming judgments, which affect us in this life as well as man's entire eternity? The Lord of Hosts, who changes not, still requires His modern called ministry servants to speak a similar message of repentance from sin to avoid a coming judgment resulting from sin.

When dealing with Christian Bible doctrine, three of the six Christian foundational doctrines listed in Hebrews 6:1–2 deal directly with repentance of sin and the results of thereof: repentance of dead works, resurrection of the dead, and eternal judgment.

Repentance from dead works is the first of six listed doctrines. This doctrine deals directly with the root that separates man from God. "But your iniquities have separated between you and your God, and your sins have hid his face from you, that he will not hear" (Isa. 59:2). One will not receive of the love of God without understanding the wrath and judgment of God, that which Christ saved us from. This is where I struggle with the love preachers who do not speak of the terrible situation man is in. Man is lost in sin and heading for judgment. There is no salvation where there is no genuine confronting of personal sins. There is no genuine liberty of faith where sin has not been confronted within. "Blessed is he whose transgression is forgiven, whose sin is covered" (Ps. 32:1).

The fifth listed doctrine is resurrection of the dead. This doctrine deals with separation at the time of Christ's second coming. This is the real awful moment of judgment. The unsaved rise in a separate resurrection one thousand years later. The "blessed" (saved) go up one thousand years before the unsaved. "And I saw thrones, and they sat upon them, and judgment was given unto them: and I saw the souls of them that were beheaded for the witness of Jesus, and for the word of God, and which had not worshipped the beast, neither his image, neither had received his mark upon their foreheads, or in their hands; and they lived and reigned with Christ a thousand years. But the rest of the dead lived not again until the thousand years were finished. This is the first resurrection. Blessed and holy is he that hath part in the first resurrection: on such the second death hath no power, but they shall be priests of God and of Christ" (Rev. 20:4–6).

The "blessed" saints arise and join our Lord in the air at the first resurrection. The resurrection blessed saints take part in heaven's wedding feast and are the bride company (1 Thess. 4:16). These "blessed saints" are judged at the judgment seat of Christ for rewards based on works (2 Cor. 5:10; Luke 12:48).

This judgment for rewards affects their eternal status in heavenly matters. Our salvation is solely based upon our faith in Christ's works (Rev. 14:13; Eph. 2:8). All of these who are judged at Christ's throne have already received eternal life (John 5:24). These beloved saved saints are tried considering their works for rewards, as though by fire. "Every man's work shall be made manifest: for the day shall declare it, because it shall be revealed by fire; and the fire shall try every man's work of what sort it is. If any man's work abide which he hath built thereupon, he shall receive a reward. If any man's work shall be burned, he shall suffer loss: but he himself shall be saved; yet so as by fire" (1 Cor. 3:13–15). The eyes of fire determine their works as to heart intent and results of same. Only saved people attend this judgment.

Whether one rises in the first resurrection or not is the major judgment. This determines whether one is part of Christ or apart from Christ. (See author's manual titled *Fivefold Ministry Church Doctrine*.)

The unrighteous, which Scripture describes as "the rest of the dead," who arise one thousand years later are judged by one criterion only: Is your name in the Book of Life? At this judgment our righteous God will demonstrate even to the unsaved why they are not in the Book of Life and why they receive whatever judgment they have for eternity (Rev. 20:12). They are not guests at the wedding feast; they are one thousand years beyond it. There will only be one wedding. The door was shut. "Afterward came also the other virgins, saying, Lord, Lord, open to us. But he answered and said, Verily I say unto you, I know you not" (Matt. 25:11–12). People like Hitler and Judas Iscariot will not be receiving the same eternal judgment as all other unbelievers (Luke 12:48; Matt. 26:24).

All who genuinely seek the living Creator God will find Him. History has many accounts of the seeking finding salvation, some in profound ways, just as Phillip's supernatural visit to a seeking Ethiopian black man in the desert (Acts 8:27). God is holy and righteous to all and meets the seeking.

May we be giants of faith under our Lord and Savior, attaining unto great works. All can be saved, although few will be. The narrow gate that leads to life eternal will see much more traffic when we God's ministry attain unto mighty ministry achievements.

## CHAPTER FOURTEEN

# MINISTRY GUNS BLAZING

*Consider the Blazing Ministry Guns*

*T*HE PROPHET JOEL declared a war cry truth for you and me when he said, "Blow ye the trumpet in Zion, and sound an alarm in my holy mountain: let all the inhabitants of the land tremble: for the day of the LORD cometh, for it is nigh at hand" (Joel 2:1). The day of the Lord is coming! We will all face and stand before our Holy God. All will render an account of our works on earth. Did we deal with the just issue of acknowledging our holy creator and His Lordship? Did we repent of personal sin and love His holy ways? Did we speak out and warn others of that impending day?

All of the called godly ministry examples in the Bible, both men or women, cried out against sin and wrong. They always directed God's people to liberty from sin and its resulting effects. All speak of the cross and the shed blood for sin. This is the focal point and subject matter of what is written within and without filling God's roll, given to Ezekiel. The roll speaks of the woes and sorrows resulting from sin in a God-separated people. These are the sorrows of God's heart due to the estate of mankind (Ezek. 2:10). He is our Creator and Father.

May we the ministry of God learn by this holy written roll since God's servants are to trumpet forth this message and truth above all worldly words and events. God is tired of the limp-wristed man-fearing and man-pleasing servants of men. Limp-wristed ministers want all men to speak well of them. Our Lord warned us about this. "Woe unto you, when all men shall speak well of you! for so did their fathers to the false prophets" (Luke 6:26). Why were these false prophets false? Some speak of peace when there is no peace. "For they have healed the hurt of the daughter of my people slightly, saying, Peace, peace; when there is no peace" (Jer. 8:11).

Jeremiah withstood false prophets, those who were telling the people not to worry about a coming judgment. Jeremiah was in contrast to the popular many as he heralded God's coming judgment. Destruction was coming upon Israel. Jeremiah's message was confronting sin to avert this destruction by preaching repentance. The false prophets only spoke of love and prosperity. The end of Jeremiah's true prophetic words fell upon the people. Destruction came, bringing Israel into captivity. Have we declared the profound truth of what lies ahead, subsequent to the grave? Have we trumpeted the coming judgment for all, affecting our eternal souls?

Jeremiah warned the people in order to prevent them from entering into captivity. After a fashion they were already in captivity, due to listening to the lies of the false prophets they followed. These false prophets did not preach or tell them what they needed to hear. The people did not believe the one voice our Lord raised up against the many false voices. They needed to discern the Jeremiah voice of God, but their ears were dulled by the "peace preachers." Jeremiah spoke of holiness, repentance, and a warning to avoid the avoidable and coming judgment. Our Lord preserved and blessed His faithful minister Jeremiah, granting him favor when the Babylonian judgment came.

I have been chastened by the Lord in this regard. The result is what the Holy Spirit prophetically spoke about to me some thirty-five years ago. He has changed me. The result is an Ezekiel type promised forehead, which is harder than flint (Ezek. 3:9). All ministry people need this forehead. "The fear of man bringeth a snare" (Prov. 29:25).

## Holy Building

You and I must tear down and destroy prior to planting and building (Jer. 1:10). This tearing down involves confronting wrong imbalanced doctrine and understandings. This involves making a conscious decision to confront untruth and half truths. Confrontation is a necessary part of holy ministry in an unholy and religious world.

We must determine whether we are "a man or woman of God" or a servant of man. This will be evidenced by the fruit of our ministry. The majority of the Bible chronicled ministers who were chosen by our Lord opened their message and writings with their guns of righteousness blazing. They attained unto turning many to righteousness and fulfilling their God-given assignment. Paul spoke by the Holy Spirit regarding truth associated with a holy sin-confronting ministry. He stated, "Yea, and all that will live godly in Christ Jesus shall suffer persecution" (2 Tim. 3:12).

There is a reason why some are popular with an unholy church and the world. They never confront sin or preach holiness! Paul did, and we should be preaching the whole counsel of God. "Wherefore I take you to record this day, that I am pure from the blood of all men. For I have not shunned to declare unto you all the counsel of God.... And when he had thus spoken, he kneeled down, and prayed with them all. And they all wept sore, and fell on Paul's neck, and kissed him, sorrowing most of all for the words which he spake, that they should see his face no more" (Acts 20:26–27, 36–38). Holy people love a holy preacher.

Holy and God-fearing preachers have a sure conviction and knowledge of what Ezekiel heard the Lord saying to him. This is very applicable to us now:

> But if the watchman see the sword come, and blow not the trumpet, and the people be not warned; if the sword come, and take any person from among them, he is taken away in his iniquity; but his blood will I require at the watchman's hand. So thou, O son of man, I have set thee a watchman unto the house of Israel; therefore thou shalt hear the word at my mouth, and warn them from me. When I say unto the wicked, O wicked man, thou shalt surely die; if thou dost not speak to warn the wicked from his way, that wicked man shall die in his iniquity; but his blood will I require at your hand. Nevertheless, if thou warn the wicked of his way to

turn from it; if he do not turn from his way, he shall die in his iniquity; but thou hast delivered thy soul.

—Ezekiel 33:6–9

Either you and I are God's watchmen, or we are only functioning as blind servants of man. We must warn the unsaved of their unbelieving destiny and the Lord's future holy court appearance. We, like the apostle Paul, must warn the church as he warned the Hebrew church, to follow after holiness, without which they shall not see God. He exhorted them to beware of the possibility of their failing the course of faith due to having "an evil heart of unbelief, in departing from the living God" (Heb. 3:12).

Jonah understood the message he was to preach: "Now the word of the Lord came unto Jonah the son of Amittai, saying, Arise, go to Nineveh, that great city, and *cry against it; for their wickedness* is come up before me" (Jon. 1:1–2, emphasis added). How many prophets today cry out, confronting wickedness? Has all of the wickedness stopped and disappeared? There has to be some reason for this changed message and ministry. But this we know. Our God has not changed!

## Micah

Micah's writing is God's message and word to Israel then and now to you and me:

> The word of the Lord that came to Micah the Morasthite in the days of Jotham, Ahaz, and Hezekiah, kings of Judah, which he saw concerning Samaria and Jerusalem. Hear, all ye people; hearken, O earth, and all that therein is: and let the Lord God be witness against you, the Lord from his holy temple. For, behold, the Lord cometh forth out of his place, and will come down, and tread upon the high places of the earth. And the mountains shall be molten under him, and the valleys shall be cleft, as wax before the fire, and as the waters that are poured down a steep place. For the transgression of Jacob is all this, and for the sins of the house of Israel. What is the transgression of Jacob? is it not Samaria? and what are

the high places of Judah? are they not Jerusalem? Therefore I will make Samaria as an heap of the field, and as plantings of a vineyard: and I will pour down the stones thereof into the valley, and I will discover the foundations thereof. And all the graven images thereof shall be beaten to pieces, and all the hires thereof shall be burned with the fire, and all the idols thereof will I lay desolate: for she gathered it of the hire of an harlot, and they shall return to the hire of an harlot.

—MICAH 1:1–7

God spoke these words directed against Jerusalem, the place of worship. Are we speaking His message against sin and wrong? Is our modern Jerusalem clean and holy? As David said to his blind unseeing brothers before confronting the blasphemous Goliath, "What have I now done? Is there not a cause?" (1 Sam. 17:29). Is there not a cause that needs to be addressed? Holy and called servants of the Lord, may we trumpet forth the need of holy righteousness, salvation from sin. May we with holy zeal reach souls in this end-time harvest and glorify our Savior and soon coming King.

## SMOOTH-WORD PREACHERS

Unfortunately some of the largest churches and congregations are rarely recipients of any messages that lead to true repentance. Some preach "just receive Jesus and His love and heaven is yours," leaving off the truth of repentance and holiness. They gather an easy crowd since they present little cost to their lifestyle. They are comparable to what Isaiah confronted and spoke of under holy anointing: "Now go, write it before them in a table, and note it in a book, that it may be for the time to come forever and ever: That this is a rebellious people, lying children, children that will not hear the law of the LORD: Which say to the seers, See not; and to the prophets, Prophesy not unto us right things, speak unto us smooth things, prophesy deceits" (Isa. 30:8–10).

Sanctification is an often used Bible word. Sanctification means set apart from something and unto something. Sanctification is being set apart from sin unto holiness. In my early ministry I was very close to being ordained by a church denomination, where one of the questions the ministry needed to answer on a monthly accountability form was, "How many people were sanctified?" This was one of two things I addressed just prior to the ordination and ultimately stopped this process. I communicated to the then pastor to whom I was accountable that I could never fill out that question with a clean conscience. I attempted to respectfully explain to him the following:

Sanctification is a term describing a continual work of the Holy Spirit within. Yes, the saved believer is positionally sanctified and pure before God by the blood of Christ. However, the work of sanctification is a continual process until the day we die. Holiness is something we are positionally given in Christ. However, we are to continually follow after holiness, and we will not see God if we believers do not (Heb. 12:14).

Repentance of our personal sin will bring us to salvation when faith in Christ is added to this repentance. Yes, we are positionally sanctified by Christ and His shed blood. However, the genuine Christian is exhorted to be experientially sanctified as to their person, so the Lord can use us in a greater manner and for our personal spiritual health (2 Tim. 2:21).

The initial repentance experienced at salvation never stops with those who desire to achieve heaven and eternal life. Repentance is not a one-time matter, but it is a continual pursuit of holiness. What man can look up to heaven and say he is now perfect in holiness and sinless? Find one, and I will call that person deceived or a liar. Who can lay claim to loving God perfectly? Who can lay claim to unselfishly loving our fellow man?

No true ministry should question this as to their experiential status. I am strongly aware of some of my failures daily, but thank God for His mercy and the blood that is sufficient for my failures. Theologically look at the spiritual man who corrects another in obvious sin, while being advised of their personal capability to give in to temptation (Gal. 6:1). Consider Job and that there was no one as righteous in all of the earth, yet at the end our God graciously corrected him as to his lack.

Smooth-word preachers ignore preaching a continual need for sanctification. They often do so by preaching a claimed salvation status based on an initial experience. Then they do not preach that this was a gateway experience into a life of repentance and holiness to be maintained and pursued. The child of God who understands this and follows this life pursuit can daily rejoice in the God of their salvation. Those who do not will always have a weak and questioning of their salvation status.

Paul who rejoiced in God's faithfulness and with joy spoke of the crown of life laid up in store for him: "And every man that striveth for the mastery is temperate in all things. Now they do it to obtain a corruptible crown; but we an incorruptible. I therefore so run, not as uncertainly; so fight I, not as one that beats the air: But I keep under my body, and bring it into subjection: lest that by any means, when I have preached to others, I myself should be a castaway" (1 Cor. 9:25–27). Paul explained that every man who looks for this crown is temperate, demonstrating a continual self-restraint in all things. This temperate is a continual walking with carefulness knowing our flesh and weakness potential. Paul summarized this with admitting to the possibility he knowingly avoided. He kept himself in a continuously spiritual training to ensure that he would not be a castaway. The Greek rendering for "castaway" means "unapproved, rejected reprobate."

May the smooth-word preachers, who speak of love and grace, include a continual exhortation to work out our salvation with "fear and trembling" (Phil. 2:12).

Ministry and people of God, may we shun smooth-word preaching. We must preach about the love of God, His mercy and grace, but not at the expense of deleting and avoiding the truths of damnation and hell. Those who avoid these truths in their preaching have never fully understood that "the law was given by Moses, but grace and truth came by Jesus Christ" (John 1:17). The law depicts righteousness. Sin is the breaking of the righteousness depicted by the law. All of mankind is guilty. Christ never came to do away with the law. He came to fulfill the law on our behalf and then died a death as a holy sacrifice in our stead. We who love Christ love holiness. He is holy! We walk in holiness as we continually desire to fulfill the righteous demands of the law, which is to love our

God and fellow man. That is the grace that we preach, but not without presenting repentance from the sin which the law exposes (Matt. 5:17).

Preaching to the church must include the exhorting of believers to continually strive for holiness. When they do not seek after this, their love for Christ is lukewarm or cold. Jesus warned the believers and churches about this: "So because thou art lukewarm, and neither cold nor hot, I will spue thee out of my mouth" (Rev. 3:16). May the believer not rest their believed salvation status on a one-time experience and event but a continually sought-after living relationship.

## Nahum

This prophet assails the fortresses of religiosity and sin. Why would the modern prophet not speak likewise to some degree and not listen to the popular request of speaking "smooth things"? I love God's Word and promises of blessings. The depths of His mercy and steadfast goodness are unsearchable. However, the Lord caused all of His prophets to speak of His judgments and vengeance along with comfort and mercy. "The burden of Nineveh. The book of the vision of Nahum the Elkoshite. God is jealous, and the Lord revengeth; the Lord revengeth, and is furious; the Lord will take vengeance on his adversaries, and he reserveth wrath for his enemies. The Lord is slow to anger, and great in power, and will not at all acquit the wicked" (Nahum 1:1–3). God's holy wrath and anger toward those who deny Him is just, who do not give Him His rightful place in their lives. Those who have made themselves to be a god of self or placed other gods before Him have denied their creator. He is holy and majestic. He is awesome and terrible in vengeance, with a righteous judgment for all. We must warn the world as Nahum did without mincing words. This message must be preached as part of God's grace, a warning to strengthen and secure your people in salvation.

## Zephaniah

In the opening verses of his writings, Zephaniah opens with God's commitment to consuming and destroying the people and all of their land due to their actions and idolatry of heart.

Should the ministry of today not speak to those who have turned back with lukewarm hearts of God's pending judgment? Have people changed? Or is it just the ministers who are changed or called to a different message of "peace, peace, when there is no peace" (Jer. 6:14)? Our Lord spoke to the church of Ephesus, where Paul had ministered for several years, about removing their candle of light in this world's darkness. The reason was because they had lots of works but had lost their first love. The warning given to this church was to change, or a drastic dealing could result: "Nevertheless I have somewhat against thee, because thou hast left thy first love. Remember therefore from whence thou art fallen, and repent, and do the first works; or else I will come unto thee quickly, and will remove thy candlestick out of his place, except thou repent" (Rev. 2:4–5).

We can become works oriented when we lose sight of our relationship of walking with God from a love basis. Yes, love has works attached to the relationship. This is why marriage is the only thing the Bible compares to the church. Marriage can degenerate to a bad roommate relationship when we do not deal with the things required to maintain the love bond. God will not tolerate a bad roommate relationship; He will have only a first place love. Candlesticks (the church) can be removed. Lukewarm souls can be spat out. Only the hot will be His bride company. "So then because thou art lukewarm, and neither cold nor hot, I will spue thee out of my mouth" (Rev. 3:16).

Beware of the loss of this. What makes one conclude that Christian churches that were on a correct path and are now ordaining homosexuals will ever be welcomed in heaven? There is no love for Christ in this practice. Yes, God loves all people, including homosexuals; He sent His Son to die on the cross for all. Regardless, He hates the sin they have embraced instead of holiness.

Oh! May we preach and teach a living holy presence relationship, with heartfelt worship at His throne. All knowledge should lead to relationship! All works are to be out of worship, due to the overflowing love of our hearts. Thou art worthy, O Lord, to receive honor and glory. We love the beauty of Your holiness and despise all that sin is.

> I will utterly consume all things from off the land, saith the LORD.
> I will consume man and beast; I will consume the fowls of the
> heaven, and the fishes of the sea, and the stumblingblocks with the
> wicked; and I will cut off man from off the land, saith the LORD.
> I will also stretch out mine hand upon Judah, and upon all the
> inhabitants of Jerusalem; and I will cut off the remnant of Baal
> from this place, and the name of the Chemarims with the priests;
> and them that worship the host of heaven upon the housetops; and
> them that worship and that swear by the LORD, and that swear
> by Malcham; *and them that are turned back* from the LORD; and
> those that have not sought the LORD, nor enquired for him.
> —ZEPHANIAH 1:2–6, EMPHASIS ADDED

Note that those whom the Lord will utterly consume are categorized in the same manner—those who are wicked and Baal worshipers, and those who slide back after walking with the Lord, knowing His grace and person. May we with holy care preach righteousness to those who are sliding and turning back. To say one cannot turn back makes a mockery of this holy writing. They had to be with the Lord to turn back! May we as Christ's ambassadors also preach what this prophet said in God's unchanging message. This called ministry, Zephaniah, spoke what adorned God's Holy Book. May we in obedience likewise speak.

## Haggai

May we as Haggai cry out in the name of our Lord with urgency as to God's message and the need of this hour. The fields are ripe unto harvest. Laborers arise.

> In the second year of Darius the king, in the sixth month, in the
> first day of the month, came the word of the LORD by Haggai the
> prophet unto Zerubbabel the son of Shealtiel, governor of Judah,
> and to Joshua the son of Josedech, the high priest, saying, Thus
> speaketh the LORD of hosts, saying, This people say, The time is
> not come, the time that the LORD's house should be built. Then
> came the word of the LORD by Haggai the prophet, saying, *Is it
> time for you, O ye, to dwell in your cieled houses, and this house*

*lie waste?* Now therefore thus saith the Lord of hosts; Consider your ways. Ye have sown much, and bring in little; ye eat, but ye have not enough; ye drink, but ye are not filled with drink; ye clothe you, but there is none warm; and he that earns wages earns wages to put it into a bag with holes. Thus says the Lord of hosts; *Consider your ways.*

—Haggai 1:1–7, emphasis added

"Consider your ways" must always be part of the preacher's message. We must consider our ways and time expenditures. The night is coming when no man can labor. Those who hear and act on this message will prosper. May we herald and trumpet God's grace through faith from judgment. May we be used to bring in the souls from the world fields of harvest. The apostle Paul taught that the unsaved need a preacher: "For whosoever shall call upon the name of the Lord shall be saved. How then shall they call on him in whom they have not believed? and how shall they believe in him of whom they have not heard? and how shall they hear without a preacher? And how shall they preach, except they be sent? as it is written, How beautiful are the feet of them that preach the gospel of peace, and bring glad tidings of good things!" (Rom. 10:13–15). May we with clarity see the end destination of the unsaved, and love them enough to tell them of the way, truth, and Life.

Church and ministry, arise. All of us are to do our part in reaping this harvest, whether we witness to the lost or invite them with love to hear from others. We must teach and train up the believers. May our Lord find us awake and burning with lots of oil when He comes for us. We must demonstrate a heart filled with living zeal by praying, planning, and doing kingdom work, burning with love and zeal in readiness when He unexpectedly comes for us.

## Zechariah

In the eighth month, in the second year of Darius, came the word of the Lord unto Zechariah, the son of Berechiah, the son of Iddo the prophet, saying, The Lord hath been sore displeased with your fathers. Therefore say thou unto them, Thus saith the LORD of hosts; *Turn ye unto me, saith the Lord of hosts, and I will turn unto you*, saith the LORD of hosts. Be ye not as your fathers, unto whom the former prophets have cried, saying, Thus saith the LORD of hosts; Turn ye now from your evil ways, and from your evil doings: but they did not hear, nor hearken unto me, saith the LORD.

—ZECHARIAH 1:1–4, EMPHASIS ADDED

Those who heard this message, whether the fathers or the sons, did not turn back to God. Some who would preside at the funerals for such will preach them into heaven at the burial. God have mercy.

Note the hard-focused message delivered with a gloves-off offensive. That is holy, inspired, hard-hitting Holy Ghost truth since five times this statement includes "saith the Lord." May men arise to become "fathers" and the women to be "mothers" in Israel. We must raise up a harvest of godly sons and daughters in the faith! May we arise from our lethargy and dwelling at ease. What makes us think that our God will act contrary to His Word? Why would He turn to those who are not genuinely turning to Him?

## Malachi

The burden of the word of the LORD to Israel by Malachi. I have loved you, saith the LORD. Yet ye say, Wherein hast thou loved us? Was not Esau Jacob's brother? saith the LORD: yet I loved Jacob, and I hated Esau, and laid his mountains and his heritage waste for the dragons of the wilderness. Whereas Edom saith, We are impoverished, but we will return and build the desolate places; thus saith the LORD of hosts, They shall build, but I will throw down; and they shall call them, *The border of wickedness, and, The people against whom the Lord hath indignation for ever.* And your eyes shall see, and ye shall say, The LORD will be magnified from the border of Israel. A son honoureth his father, and a servant his master: if then I be a father, where is mine honour? and if I be a master, where is my fear? saith the LORD of hosts unto you, O priests, that despise my name. And ye say, Wherein have we despised thy name? Ye offer polluted bread upon mine altar; and ye say, *Wherein have we polluted thee? In that ye say, The table of the Lord is contemptible.* And if ye offer the blind for sacrifice, is it not evil? and if ye offer the lame and sick, is it not evil? offer it now unto thy governor; will he be pleased with thee, or accept thy person? saith the LORD of hosts.

—MALACHI 1:1–8, EMPHASIS ADDED

Malachi opened His anointed message with what was foremost on his heart, a heart filled with God's seeing and message. He spoke of the stereotype Jacob, whom God loved, as well as Esau, whom God hated. Birthright and holy promises meant little to Esau. Entering into a marriage covenant with ungodly idol-worshipping wives was all right in his opinion. Malachi continues with describing the path leading to Esau's road, demonstrated by what offerings the people gave. We the church of today can also be treading the wrong path, where the things we offer the Lord are our second best as to seeking Him. This applies to our prayer time, heartfelt witnessing of Him, plus time and financial focus. Again we see that our God will have indignation forever against these circumcised Israelites herein addressed.

We are easily drawn into an "I must" law and works relationship, birthed out of fear and duty, instead of a heart of love for God and man. "O foolish Galatians, who hath bewitched you, that ye should not obey the truth, before whose eyes Jesus Christ hath been evidently set forth, crucified among you? This only would I learn of you, Received ye the Spirit by the works of the law, or by the hearing of faith? Are ye so foolish? having begun in the Spirit, are ye now made perfect by the flesh?" (Gal. 3:1–3).

We must preach righteousness. We must present God's holiness. We must lead people into a holy, fervent love relationship, encouraging them to seek the Lord. We cannot do this unless we have an intimate personal prayer life relationship. Our ministry hearts and fires must burn brightly.

## CONCLUSION

Both the people of God and the world need to hear God's message. His message reveals His love as shown by the incarnation of the virgin birth ending in a post Calvary tomb. We must labor, preach, teach and minister while it is day: "I must work the works of him that sent me, while it is day: the night cometh, when no man can work" (John 9:4). We must see the harvest which is now ripe, telling the world we live in of His love. We must share about the cross, forgiveness of sin, and a heaven to win. But also that the wrath of God abides on those who are without Christ. "He that believeth on the Son hath everlasting life: and he that believeth not the Son shall not see life; but the wrath of God abideth on him" (John 3:36). We must preach and cry out to those who deny holiness by exposing sin for what it is and where it leads to. We preach this by teaching the reality of God and the holiness He is (Heb. 12:14).

In Isaiah's vision of the seraphims above the throne, their utterance was of what they were consumed with while they looked upon God's throne. All they could unceasingly say was, "Holy, holy, holy!" Holiness is the perfection and fullness of love. True love is more than a feeling; it is also a moral matter of righteousness. The perfection of righteousness is HOLY.

PLEASE NOTE: One cannot love God and not love holiness, for He is holy!

PLEASE NOTE: One cannot love God and not love holiness, for He is holy!

PLEASE NOTE: One cannot love God and not love holiness, for He is holy!

The called servant of the Lord must have this knowledge. We must speak forth God's message to the church and a dying world. We are His messengers! "For the priest's lips should keep knowledge, and they should seek the law at his mouth: for he is the messenger of the LORD of hosts" (Mal. 2:7).

May the genuine called ministry hear His words and speak them forth, proclaiming the message "OUR GOD REIGNS!"

May we build His church, which is constructed on the foundation of apostles and prophets, Christ being the chief cornerstone. All of the building is measured from Him. We in the ministry must give glory to our God in the highest and speak out peace on earth and good will toward men. If we do not see this truth, we should get out of the ministry, as we are demonstrating and abetting a lie by our words and lives.

We are the most honored people in the entire world. We are ambassadors of heaven's throne. We represent THE KING!

—APOSTLE JOHN DEVRIES

# ABOUT THE AUTHOR

*W*HILE OCCASIONALLY ATTENDING a Calvinistic denominational church, John DeVries, due to a mountainside experience, was immediately drawn into intensive Bible reading as a closet Christian and was "saved." A radically changed life resulted. He was immediately thrown into doctrinal issues and debate due to attending a different church where he could be baptized in water. This resulted in a public excommunication by the denomination due to not repenting for having done so and thereby refuting his infant baptism. He immediately started in ministry pursuits—passing out tracts, ministering in teen centers, being an assistant pastor, church planting, and being involved in overseas ministry, crusades, Bible school seminars, and conferences. This especially involved numerous trips to the Philippines, including taking teams with him. He experienced many things in church and ministry dealings, both good and bad, learning through them all. He was also blessed to continually see the Lord's blessings in all ways, including constant miracles and healings while ministering.

Seeing the great need of establishing biblical ministry in churches and the need for ministry to mature in knowledge, wisdom, hearing the voice of God, servant demeanor, and multiple ministries submitting one to another, he started writing. His writing mandate has prophetically been spoken by a number of ministries and is a great burden on his heart. He also currently mentors a number of ministries.

# Contact the Author

## Fivefold Foundation Ministries Inc.

PO Box 1119
Post Falls, ID 83877-1119